Refactoring to Rust

Refactoring to Rust

LILY MARA
JOEL HOLMES

MANNING
SHELTER ISLAND

For online information and ordering of this and other Manning books, please visit www.manning.com. The publisher offers discounts on this book when ordered in quantity. For more information, please contact

> Special Sales Department
> Manning Publications Co.
> 20 Baldwin Road
> PO Box 761
> Shelter Island, NY 11964
> Email: orders@manning.com

©2025 by Manning Publications Co. All rights reserved.

No part of this publication may be reproduced, stored in a retrieval system, or transmitted, in any form or by means electronic, mechanical, photocopying, or otherwise, without prior written permission of the publisher.

Many of the designations used by manufacturers and sellers to distinguish their products are claimed as trademarks. Where those designations appear in the book, and Manning Publications was aware of a trademark claim, the designations have been printed in initial caps or all caps.

∞ Recognizing the importance of preserving what has been written, it is Manning's policy to have the books we publish printed on acid-free paper, and we exert our best efforts to that end. Recognizing also our responsibility to conserve the resources of our planet, Manning books are printed on paper that is at least 15 percent recycled and processed without the use of elemental chlorine.

The author and publisher have made every effort to ensure that the information in this book was correct at press time. The author and publisher do not assume and hereby disclaim any liability to any party for any loss, damage, or disruption caused by errors or omissions, whether such errors or omissions result from negligence, accident, or any other cause, or from any usage of the information herein.

Manning Publications Co. 20 Baldwin Road PO Box 761 Shelter Island, NY 11964	Development editor: Elesha Hyde Technical development editor: Mark Elston Review editor: Kishor Rit Production editor: Aleksandar Dragosavljević Copy editor: Alisa Larson Proofreader: Katie Tennant Technical proofreader: Jerry Kuch Typesetter and cover designer: Marija Tudor

ISBN 9781617299018
Printed in the United States of America

To anyone who thought that they couldn't
—Lily Mara

*To my Grandma Jo and my Aunt Alisha who inspired
my love of reading and technology*
—Joel Holmes

brief contents

1 ■ Why refactor to Rust 1
2 ■ An overview of Rust 15
3 ■ Introduction to C FFI and unsafe Rust 60
4 ■ Advanced FFI 93
5 ■ Structuring Rust libraries 138
6 ■ Integrating with dynamic languages 164
7 ■ Testing your Rust integrations 187
8 ■ Asynchronous Python with Rust 212
9 ■ WebAssembly for refactoring JavaScript 229
10 ■ WebAssembly interface for refactoring 249

contents

preface xi
acknowledgments xii
about this book xiv
about the authors xvii
about the cover illustration xviii

1 Why refactor to Rust 1

1.1 What is refactoring? 2

1.2 What is Rust? 4

1.3 Why Rust? 4

1.4 Should you refactor to Rust? 5

Performance 5 ▪ *Memory safety 7* ▪ *Maintainability 7*

1.5 When not to refactor to Rust 9

1.6 How does it work? 9

1.7 What will you learn in this book? 11

Calling Rust functions directly from your program 11
Communicating with a Rust service over the network 12

1.8 Who is this book for? 13

1.9 What tools do you need to get started? 13

2 An overview of Rust 15

- 2.1 Ownership and borrowing 16
- 2.2 Memory management in other languages 19
- 2.3 Lifetimes 23

  *References and borrowing 26 • Controlling mutability 28
  References and lifetimes 30*

- 2.4 Rust's string types 33

  Mutable strings 34

- 2.5 Enums and error handling 37

  *Enums 37 • Error handling with enums 41 • The unit
  type 43 • Error types 45 • Transforming errors 49
  Panicking with errors 53*

3 Introduction to C FFI and unsafe Rust 60

- 3.1 Unsafe Rust 61

  Raw pointers 61

- 3.2 C Foreign Function Interface 64

  *Including a crate 68 • Creating a dynamic library with
  Rust 70 • Solving arithmetic expressions in Rust 77
  The Display trait 87*

4 Advanced FFI 93

- 4.1 Downloading the NGINX source code 94
- 4.2 Creating the NGINX module 94
- 4.3 Linking C to Rust 98

  Build scripts 100 • bindgen 103

- 4.4 Reading the NGINX request 109

  *Lifetime annotations 115 • Lifetime annotations in our
  NGINX plugin 120*

- 4.5 Using our calculator library 124
- 4.6 Writing the HTTP response 128

5 Structuring Rust libraries 138

- 5.1 Modules 138

  Who cares? 142 • Multiple files 143

- 5.2 Paths 146

  Relative vs. absolute pathspaths 147 • Path aliases 155

- 5.3 Upward visibility 159

6 Integrating with dynamic languages 164

- 6.1 Data processing in Python 164
- 6.2 Planning the move 165
- 6.3 JSON Parsing 166
- 6.4 Writing a Python extension module in Rust 171
- 6.5 Benchmarking in Rust 176
- 6.6 Optimized builds 184

7 Testing your Rust integrations 187

- 7.1 Writing tests with Rust 187

    Documentation tests 193 • Adding tests to existing code 198

- 7.2 Testing Rust code using Python 202

    Monkey patching 206

8 Asynchronous Python with Rust 212

- 8.1 Generating a Mandelbrot set in Python 213
- 8.2 Scaling 215
- 8.3 Asyncio 218
- 8.4 Threading 220
- 8.5 Global Interpreter Lock 223
- 8.6 PyO3 224

9 WebAssembly for refactoring JavaScript 229

- 9.1 What is WebAssembly? 230
- 9.2 Moving from JavaScript to Rust 231
- 9.3 Rust in the browser 232

    Requesting data 232 • Compiling to Wasm 235 Loading Wasm in the browser 237

- 9.4 Creating a React component 238
- 9.5 Web components entirely in Rust 241
- 9.6 Refactoring JavaScript revisited 247

10 WebAssembly interface for refactoring 249

- 10.1 WASI universal runtime 252
- 10.2 From the browser to the machine 255
- 10.3 Wasm library 261

10.4 Consuming Wasm 262
10.5 More Wasm 267
10.6 Wasm memory 270
10.7 Just the beginning 275

index   277

preface

Throughout our software careers, we've had the opportunity to participate in several refactoring projects. The narrative is often the same: products need to scale, but time is limited. This situation leads to extensive development efforts over months, filled with discussions about patterns and languages.

Refactoring with Java and Go involved significant challenges, including constant file moving, package exports, system wrappers, and outright rewrites of existing systems. The paths to success were rarely clearly defined. This book aims to provide you with many of these patterns, using a language designed for breaking down and rewriting existing systems. *Refactoring to Rust* demonstrates how Rust can seamlessly integrate into your ecosystem, delivering scaling benefits from day one due to the nature of the language.

Rust brings advantages, such as type safety and memory safety, along with performance gains attributed to these properties. In this book, you will learn how Rust can enhance nearly any project. Positioned to replace existing languages like C and C++, Rust stands out for its robust toolchain and memory safety features. We will also explore how Rust can interact with languages like Python, revealing performance improvements when building libraries and modules that work across both languages. Additionally, we'll discover unexpected uses for Rust, such as in web browsers and as a universal runtime.

Overall, this book aims not only to showcase the power of Rust but also to equip you with the skills to refactor large systems with confidence.

acknowledgments

I thank my partners for encouraging me to get this book over the finish line after I let it languish for so long.

To my mother, whose love of reading kept my nose in books for years and who edited some early drafts, thank you.

I thank my parents and grandparents for always encouraging me to pursue a technical education and making that possible.

Thank you, the trans community, everywhere that you are. There is no world without us.

To my Uncle Conrad, thank you for helping me develop my curiosity in the way things work.

To everyone at Manning, thank you. This book would not exist without the dedication of many editors, technical editors, graphics editors, marketers, proofreaders, and more. I thank Andy Waldron for the chance to write my first book.

A special thank you goes to the editors of this book, Elesha Hyde and Susan Ethridge. Your guidance led this book out of the vagaries of my thought into the real world.

To OneSignal, thank you for giving me the time and freedom to write this book.

I thank the teachers and professors who nurtured an appreciation for the written word within me—Kristen Schumacher, Paul Hebert, and the late Jean Lutz.

Thank you, Norm Krumpe, for feeding my technical curiosity, and Dr. Paris Franz for encouraging me to do something as big as writing a book.

Thank you, Jan Pascual, for being the guinea pig behind the technical communication skills that underpin this writing, and for your encouragement throughout the process.

Writing a book is a herculean effort, and I also thank everyone who was an early reviewer or a MEAP customer who left feedback in the online forums for the book.

—LILY MARA

First, I would like to thank my wife and partner, Chelsea, who encourages me to pursue my dreams of writing and learning.

I also thank my two sons, Eli and Abel, who are an endless source of inspiration.

My dedication of this book is to two important women in my life. The first is my grandmother, who instilled my love of books and reading, and second is my Aunt Alisha, who influenced my love of computers at an early age.

This book could not have been written without the immense support of Manning's publishing team. Thank you, Andy Waldron, for this opportunity to write a book on such an exciting subject.

As a reviewer of many Manning books myself, I especially appreciate all those who provided feedback in the book reviews: Alain Couniot, Alfred Thompson, Amit Lamba, Ariel Otilibili, Chris Kardell, Christopher Villanueva, Clifford Thurber, Dan Sheikh, Daniel Tomás Lares, Diego Alonso, Federico Kircheis, Foster Haines, Gabor Laszlo Hajba, Gilles Iachelini, Havard Wall, Jahred Love, James Blachly, John Kasiewicz, Jon Riddle, Jonathan Reeves, Julien Castelain, Kent R. Spillner, Krzysztof Kamyczek, Maciej Przepióra, Marcus Geselle, Matthew Sarmiento, Max Sadrieh, Michal Rutka, Mohsen Mostafa Jokar, Ramon Snir, Rani Sharim, Richard Randall, Salvador Navarrete Garcia, Sam Van Overmeire, Sambasiva Andaluri, Seung-jin Kim, Seyi Ogunyemi, Tim McNamara, Troi Eisler, Walt Stoneburner, William E. Wheeler, and Yerkebulan Tulibergenov. And I appreciate those who purchased this book early via MEAP and provided feedback and support.

I am very grateful for all the help, guidance, and patience that Elesha Hyde provided. She had the difficult task of shepherding this book throughout the process with immense grace. Her patience and support are greatly appreciated.

Thanks also go to Regrow.ag, who gave me the freedom and encouragement to write this book; my friend Cody, who has been there for me since elementary school; my high school English teachers, who encouraged my writing and helped me establish my voice; and Otto, for always being there to listen and never to judge.

—JOEL HOLMES

about this book

Martin Fowler's renowned book *Refactoring* emphasizes the primary goal of refactoring: to enhance the design of existing code. Readers familiar with the book will recognize its method of presenting various code segments, followed by improved alternatives that enhance readability, efficiency, or simplicity. While the strategies have evolved in the second edition, the core message remains unchanged: functional code can always be improved.

Refactoring to Rust outlines strategies for transitioning from one programming language to another while preserving the external behavior of the code. How is this achieved? As we will examine, Rust is designed to gradually replace other languages by integrating and decomposing existing code—much like the process of rusting iron—and substituting it with Rust code. Initially focused on replacing C++, the project has expanded to include JavaScript and Python.

Who should read this book

This book is focused on developers who specialize in other languages, such as C, C++, Python, and JavaScript, but want to learn Rust. While this book does not give you an in-depth view of the language, it does provide practical examples and use cases to change your code to Rust. No formal understanding of Rust is needed, although it is helpful.

How this book is organized: A roadmap

In line with Fowler's approach, we will present challenges in one language and demonstrate how to refactor these complexities in Rust. The goal is to maintain the underlying functionality of the application while using Rust's speed and safety to enhance the overall system.

Our exploration begins with an introduction to the Rust language, discussing its mechanics and comparing it to languages like C, C++, and Python. This information is framed within the context of refactoring, emphasizing how we can systematically improve our systems instead of allowing them to devolve into unmanageable code. We will also delve into Rust's advanced features, such as variable lifetime and ownership, which are crucial to mastering the language.

The first major focus will be on C, the foundational language for many others. In chapter 3, we will examine Rust's ability to create both safe and unsafe code, explore wrapping dangerous code in Rust, and utilize debugging tools. This foundation will prepare us for chapter 4, where we will integrate Rust into an existing C codebase, manipulate memory, and add new functionality to an NGINX server.

After our initial integration into another system, in chapter 5, we will consider Rust as a library tool. Creating packages compatible with other projects is an effective way to refactor applications, provided that these libraries offer enhanced functionality. We will also explore benchmarking and performance metrics to justify the transition from older languages to Rust. In chapters 6, 7, and 8, we will demonstrate how these packages can be used to refactor Python code, either by executing Python within Rust or by embedding Rust into Python.

The final two chapters will challenge us with advanced applications of Rust. Chapter 9 will focus on compiling Rust to run in web browsers using a new format called Wasm. Chapter 10 will use this technology to build a universal runtime, providing a flexible (yet complex) method for refactoring or interacting with existing code.

The chapters are not required to be read in order, and if you are already familiar with Rust, you can probably skip the first two chapters unless you want a refresher. If you are eager to jump into a particular language, chapters 3 and 4 focus on integrating with C and C++, and chapters 6 through 8 focus on Python, while chapter 9 focuses on JavaScript.

Chapter 10 can also be read on its own and offers a different way to refactor by changing the environment in which an application runs rather than changing the code itself.

Refactoring is more art than science. Both Martin Fowler's book and ours offer patterns to follow; it will be your responsibility to apply these techniques effectively.

About the code

The code covered in this book mostly focuses on Rust, but within the context of other languages. The basics of Rust are covered at the beginning, and then integration with C, Python, and JavaScript occurs throughout the remainder of the book. These languages are not taught but are expected to be known by the reader if they are refactoring code in that language.

There are no limitations on hardware or the software used. Nothing in the text is specific to a particular operating system or requires any special setup other than an installation of Rust. Additional libraries and tools are mentioned in the chapters, but the text is dedicated to this setup and is not required by the reader to do beforehand.

In addition, Rust is a growing language, and therefore, the syntax and libraries may shift over time. We have taken care to select stable libraries in our examples to accommodate this as much as possible.

The book contains many examples of source code in numbered listings and in line with normal text. In both cases, source code is formatted in a `fixed-width font like this` to separate it from ordinary text.

In many cases, the original source code has been reformatted; we've added line breaks and reworked indentation to accommodate the available page space in the book. In some cases, even this is not enough, and listings include line-continuation markers (➥). Additionally, comments in the source code have often been removed from the listings when the code is described in the text. Code annotations accompany many of the listings, highlighting important concepts.

You can get executable snippets of code from the liveBook (online) version of this book at https://livebook.manning.com/book/refactoring-to-rust. The complete code for the examples in the book is available for download from the Manning website at https://www.manning.com/books/refactoring-to-rust, and from GitHub at https://github.com/lily-mara/refactoring-to-rust.

liveBook discussion forum

Purchase of *Refactoring to Rust* includes free access to liveBook, Manning's online reading platform. Using liveBook's exclusive discussion features, you can attach comments to the book globally or to specific sections or paragraphs. It's a snap to make notes for yourself, ask and answer technical questions, and receive help from the author and other users. To access the forum, go to https://livebook.manning.com/book/refactoring-to-rust/discussion.

Manning's commitment to our readers is to provide a venue where a meaningful dialogue between individual readers and between readers and the authors can take place. It is not a commitment to any specific amount of participation on the part of the authors, whose contribution to the forum remains voluntary (and unpaid). We suggest you try asking the authors some challenging questions lest their interests stray! The forum and the archives of previous discussions will be accessible from the publisher's website as long as the book is in print.

about the authors

LILY MARA is a software developer based in San Francisco, California. She speaks domestically and internationally about Rust software development. She has been writing Rust since 2015 and uses it professionally for writing high-performance, scalable systems. She is currently writing software at Discord.

JOEL HOLMES is a software developer who has been focused on building cloud-native applications. He has worked at several startups to architect, design, and develop new products and services to help those companies develop and grow. Along the way, he was able to help establish tools and processes that helped development and increase quality. He lives in Pittsburgh with his family and currently works building cloud applications at Regrow.ag.

about the cover illustration

The figure on the cover of Refactoring to Rust is "Piemontoise d'Asti," or "A Woman from City of Asti in Piedmont," taken from a collection by Jacques Grasset de Saint-Sauveur, published in 1788. This illustration is finely drawn and colored by hand.

In those days, it was easy to identify where people lived and what their trade or station in life was just by their dress. Manning celebrates the inventiveness and initiative of the computer business with book covers based on the rich diversity of regional culture centuries ago, brought back to life by pictures from collections such as this one.

Why refactor to Rust

This chapter covers
- Why you may want to refactor an application
- Why Rust is a good choice for refactoring
- When it is and is not appropriate to start a refactoring project
- A high-level overview of methods you can use to refactor your code into Rust

If you have ever heard of the Rust programming language, you may have heard of software companies rewriting their code in Rust from a slower, interpreted language. A few of these companies have published blog posts lauding the performance benefits of Rust over their previous systems, and they tell a very tidy story: other languages are slow, and Rust is fast. Therefore, rewrite your code in Rust, and your systems will be fast.

While it may be tempting to think that we can all just rewrite our code when something better comes along, we all know the reality that software does not exist in a bubble of infinite resources. Performance improvements and technical debt payments need to be balanced with feature development, user requests, and the million other things that come along with modern software work. While reimplementing functionality in a new language, you also need to ensure that you are providing a consistent and reliable service to your users. How, then, can a developer hope to improve their code base while maintaining the rapid pace of development and reliability expected? The answer lies not in big bang–style rewrites but in incremental refactoring.

1.1 What is refactoring?

Refactoring is the process of restructuring code so that it performs better, is easier to maintain, or meets some other definition of "better." There is a distinction, however fuzzy, between refactoring and rewriting. The difference between the two comes down to the size of the operation.

Rewriting is taking a whole application or a large part of an application and reimplementing it from scratch. We might rewrite to take advantage of a new programming language or data storage model or just because the current the system is difficult to maintain, and it seems easier to throw it out and start over than to improve it.

Refactoring is rewriting on a much smaller scale. Instead of aiming to replace the current system wholesale, we want to find the parts of the system that need the most help and replace the smallest amount of code possible to improve the system. The benefits of refactoring over rewriting are numerous:

- Because the current system is the "new system," it can continue to run and serve customers while the refactoring is in progress. We can deploy a series of very small code changes to ensure that we know what change caused a problem. If we rewrite and deploy a whole new system all at once, how would we know what part of the system is causing errors if we see them?
- Existing code probably already has years of production experience and monitoring around it. The experience others have of operating and debugging existing code should not be undervalued. If a new system has a problem that you have no experience dealing with, how are you going to find it?
- Ideally, existing code will have automated testing associated with it. These tests can be reused to verify that our refactored code fulfills the same contract as the existing code. If your existing code does not have automated tests, refactoring is a great impetus to start writing them!

Figure 1.1 displays how deploys over time might be different in a rewrite versus a refactor.

When rewriting a system, changes must often be bundled and deployed together. This decreases velocity and increases the risk of errors in deployments. The longer features sit on a branch or in a stale staging environment, the more difficult it will be to debug that code when it is deployed. If all software has some risk of a bug, increasing the frequency of changes and decreasing the lines of code changed in deployments will help us find and eliminate bugs in the least amount of time.

When refactoring, we want to make small, independent changes that can be deployed as soon as possible. We add metrics and monitoring around our changes to

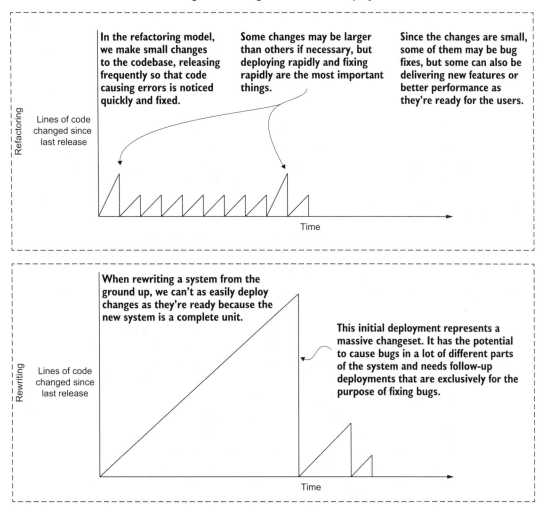

Figure 1.1 How refactoring and rewriting affect the size of deployments

ensure that when they are deployed, results remain consistent. This process allows us to quickly and consistently deploy small changes that fix bugs, add features, or improve the performance of our system.

That being said, we must consider a number of factors when refactoring code that's already doing its job:

- Ensuring that behavior is consistent between the old and new code
  - Using existing automated testing
  - Writing new tests that deal with new data structures introduced by the refactoring

- Deploying the new code
  - Determining the level of separation between the old and new code's deployment environments
  - Deciding how to compare the performance of the systems while they are both running
  - Controlling the rollout of the new system so that only a small percentage of customers access the new code paths

In this book, we will explore techniques and approaches that can be used to refactor code that is slow or difficult to reason about into Rust. We'll cover how to find the most critical parts of your code in need of refactoring, how to make your existing code talk to Rust, how to test your newly refactored code, and more.

1.2 What is Rust?

Rust is a programming language that emphasizes fast run time, high reliability, and memory safety. According to rust-lang.org, Rust is "a language empowering everyone to build reliable and efficient software." What does that mean?

- *Empowering*—Rust aims to give developers abilities that they would not otherwise have.
- *Welcoming*—The Rust community is extremely welcoming to everyone regardless of background. Rust developers span every skill level; some have Rust as their first programming language, and others know many. Some are coming from low-level programming, while others are application developers in languages like Python, Ruby, and JavaScript.
- *Reliable*—Rust software aims to be fault tolerant and explicit about how errors are handled so that nothing slips through the cracks.
- *Efficient*—Due to being compiled directly to machine code and the lack of a run-time garbage collector, Rust code is much faster right out of the box than code written in interpreted languages like Python, Ruby, and JavaScript. In addition, Rust provides developers with the tools to control lower-level details like memory allocations when required, which can lead to massive speedups while still keeping your application easy to understand.

1.3 Why Rust?

Rust combines memory safety, performance, and a fantastic type system; these features act together to keep your applications working correctly. The strong type system ensures that data exchange follows the correct contract, and unexpected data will not cause unexpected results. The lifetime and ownership systems permit you to share memory directly across Foreign Function Interface (FFI) boundaries without questions of where the responsibility for freeing resources lies. The strong guarantees around thread safety allow you to add parallelism that would have previously been impossible or highly risky. When you combine these features, which were initially designed to help developers write better Rust programs, you will see that they are ideal for aiding in incremental refactoring of almost any language into Rust.

1.4 Should you refactor to Rust?

There are a variety of reasons that you may want to refactor parts of your application into Rust, but the two primary goals that we will discuss in this book are performance and memory safety.

1.4.1 Performance

Let's imagine that you're working on an application written in a language like Python, Node.js, or Ruby. You've been adding new features to your application for a while, and you have a large codebase. However, as your user base grows, you have started to notice that you're paying a lot to scale your service with the required compute resources. Your application is being slowed down by some part of the request handling, but you're not quite sure where yet.

This book will guide you through techniques, like benchmarking and profiling, that will lead you to the places in your code that will benefit the most from a performance-oriented refactoring. Once we find these places, we will explore techniques to implement the same functionality in Rust, along with some performance tuning that can make your code as fast as possible.

Let's look at a small example. Imagine that the CSV-parsing code in the following listing is in your web application.

Listing 1.1 Python function: The sum of values from a column in a CSV string

```python
def sum_csv_column(data, column):
  sum = 0

  for line in data.split("\n"):
    if len(line) == 0:
      continue

    value_str = line.split(",")[column]
    sum += int(value_str)

  return sum
```

This Python function is fairly trivial; it returns the sum of all values from a given column in a CSV string. Writing the same function in Rust looks very similar.

Listing 1.2 The same CSV column summing function written in Rust

```rust
fn sum_csv_column(data: &str, column: usize) -> i64 {
  let mut sum = 0;

  for line in data.lines() {
    if line.len() == 0 {
```

The mut keyword indicates that a variable is mutable and its value can change over time.

Functions in Rust always have their parameter and return types explicitly labeled.

```
        continue;
    }
    let value_str = line
        .split(",")
        .nth(column)
        .unwrap();
    sum += value_str.parse::<i64>().unwrap();
}
sum
}
```

> The unwrap function at the end of these lines indicates that the functions used could possibly fail, and we're just going to panic if they do.

> This syntax (::<i64>) is called the "turbofish" operator in Rust; it is used when the compiler needs a hint about what type a function should return. Since the parse function can return different types depending on context, it is required for disambiguation (for more information, see chapter 3).

The Rust version of the function may look slightly more intimidating at first, but it is quite similar to the Python version:

- Both functions take two variables: a string of CSV and a column number to sum. The Rust version has explicitly labeled types, but the Python version still expects variables to have those types too, even if they're not labeled.
- Both functions return numbers; once again, Rust explicitly labels these at the top of the function declaration, while Python does not.
- Both functions raise errors if the data they are given does not match expectations. The Python version raises exceptions, and the Rust version panics (for more on error handling, see chapter 2).
- Both functions use the same naive CSV parsing algorithm to accomplish their goals.

Despite their similar appearance, these two functions have quite different performance characteristics. The Python version will allocate a list of strings containing each line in the CSV input string, put those strings in a list, and allocate a new list of strings for each row of comma-separated values in the data. Because of the strong guarantees that the Rust compiler can make about when memory is allocated and deallocated, the Rust version safely uses the same underlying string memory for the whole function, never allocating. Additionally, Rust's .split function on strings creates an Iterator, not a list. Consequently, the whole sequence of substrings is moved over one at a time instead of allocating the whole thing up front as the Python version does. This distinction is discussed in more detail in chapter 3. If the input data is many millions of lines long or has many fields, it will have a huge effect on performance.

We ran both of these examples with the same input file of 1 million rows and 100 columns. Table 1.1 highlights their respective time and maximum memory usage.

Table 1.1 Performance differences between Python and Rust CSV aggregation functions

Version	Run time	Max memory used
Python	2.9 s	800 MiB
Rust	146 ms	350 MiB

The Rust version represents a speedup of approximately 20 times, and it uses less than half the memory. These are significant performance gains without a significant increase in the complexity of the code. We cherry-picked this example; Rust may perform better or worse in your use case.

1.4.2 Memory safety

Alternatively, you may be working on a C or C++ project and want to utilize Rust for the benefits in safety that it provides over those languages. At compile time, Rust can verify that your application is safe from memory bugs like data races, dangling pointers, and more. By incrementally refactoring the critical parts of your codebase into Rust, you can ship software more quickly with less time spent worrying about the memory invariants of your code. Let the compiler do the worrying for you!

Many common bugs in C and C++ code are simply impossible to express in normal Rust code. If we try to write code that exhibits these bugs, the compiler will not accept the program because the Rust compiler manages one of the most difficult parts of programming in C and C++— memory ownership.

> **NOTE** Experienced C++ developers may wonder about developing with frameworks, like the popular Boost C++ framework. These kinds of library ecosystems do not exist in Rust in the same way that they do in C++, as most crates interface using standard library types and are compatible with one another.

Experienced C and C++ programmers will probably be familiar with the concept of memory ownership, but all these developers have to deal with it eventually. It will be discussed in more detail in later chapters, but the bottom line is that one handle always controls when a piece of memory is allocated and deallocated, and this handle is said to "own" that memory. In a typical C or C++ program, the programmer is totally responsible for maintaining the state of memory ownership in their heads. The languages provide very few tools to annotate what values are owned by what handles. The Rust compiler, on the other hand, requires that programs adhere strictly to its memory ownership model.

Memory ownership is one of the largest benefits of Rust development. Rust takes errors that were traditionally run-time errors with unpredictable or dangerous consequences and turning them into compile-time errors that can be resolved before the code is ever executed.

1.4.3 Maintainability

When projects written in dynamically typed programming languages start to reach into the tens of thousands of lines, you may find yourself asking questions like "What is this object?" and "What properties are available?" Rust aims to solve these questions about strong, static type systems. Static typing means that the type of every single value in your Rust program is known at compile time. Static typing is coming back in a big way these days. Projects like Typescript, Mypy, and Sorbet add type checking to

JavaScript, Python, and Ruby, respectively. These programming languages never had support for type checking, and the amount of effort that has gone into developing these systems highlights how helpful it is to *know* a value's type ahead of time.

The type system in Rust is very powerful, but in most cases, it stays out of your way. Functions must have their input and output types annotated explicitly, but the types of variables inside of functions can usually be determined statically by the compiler without any extra annotations. Just because the types are not labeled explicitly does not mean that they are not known. If a function is declared to only accept a Boolean as its input, you cannot give it a string. Many IDEs and editor plugins exist that can show you these implicitly defined types to aid in development, but you, as a developer, don't need to write them yourself. Some developers may be nervous about static typing, having last seen it when Java required you to use the following Kafkaesque syntax.

Listing 1.3 Initializing a map of numbers to lists of numbers in Java 1.6

```
HashMap<Integer, ArrayList<Integer>> map
  = new HashMap<Integer, ArrayList<Integer>>();

ArrayList<Integer> list = new ArrayList<Integer>();
list.add(4);
list.add(10);

map.put(1, list);
```

Specifying the type of every single local variable in each function is exhausting, especially when the language requires you to do it more than once. The same operation in Rust takes only two lines, with no explicit types required.

Listing 1.4 Initializing a map of numbers to lists of numbers in Rust

```
let mut map = HashMap::new();
map.insert(1, vec![4, 10]);
```

How does the compiler know what type of values go into `map`? It looks at the call to `insert` and sees that it is passed an integer as the key and a list of integers as the value. The same code can be written with explicit type annotations in Rust, but it is completely optional in most cases. We will cover some of these cases in chapter 2.

Listing 1.5 Initializing a map of numbers to lists of numbers in Rust with explicit types

```
let mut map: HashMap<i32, Vec<i32>> = HashMap::new();
map.insert(1, vec![4, 10]);
```

This strong type system ensures that when you revisit the code later, you can spend more time adding new features or improving performance and less time worrying about what the fifth untyped parameter to the `perform_action` function means.

1.5 *When not to refactor to Rust*

If you are looking at a greenfield project, you don't need to refactor it to Rust; you can write your initial solution in Rust! This book primarily assumes that you have an existing software project that you want to improve. If you're just starting out, you may benefit more from a general-purpose Rust programming book. Also, if your project is running in an environment that you don't have very strong control over, such as a PHP shared hosting service or tightly controlled enterprise servers where you don't have the ability to install new software, you may run into problems with some of the techniques outlined in this book.

A plan is always necessary when deploying any software project. How are you going to get it in front of users? The type of refactoring discussed in this book assumes that deploying new code is fairly low cost and can be done frequently. If you need to ship physical media to customers for new versions or your organization has a very rigid release structure, this book may not fit your needs.

When writing new software, you should always plan for how it will be maintained for years to come. If you are the only one excited about Rust development in your large company, you may be setting yourself up to be "the Rust person" for when this system inevitably has problems down the line. Do you want to be the only one responsible for maintaining this system?

1.6 *How does it work?*

Incremental refactoring of a mature production system is no simple task, but it can be broken down into a series of a few key steps:

1. Planning
   - What do I hope to improve by refactoring to Rust?
     - If existing code is written in C or C++, you should be thinking of how Rust can improve the memory safety of your application.
     - If existing code is written in an interpreted, garbage-collected language like Python, you will be mostly concerned with improving the performance of your application.
   - What parts of my code should be refactored?
   - How should my existing code talk to the new code?
2. Implementation
   - Mirroring the functionality of existing code in new Rust code.
   - Integrating Rust code into the existing codebase.
3. Verification
   - Using testing facilities of the Rust language to test new functionality.
   - Using your existing tests to compare results between the two code paths.
4. Deployment
   - Depending on the decisions you made earlier, there are different ways that your Rust code will need to be run when it is serving your customers.

- How can you effectively roll out your refactored code without affecting your end users?

Figure 1.2 lists these steps and some of their finer parts in more detail.

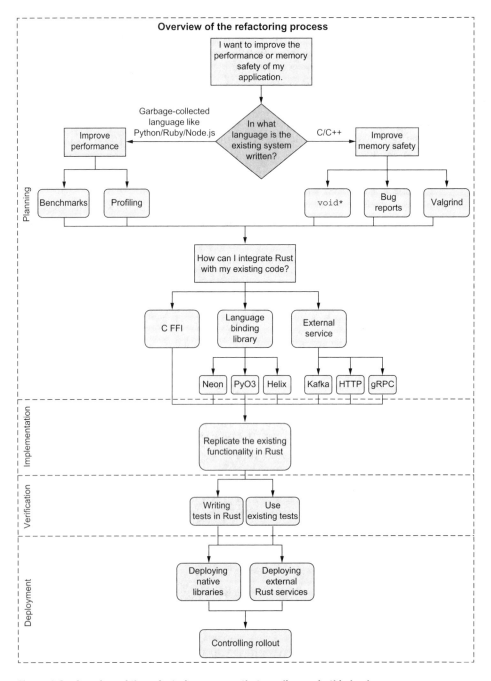

Figure 1.2 Overview of the refactoring process that we discuss in this book

As you can see from figure 1.2, the largest part of this process is planning. Performing this type of refactoring work is complex, and it requires you to know the effects of replacing code before that code is replaced. You must also carefully consider the performance and maintainability that comes with introducing new code patterns. After planning, the largest section is deployment, where you control which users access the new functionality instead of the old.

1.7 What will you learn in this book?

This book covers incremental refactoring in an abstract sense and then moves into how Rust can specifically help an incremental refactoring approach and how it can be incorporated into your applications. There are two main techniques for integrating Rust code into existing applications, and each has a few variations.

1.7.1 Calling Rust functions directly from your program

In this model, you write a Rust library that acts like a library written in your existing programming language. The various techniques are discussed at a high level in this section and will be discussed at length in later chapters. Figure 1.3 illustrates this model.

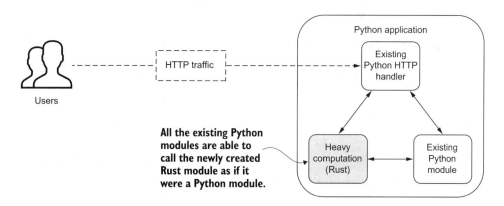

Figure 1.3 When calling Rust directly from your existing application, your Rust code looks like a normal module.

If you're refactoring a Python project, for instance, your Rust library will expose functions and classes that act like Python functions and classes. This method will have the lowest possible overhead for communication between your existing code and the new Rust code since they are both running as a part of the same OS process and can directly share memory with each other.

There are a few branches of this approach:

- Using the C FFI
  - This topic is discussed at great length in chapter 3, but the bottom line is that Rust will let you write a function that looks like a C function, and many other languages know how to call C functions.

– This approach is the most universal since most commonly used programming languages understand C FFI.
– This approach has the most potential for memory bugs, as the programmer will be directly responsible for ensuring that memory is allocated, deallocated, and passed back and forth correctly, and ownership is always clear.
– If your projects are in C or C++, you will use this integration technique.

- Using Rust libraries to bind directly to the other language's interpreter
  – Using this technique, you can write a Rust library that looks just like a Python, Ruby, or Node.js library, for instance.
  – This technique, which is often easier to implement than the C FFI approach, breaks down if no Rust bindings are available for the language that you want to use.

- Compiling Rust to WebAssembly (WASM) and using WASM FFI
  – WASM is a bytecode format for JavaScript engines, similar to Java bytecode. Many languages (Rust included) can compile to WASM instead of native machine code.
  – This approach is useful when using Rust with in-browser JavaScript engines or Node.js.

1.7.2 Communicating with a Rust service over the network

This technique relies on using a network protocol to communicate with a newly created Rust service. Figure 1.4 illustrates this concept.

This approach has several advantages and disadvantages compared with the previously discussed model:

- Advantages
  – Because this technique has no direct access to memory, you don't run the risk of memory corruption in the interop between the two languages.

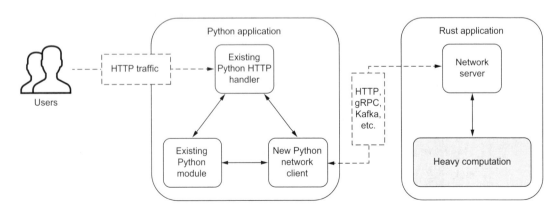

Figure 1.4 When Rust code is in an external service, there is additional overhead due to the network hop.

- This approach allows your Rust system to be scaled independently of your existing application.
- More developers have experience with networked communication between applications, so it is less of a conceptual jump than the idea of multiple programming languages coexisting in one application.
- Disadvantages
  - As alluded to in the last section, you will lose out on some performance due to the extra time it takes for data to be sent across the network.
  - There is additional operational overhead for adding an extra service with its own independent logging, monitoring, and deployment logic.

1.8 Who is this book for?

This book is written for programmers who already have several years of experience working with applications in a language other than Rust and are looking for ways to improve their applications' performance, safety, or maintainability.

This book will also benefit Rust programmers who want to apply their knowledge to help improve the performance or memory safety of existing applications written in other languages. There's a lot more code out there that isn't written in Rust than there is code written in Rust.

The code examples will, of course, mainly be Rust, but since this book covers moving from other languages to Rust, we need something to compare to. Chapter 3 has many C and C++ code examples, and many of the remaining chapters have code examples in Python to highlight the differences between it and Rust and show how the integration methods work. You do not need to be an expert in these languages; experience with other procedural languages in the C family should suffice.

Chapter 3 discusses many topics around memory safety that may be foreign to developers that primarily work in languages that have run-time garbage collection. These topics are not required for refactoring from these garbage-collected languages; they are mainly for the benefit of the readers coming from a C and C++ background.

1.9 What tools do you need to get started?

All of the software tools that you need to get started are readily and freely available. You will need

- A *recent Rust compiler*—Instructions for installing Rust can be found at https://www.rust-lang.org/tools/install.
- A *text editor suitable for programming*
- A *computer or virtual machine running a GNU/Linux operating system*—Most strictly Rust programming examples in this book will work on any operating system, but some of the examples are written assuming a GNU/Linux operating system:
  - If you are using Microsoft Windows, the Windows Subsystem for Linux (WSL) provides a convenient way to run Linux programs that integrate with your normal Windows environment.

- All examples in the book are tested on Ubuntu 20.04 running under WSL.
- *Libclang development packages*—Again, this is not strictly required for the Rust-only coding exercises, but many of the chapters use Libclang (indirectly) to generate code to talk between Rust and C/C++ code.
- *Python 3,* `virtualenv`, *and* `pip`—These are required to run the Rust-based Python extension modules in later chapters.

Summary

- Refactoring can be used to replace small parts of your code at a time. Making smaller changes more often can help improve performance without the pain and time investment of a large rewrite.
- Rust has a strong static type system that ensures inputs and outputs are clearly defined and edge cases are handled.
- Rust provides easy parallelism, meaning you can take already fast Rust code and use every bit of available CPU power to maximize performance.
- Rust can easily integrate with other languages and allows you to focus on delivering value without worrying about reinventing the wheel.
- Refactoring to Rust can improve performance, memory safety, and maintainability, which can help your software systems scale faster and with less expense in the long term.

An overview of Rust

This chapter covers

- Designing systems that properly utilize Rust's ownership system
- Visualizing Rust's lifetime system to aid in debugging
- Controlling allocations of strings for fast performance
- Enums and basic error handling

Before we can integrate a Rust library into an existing application written in another language, we first need to understand the basics of Rust programming. This chapter guides us through a simple application to manage digital artworks for an art museum and teaches us about how the ownership system works. Ownership and borrowing are considered by many to be some of the most challenging things for new Rust developers to learn. We're starting with them here instead of something simpler because these are the areas where Rust differs most from other programming languages, and they're at the core of all Rust programs. If we don't take the time to cover these important ideas now, it will make the rest of the book far more difficult. We're going to use an example that ties the ownership and borrowing components of Rust programs to ownership and use of digital artwork. This process should make reasoning about ownership easier, and we'll introduce tools for visualizing changes to ownership over time.

2.1 Ownership and borrowing

One of the biggest differences between Rust and other programming languages is the enforcement of a few very important rules about how data can be accessed and dependencies between different forms of data access. These rules are not overly complicated, but they are different from many other languages, which have no enforcement of such rules. The rules for ownership are as follows:

- Each value in Rust has a variable that's called its owner.
- There can only be one owner at a time.
- If the owner goes out of scope, the value is dropped.

When looking at Rust code for the first time, it may not be obvious that these rules are being followed. Procedural Rust code can look very similar to code written in other languages, and you may be able to follow along without any problems. However, you may find that when trying to edit existing Rust code or write your own, you have difficulty getting code that seems perfectly reasonable to compile. This difficulty is because the Rust compiler is enforcing these rules, which you have not fully internalized yet.

We will walk through a simple example problem to showcase how the ownership and borrowing rules can affect a Rust program. Let's imagine that you're approached by an art museum; they want you to design a system in Rust that allows them to manage their catalog of artwork digitally. The system should allow patrons to purchase tickets that give them the right to view works.

We'll start out by creating a new Rust project using Rust's package manager, Cargo. To start a new project with Cargo, we use the command `cargo new`, followed by the name of the project that we want to create:

```
$ cargo new art-museum
```

This code creates a new directory called `art-museum`; it has all the files we need to get started writing Rust. For now, we'll focus on the main Rust code file that is generated, `art-museum/src/main.rs`. Open that file in your favorite text editor, and we can get started.

When you first open the file, you may be surprised to find that it's not empty, and, in fact, it already contains what is perhaps the most famous of all programming example problems, the "Hello world!" program.

Listing 2.1 The "Hello world!" program in Rust

```
fn main() {
    println!("Hello world!");
}
```

The ! after println is an indication that this is a macro, not a function.

Most Rust programs have a main function as their entry point. All Rust function definitions contain the fn keyword, followed by the name of the function being defined.

We can run this program to verify that it prints out what we expect by using another Cargo command; `cargo run`. The `run` command instructs Cargo to compile our Rust application and run the resulting executable. `cargo run` will be one of our most frequently used commands:

```
$ cargo run
Hello world!
```

Let's replace the code in the "Hello world!" program with the beginnings of our art museum code. We'll start by defining a type that represents artwork in the museum.

Listing 2.2 Struct representing an artwork

```rust
struct Artwork {
  name: String,
}

fn main() {
  let art1 = Artwork {
    name: "Boy with Apple".to_string()
  };
}
```

Structs are collections of fields that represent single logical values. Rust structs are similar to classes in object-oriented programming languages, but they do not support inheritance as classes do. They are more similar to structs in languages like C++ or Go, as they allow developers to combine data with functionality.

When initializing a new variable in Rust, we use the `let` statement. The compiler is able to infer the type of the variable that we're creating based on the value on the right-hand side of the equals sign.

It may appear odd that `"Boy with Apple"` is not good enough to be a string on its own and requires the extra function call to be considered a `String`; we discuss this situation in more detail in section 2.3. For now, know that calling `to_string()` is required to turn a string literal into a `String`. The first operation that we might want to model is viewing a piece of art.

Listing 2.3 Allowing our art to be admired

```rust
struct Artwork {
  name: String,
}

fn admire_art(art: Artwork) {
  println!("Wow, {} really makes you think.", art.name);
}

fn main() {
  let art1 = Artwork { name: "La Trahison des images".to_string() };
  admire_art(art1);
}
```

The curly braces in the string literal passed to the `println!` macro will be substituted with the values given after the initial string argument. This process is similar to the format string style substitutions that languages like C and Go make available in the `printf` function and languages like Python provide in the `.format` method on strings.

We now have a function called `admire_art` that accepts a single `Artwork` as its only argument and prints a message about how fantastic the art is. This program should print the following:

```
$ cargo run
Wow, La Trahison des images really makes you think.
```

So far, this system seems pretty great: we have art, and we have quiet admiration. Both are key elements in any art museum. Since we're not running the world's smallest art museum, let's add in a second work of art!

Listing 2.4 A program where two pieces of art can be admired

```
struct Artwork {
  name: String,
}

fn admire_art(art: Artwork) {
  println!("Wow, {} really makes you think.", art.name);
}

fn main() {
  let art1 = Artwork { name: "Las dos Fridas".to_string() };
  let art2 = Artwork { name: "The Persistence of Memory".to_string() };

  admire_art(art1);
  admire_art(art2);
}
```

This program should have very unsurprising output for everyone following along:

```
$ cargo run
Wow, Las dos Fridas really makes you think.
Wow, The Persistence of Memory really makes you think.
```

Now, admiring two pieces of art is all well and good, but let's imagine that this museum has multiple patrons who want to look at the same piece of art. Listing 2.5 shows what this code might look like.

Listing 2.5 A program attempting to admire the same art twice

```
struct Artwork {
  name: String,
}

fn admire_art(art: Artwork) {
  println!("Wow, {} really makes you think.", art.name);
}
```

```
fn main() {
    let art1 = Artwork { name: "The Ordeal of Owain".to_string() };

    admire_art(art1);
    admire_art(art1);
}
```

If we try to run this seemingly reasonable program, we'll get a compiler error—a compiler error that will probably look quite foreign to those who have not developed in Rust before. Let's take a look at it:

```
$ cargo run
error[E0382]: use of moved value: `art1`
  --> src/main.rs:11:16
   |
8  |         let art1 = Artwork {};
   |             ---- move occurs because `art1` has type `Artwork`, which
   |                  does not implement the `Copy` trait
9  |
10 |         admire_art(art1);
   |                    ---- value moved here
11 |         admire_art(art1);
   |                    ^^^^ value used here after move

error: aborting due to previous error; 1 warning emitted
```

What's going on here? What does `use of moved value` mean? What is the `Copy` trait? What is Rust trying to tell us?

The Rust compiler is trying to tell us that we have violated the ownership rules and, therefore, our program is invalid. But before we can discuss the reasons why this code doesn't work in Rust, we need to take a brief detour to look at how memory is managed in other programming languages.

2.2 Memory management in other languages

Generally, computer programs store the data that they use or generate at run time in the computer's memory. Memory is usually divided into two parts: the stack and the heap.

The stack is used to store local variables created inside the currently running function and the functions that led to the current function being called. It has a small limit on its maximum size, often 8 MB. It always grows like a stack of papers, meaning whenever values are added or removed, they are added or removed from the top. As a result, the stack does not have gaps.

The heap, on the other hand, is only limited by the memory size of the computer on which the program is running, which may be gigabytes or terabytes. Consequently, the heap is used to store much larger data or data where the exact size is not known before the program runs. Things like arrays and strings are commonly stored on the heap. Memory associated with the heap is also referred to as *dynamic memory* because the size of the values on the heap will not be known until the program is running.

Let's imagine that we want to welcome a patron when they enter our art museum by saying "Welcome {name}." To do so, we need to first request that the computer set aside enough space in memory to store a patron's name, which we store in the variable name. This process is called *allocation*. Nothing else can be stored in that area of memory other than this patron's name value. We can replace or alter the value in memory by assigning a new value to name, but name will still always refer to the same area in memory.

We need to clean up the memory of our program periodically, or it will eventually fill with name values that we're not using. When we're no longer using name, after we've successfully printed our welcome message, we need to tell the computer that it's OK to reuse the memory that was associated with name for other purposes because we're not using it anymore. Rust refers to this clean-up process as drop-ing a value, but the more generic term is *deallocation*. In the past, there have been two common ways different programming languages allowed developers to allocate and deallocate memory:

- The developer can write code that explicitly requests the amount of memory required and marks the point at which the memory is no longer used and can be cleaned up. This process is called *manual memory management* because it requires manual effort by the developer to ensure that memory is allocated and deallocated when appropriate. Many languages with manual memory management automatically deallocate values from the program's *stack* memory when the function that allocated it returns, and the stack frame exits. The larger concern with these languages is the management of *heap* memory.
- The language can have extra code that runs in the background of all programs to periodically check to see when no variables are left that refer to allocated blocks of memory and deallocate them. This process is called *garbage collection* or *automated memory management*, because there is no manual step required from the developer to deallocate memory. These languages generally also have much simpler methods for performing allocation, preventing the developer from asking for too much or too little memory to store a value of a given type.

If you are interested in writing very high-performance programs, you are generally stuck using languages that provided manual memory management tools to the developer. Languages like C and C++ require the programmer to figure out how much memory is required and ask the computer to allocate exactly that amount of memory. Asking for too much can result in slow allocation times or overly high memory use. Asking for too little and erroneously using memory outside of your allocated block can cause massive problems. These problems can lead to things like programs crashing, exposing areas of memory that should be secret (think passwords, encryption keys, etc.), or allowing malicious users to inject code into your running program and hijack it. Trying to write a large program in a language that requires the developer to manage memory manually requires a lot of mental effort on the part of the developer—or at least a lot of documentation.

One of the most common problems that occurs with manual memory management is the idea of "use after free," which is what happens when you try to use an area of memory after it's been deallocated. It may have been repurposed to hold something else, it may have been zeroed, or it may still contain the data that you think it does. It's completely up to the compiler to do whatever it wants to do with deallocated memory.

Let's imagine that you want to write a simple program using an imaginary programming language, which we'll call "K." The K programming language is very similar to the Python programming language, with the exception that K requires the developer to explicitly deallocate dynamic memory by calling the `free` function on values. You must call `free` on every value allocated in dynamic memory, and you must call it exactly one time. If you attempt to use a freed value, your program will crash. Let's try to write our welcoming program using K.

> Listing 2.6 The welcome program written with K

```
def welcome(name):
  print('Welcome ' + name)

name = input('Please enter your name: ')
welcome(name)
free(name)
```

This code asks a user for their name, gives them a personalized welcome message, and then deallocates the memory used to store their name. This program is perfectly fine, you think to yourself, but most of the time when you're calling `welcome`, don't you need to `free` the string on the next line anyway? Let's move the call to `free` inside of the `welcome` function so we don't need to remember to call it.

> Listing 2.7 The welcome program with deallocation inside the `welcome` function

```
def welcome(name):
  print('Welcome ' + name)
  free(name)

name = input('Please enter your name: ')
welcome(name)
```

Moving the call to `free` inside of the `welcome` function saves us from needing to remember to call `free` each time `welcome` is called. It's quite obvious in this small example that the program is still valid, but we created a subtle undocumented behavior of the `welcome` function. Any string given to the `welcome` function is now unusable after it's called. If we have 10,000 lines of code, we now need to inspect each call to the `welcome` function to ensure that strings passed to it are never reused, or we risk crashing our program.

If we updated the `welcome` logic to keep a log of the patrons who entered the museum from a specific entrance, we would need to change the `welcome` function to once again not deallocate the strings passed to it. This process again requires us to examine the codebase, look at all calls to `welcome`, and determine if the name should be deallocated immediately after or put onto the log. The programmer must make all these decisions before the program runs, but the K language provides no tools to verify that the program is correct other than by running it.

Here, we can start to see the benefits of Rust's ownership system. With Rust, we have encoded at the type level information about when memory is allocated, when it is valid to use, and when it is deallocated. Knowing this information protects us from use after free errors and many other classes of memory corruption errors. They're simply not possible to express in Rust. The compiler will stop our programs from ever running if they violate the rules of Rust.

We can also see that Rust programs have a bit of the best of both worlds of garbage collection and manual memory management. We have the speed of manual memory management because no extra process is running in the background to scan memory in the Rust program, and we can rest easy knowing that the compiler will protect us from making memory errors that will cause our program to crash or worse.

Recall the code in listing 2.5. It is repeated here.

Listing 2.8 Repeating the code in listing 2.5

```
struct Artwork {
  name: String,
}

fn admire_art(art: Artwork) {
  println!("Wow, {} really makes you think.", art.name);
}

fn main() {
  let art1 = Artwork { name: "The Ordeal of Owain".to_string() };

  admire_art(art1);
  admire_art(art1);
}
```

When we defined our `admire_art` function, we told Rust that to call the function, the caller would need to provide an owned value of type `Artwork` to the function and that the function would take ownership of the value. Remember, in all Rust programs, each value can only ever have a single owner. Since our variable `art1` owns the `Artwork` value that it refers to, when we call `admire_art` with `art1` as the parameter, Rust removes the ownership of the value from `art1`, and moves the ownership of the artwork to the `art` variable inside of our `admire_art` function. This step is very important: after the initial call to `admire_art`, the `art1` variable is no longer valid because it no longer refers to anything and thus cannot be used. When we call the `admire_art` function with any `Artwork`, the memory associated with that artwork is deallocated at the time that the function completes.

Understanding ownership and movement is critical in writing Rust code, but equally important is the understanding of lifetimes.

2.3 Lifetimes

The concept of lifetimes in Rust is at the core of understanding the memory management process. All values in all programming languages have lifetimes, although most are not as explicit about it as Rust. The lifetime of a value describes the period of time when that value is valid. If it's a local variable in a function, its lifetime might be the time that the function is being called. If it's a global variable, it might live for the entire run time of the program. A value is valid in the time after its memory is allocated and before it is dropped. Trying to use a value at any time outside of this range is invalid. In languages like C and C++, using a value outside its lifetime may result in crashes or memory corruption errors. In Rust, it results in your program not compiling.

To aid in understanding, let's introduce a new type of visualization that we'll call the "lifetime graph." These graphs appear frequently in this chapter and periodically throughout this book. Before we try to visualize the error from listing 2.5, let's first look at a simpler example from earlier in the chapter. Figure 2.1 shows the lifetime graph for listing 2.2; the code is included for convenience.

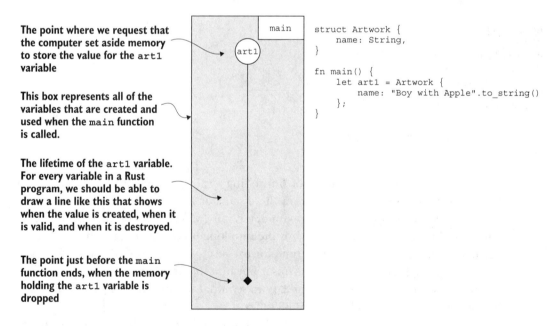

Figure 2.1 The lifetime graph for listing 2.2

Notice that the art1 variable has a single line that shows when the variable is created, when it is usable, and when it is destroyed. In Rust, values are dropped when they go out of scope. Local variables in a function are dropped just before the function ends. When we're having difficulty sorting out problems with Rust's memory management system, we rely on these graphs to help understand what's going on.

Now, let's take a look at what the lifetime looks like for listing 2.3.

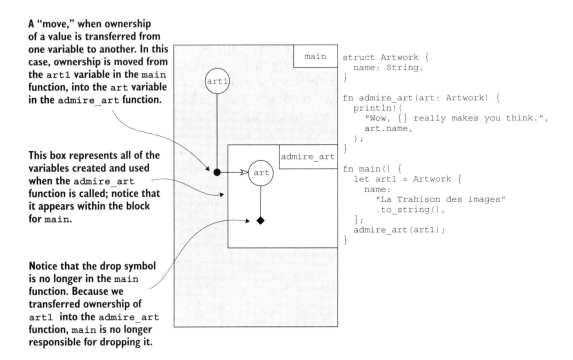

Figure 2.2 The lifetime graph for listing 2.3

Figure 2.2 introduces the concept of "move"-ing a value or transferring its ownership to another variable. As we know from the discussion of listing 2.3, when we call the admire_art function with our art1 parameter, it is "move"-d out of the main function and into the admire_art function. It is then no longer accessible from the main function. The disappearance of the lifetime for the art1 variable from the main function as soon as the admire_art function runs is our hint that it has been moved.

If we visualize the code in listing 2.4, we see what it looks like for two variables to coexist, with their own independent lifetimes.

We can see in figure 2.3 that each of the two Artwork variables is created in the main function and then moved into different call sites of the admire_art function. Each variable has its own independent lifetime, and each has an appropriate start, middle, and end.

2.3 Lifetimes

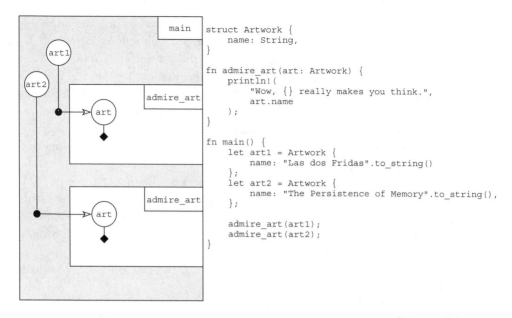

Figure 2.3 The lifetime graph for listing 2.4

When we try to construct a lifetime for listing 2.5, we begin to run into some problems. Let's see whether we can gain any insights into what's happening by looking at that visualization in figure 2.4.

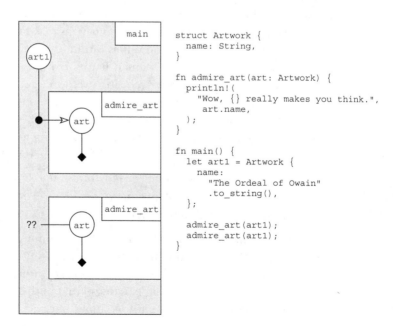

When we try to call `admire_art(art1)` the second time, `art1` has already been moved out of the `main` function and dropped. There is no value left in `art1` to use!

Figure 2.4 The lifetime graph in listing 2.5

Let's dissect what's happening. Notice that `art1` is moved into the `admire_art` function and is no longer reachable from the `main` function. When we try to call `admire_art` a second time, the value is gone; there's nothing there, which is what the error message Rust provided is trying to tell us. Remember that the headline of that error message is `use of moved value`. In the code, `art1` has moved out of the `main` function, but we tried to use it from the `main` function. In other words, we're trying to use a value after it's been moved, making it invalid.

At this point, you may be asking yourself, "So what? Why should values basically disappear when I pass them to a function? This seems like a waste of time to keep track of!" It may seem like an extra burden Rust places on the programmer just to make our lives more difficult, but the truth is that programmers using languages with manual memory management like C or C++ need to follow rules like this constantly. The only difference is that the compiler doesn't enforce the rules; it's up to the programmer to remember to follow them!

Let's briefly discuss how we can write functions that don't take ownership of the values they use.

2.3.1 References and borrowing

Unless you're writing a program that only uses every piece of data a single time, you'll find passing values by moving them to be extremely constraining. At some point, you will want to use the same value from multiple places or use a value without transferring its ownership. In Rust, you can *borrow* values instead of owning them. Borrowing a value in Rust always results in having a *reference* to the thing you are borrowing. References can be thought of as values that tell Rust how to find other values. If you imagine your computer memory as an enormous array of values, references are like indices in that array that allow you to find values within it.

Borrowing a value in Rust is much like borrowing a physical object in real life. Since we don't own the value we're using, we don't get to destroy it when we're finished with it. We may use it temporarily, but we always need to return it to the owner before the owner is destroyed. Borrowing comes with some rules. Like with ownership, these rules define the way that data moves through a Rust program, and they will eventually become second nature to you. Let's take a look at them:

- Each value may have either exactly one mutable reference or any number of immutable references at any time.
- References must always be valid.

The first rule may seem a bit odd to developers coming from languages that do not have a concept of controlled mutability. We discuss this concept in more detail in section 2.2.2, but first let's take a look at how references work more generally by applying them to our art program in listing 2.5. Recall that in that listing, we attempted to pass a variable to the same function multiple times but had difficulty because passing the variable moved it out of the `main` function. If we change the signature of the `admire_art` function from that example to take a reference to an artwork instead of the owned artwork, it works the way we expect.

> **Listing 2.9 A program admiring the same art twice**

```
struct Artwork {
  name: String,
}

fn admire_art(art: &Artwork) {      ◁──┐  Notice the use of the ampersand (&) on this
  println!("Wow, {} really makes you think.", art.name);
}                                          line. When this symbol appears in a type
                                           declaration, like &Artwork, it means that the
                                           type referred to is a reference to the type
                                           following the ampersand. Consequently, the
                                           function admire_art will only work with a
                                           reference to an artwork, not an owned one.

fn main() {
  let art1 = Artwork { name: "The Ordeal of Owain".to_string() };

  admire_art(&art1);    ◁──┐  When the ampersand appears in an
  admire_art(&art1);       │  expression, it is called the "borrow operator."
}                             As a result, the expression &x evaluates to a
                              reference to whatever is in the expression x.
```

Listing 2.9 looks very similar to listing 2.5. The only difference is a change to the type that `admire_art` accepts. Instead of requiring an owned `Artwork` to be passed to it, `admire_art` now accepts a reference to an `Artwork`. If we think about this from the perspective of the museum, it makes sense. We don't want to be creating and destroying artwork just so it can be admired one time; we want to be able to share the admiration of artwork with many people at many times. It also makes sense from a memory perspective: thrashing memory by creating and destroying values constantly is inefficient. It's much better to reuse memory when possible. If we compare the lifetime graph for listing 2.9, it's immediately apparent that it makes more sense. Let's look at the lifetime graph for this example to see how we can represent immutable borrows like this.

In figure 2.5, we can see that `art1` is no longer moved into either of the calls to `admire_art`. We pass in a reference, but `art1` remains owned by the `main` function. The memory associated with `art1` is not deallocated until the end of `main`, and since the references to it are dropped when their function calls end, that is perfectly fine.

So that we understand the difference between mutable and immutable references in Rust, let's take a look at the way that Rust handles mutable and immutable variables differently.

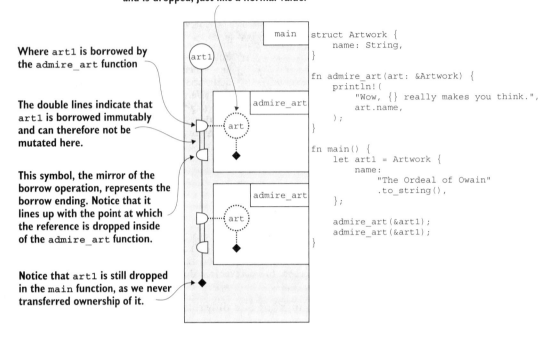

Figure 2.5 The lifetime graph for listing 2.9

2.3.2 Controlling mutability

All variables in Rust are tagged with a bit of extra information to help the developer (and the Rust compiler) reason about how the program will behave at run time. This information determines whether the variable is mutable, meaning it can be changed, or immutable, meaning it cannot be changed.

All variables in Rust are immutable unless explicitly labeled as mutable when they're declared. The following listing shows what it looks like to declare and use an immutable variable and a mutable variable.

Listing 2.10 Using immutable and mutable variables in Rust

```
fn main() {
    let x = 0;            ◁── The x variable's declaration has no annotation, meaning
    let mut y = 0;              that it is immutable and cannot be changed.
                          ◁── The mut keyword here before the variable
    println!("x={}, y={}", x, y);   name tells the compiler that the y variable
                                    is mutable and can be changed.
    y += 10;
    println!("x={}, y={}", x, y);   ◁── Because we want to mutate the value stored
}                                       in y, it must be declared as mutable. What
                                        happens if we change the y on this line to x?
```

It may seem odd at first that Rust requires that you specify up front whether a value will be changed later, but you will be surprised by how often mutations can be avoided in most Rust code. In addition, the Rust compiler knows about mutations, which means that it can statically verify some code that would otherwise be tricky to get right in other languages. We'll get into some more specifics in chapter 8, when discussing concurrent Rust code. For now, know that this is a small change to the way you declare variables in exchange for a big payout on your ability to reason about the code that you're running.

As we can see from listing 2.10, it's very easy to mark a variable as mutable. Making a variable mutable allows us to reassign its value. In an example this small, it may not be obvious why it's beneficial to have this control over mutability, but when we combine it with references, the benefits should become very clear. Let's return to our art museum code and see whether we can use the concept of mutability.

The current version of `admire_art` accepts an immutable reference, but what if we wanted each artwork to have a view counter that is incremented each time it is admired? In that case, we would need to edit the function to accept mutable references.

Listing 2.11 Incrementing a view counter on an artwork using mutable references

```
struct Artwork {
  view_count: i32,
  name: String,
}

fn admire_art(art: &mut Artwork) {
  println!("{} people have seen {} today!",
    art.view_count, art.name);
  art.view_count += 1;
}

fn main() {
  let mut art1 = Artwork {
    view_count: 0, name: "".to_string() };

  admire_art(&mut art1);
  admire_art(&mut art1);
}
```

The types changes from &Artwork to &mut Artwork, indicating that the artwork may be modified within this function.

This line requires a mutable reference. Since view_count is mutated here, we need a mutable reference to the owner of view_count, which is the Artwork that contains it.

Even though art1 is not mutated inside the main function, we create mutable references to it, which requires that we annotate the declaration with the mut keyword.

The expression to create a mutable reference also requires the addition of the mut keyword. &mut x creates a mutable reference to x.

In listing 2.11, it appears that we have achieved our goal of incrementing a number and reading it each time that an artwork is viewed. "But wait!" you might be saying, "I thought that there could only be one mutable reference to a value at any one time! Doesn't this program violate that rule?" If we take a moment to consider what happens in the program, we see that two mutable references never point to the same value. Figure 2.6 illustrates this point.

Notice the references we create have drop points after which they no longer exist. When we call `admire_art`, we give it a reference, and when the function ends, that reference goes out of scope and is dropped. In the time between the two function calls, there are zero references to `art1`. Consequently, our program is legal Rust.

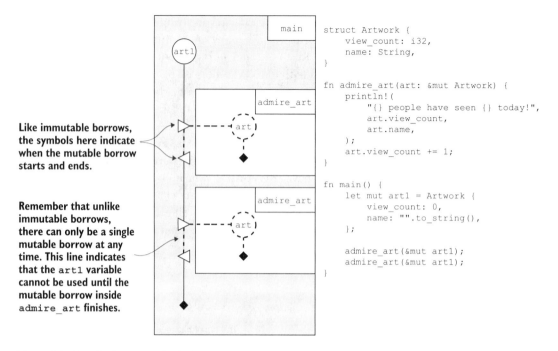

Figure 2.6 The lifetime graph for listing 2.11

Going back to the code in listing 2.9, we can see the value of the explicit mutable annotations. We know by looking at the type declaration of the admire_art function that it will not modify the Artwork value that is passed into it. Why? Because it accepts an &Artwork, not an &mut Artwork. You can look at a function declaration from library documentation and know, not guess, which functions will modify the values given to them and which functions will only view the values they are given. This structure has large, overlapping implications for security, performance, and debugging purposes. We'll explore that more in chapter 3 during our discussion of integrating Rust code with C and C++.

2.3.3 References and lifetimes

Just like values have lifetimes in Rust, so do references. References point to values, but they are also values themselves and are dropped when they go out of scope. In addition, references have an extra rule placed on them by Rust. Remember from our initial discussion of references that all references must be valid. What does that mean? Simply put, all references must point to valid values. Also, recall that lifetimes are the Rust compiler's way of determining whether a value is valid or invalid. Thus, references and lifetimes are very strongly tied together. Not only do references have lifetimes, but they must also be concerned with the lifetimes of the values to which they point. Let's take a look at a concrete example.

2.3 Lifetimes

Listing 2.12 A program attempting to use a value after it's been moved

```
struct Artwork {
  name: String,
}
fn admire_art(art: Artwork) {          ⟵  admire_art was changed
  println!("Wow, {} really makes you think.", art.name);     here to take an owned
}                                                            Artwork, not a reference.

fn main() {
  let art1 = Artwork { name: "Man on Fire".to_string() };

  let borrowed_art = &art1;      ⟵  borrowed_art is a
                                     reference to art1.
  admire_art(art1);

  println!("I really enjoy {}", borrowed_art.name);
}
```

When we try to run this code, we get a compiler error! Let's try to construct a lifetime graph and see where we went wrong.

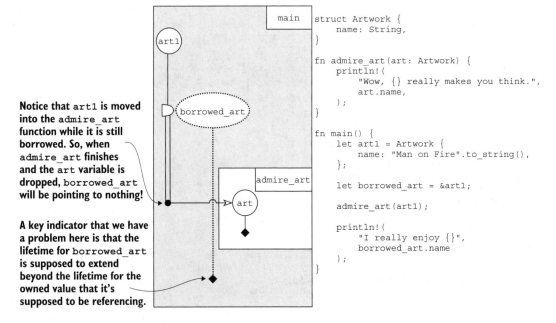

Notice that art1 is moved into the admire_art function while it is still borrowed. So, when admire_art finishes and the art variable is dropped, borrowed_art will be pointing to nothing!

A key indicator that we have a problem here is that the lifetime for borrowed_art is supposed to extend beyond the lifetime for the owned value that it's supposed to be referencing.

Figure 2.7 The lifetime graph for listing 2.12

As we can see from figure 2.7, our program is invalid because the borrowed_art reference is invalidated after the admire_art function is called. Let's look at another common pitfall of reference lifetimes.

Listing 2.13 A function trying to return a reference to a dropped value

```
struct Artwork {
  name: String,
}

fn build_art() -> &Artwork {
  let art = Artwork { name: "La Liberté guidant
    le peuple".to_string() };

  &art
}
fn main() {
  let art = build_art();
}
```

The return keyword is optional in Rust. The last expression in a function is used as a return value when there is no semicolon at the end of the line.

The build_art function in listing 2.13 is invalid for a slightly different reason. art is never moved; however, we try to return a reference to it, even though it is dropped at the end of the function. Let's look at the lifetime graph for this program in Figure 2.8.

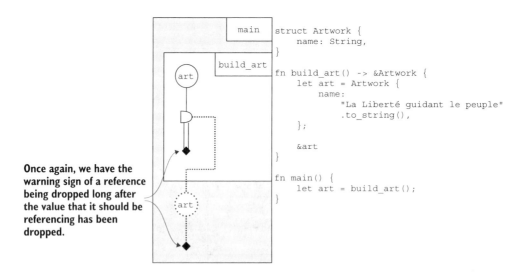

Once again, we have the warning sign of a reference being dropped long after the value that it should be referencing has been dropped.

Figure 2.8 The lifetime graph for listing 2.13

The lifetime graph in figure 2.8 shows the same common warning sign as the graph in figure 2.7. A reference extends past the drop point for the value that it should be referencing. It is possible to write Rust functions that return references, but those functions will usually also take references as inputs. If a function returns a reference but has no parameters or only takes in owned parameters, that's usually a sign that you will see a lifetime error when you to compile it.

2.4 Rust's string types

Nearly every programming language has some kind of support for string operations. They're just so useful; how could they not? Many programming languages have a `String` type, but Rust differs from the pack slightly: it has multiple types that are used to represent strings. The most common types are `String` and `&str`. Let's take a look at how they're both used.

`&str`, also called a string reference, is the simpler of the two types, consisting only of a pointer to a starting position in memory and a length. Due to its simplicity, `&str` is the more flexible of the two types because the reference can point to any string data anywhere in memory. It may be backed by a stack-allocated array buffer, a `String`, or even a string literal compiled into the program binary itself. If you're coming from C or C++, you may be aware that string literals in these languages are subtly different from other string values, even though they have the same types. String literals in C and C++ are read-only because they are compiled into the binary and live in read-only memory. If you try to run this C program, you will most likely get a segmentation fault (illegal memory access error at run time).

Listing 2.14 A C program attempting to write to read-only memory

```
int main(void) {
  char *str = "hello, world!";
  str[0] = '!';                    ◁── This line causes the
                                        segmentation fault.
  return 0;
}
```

The code in listing 2.14 is invalid because it attempts to write data into a read-only location. The C compiler doesn't know that `str` points to read-only memory because C types provide no information about whether values can be mutated. The equivalent type for string literals in Rust is `&'static str`. The new syntax here, the `'static` part, is a *lifetime annotation*. This marker to the compiler explicitly calls out how long this reference will be valid. We'll discuss this topic in more depth in chapter 4, but for now, you should know that `&'static` anything means the reference will live for the entire runtime of the program. Since string literals are compiled into the binary, `&'static str`s can reference them at any point without worrying about if they've been dropped (because they cannot be dropped). It's also legal in Rust to have a nonstatic reference to a string literal. Let's see what that might look like.

Listing 2.15 Nonstatic reference example

```
struct Artwork {
  name: &'static str,
}

fn admire_art(art: &Artwork) {        When we pass the &'static str into a
  print_admiration(art.name);         function that takes &str as its argument,
}                                ◁──  we turn a &'static reference into an &
```

```
fn print_admiration(name: &str) {
  println!("Wow, {} really makes you think.", name);
}

fn main() {
  let art1 = Artwork { name: "The Ordeal of Owain" };    ⟵  We no longer need to call
                                                             to_string() because the
                                                             expected type for name is
                                                             not String but &'static str.
  admire_art(&art1);
}
```

The fact that string references are immutable is relevant. Since they only point to memory buffers, with no knowledge of how those buffers are constructed or what extra capacity they might have, they can never be modified. If we want to modify our string values, we need to look at the other type of string in Rust, `String`.

2.4.1 Mutable strings

If you're coming from a language like Java, JavaScript, or Python, you may have first heard of mutability in the context of strings. In these languages and many like them, all strings are immutable; they cannot be changed after they are created. You may be telling yourself that you frequently change the values of strings by using += operations in these languages to concatenate a string onto another string, but you're not quite right. In languages with immutable strings, you cannot edit the memory of a string after it is created; you may only edit the string by creating a new string that contains the newly requested content.

Let's imagine that we need to create a program that adds a dot "." character onto a string each time some action occurs, which we will approximate with a `for` loop of 10 million iterations.

Listing 2.16 Creating a very large string one character at a time in Python

```
x = ""

for _ in range(0, 10_000_000):
  x += "."

print(len(x))
```

Each time the `for` loop in listing 2.16 iterates, it creates a new string that holds a copy of all the data in the current string plus one dot character. Consequently, to build our string of 10 million dots, our program needs to perform 10 million allocations, resulting in 9,999,999 copied strings that aren't useful. The process of copying memory to a larger storage area is referred to as *reallocation*. Let's contrast this process with Rust, which provides the developer with the ability to mutate strings.

In Rust, a `String`, or owned string, is made up of a growable, heap-allocated buffer that stores the character data. If you want to add extra characters to the end of the string, you can add them to the end of the buffer. If you want to swap characters out of the middle, you can move them around in the middle. These buffers have both a length and a capacity. The length represents the number of valid elements in the buffer, and the capacity represents the number of elements that the buffer can hold when it's full. The only time that Rust `String` values need to do the extra allocation and copying step like Python is when mutating the string would cause the length of the buffer to exceed its capacity. In these instances, the buffer will be reallocated with a capacity at least as large as would be required to store the new data. The Rust standard library does not guarantee any particular strategy for how the buffer will increase, but it is possible for the buffer's capacity to, for instance, double when pushing a single character onto a string, so that future character pushes will not require reallocation.

Let's see how to use a string to mimic the functionality of listing 2.16.

Listing 2.17 Creating a very large string one character at a time in Rust

```
fn main() {
    let mut x = String::new();

    for _ in 0..10_000_000 {
        x.push('.');
    }

    println!("{}", x.len());
}
```

String::new creates a new string with a buffer that has a capacity of zero. This function does not perform any allocations.

As you can see in listing 2.17, most of the buffer maintenance is hidden from the developer. Generally, the only interaction that you will have with it directly is to set its capacity to some predetermined size to try to limit the number of allocations that your code does. If we want to make the fewest allocations possible to have the fastest run time possible for our program, we can use the `String::with_capacity` function to explicitly set the capacity up front. In this way, our 10 million dots program could run with just a single allocation! If you're working with large strings, this ability can lead to a large performance gain.

The following listing demonstrates how to use `with_capacity`.

Listing 2.18 Preallocating strings to aid performance

```
fn main() {
    let mut x = String::with_capacity(10_000_000);

    for i in 0..10_000_000 {
        x.push('.');
    }

    println!("{}", x.len());
}
```

This line is the only one that needed to change to drop to a single allocation. The code using the string remains the same.

`String::with_capacity` is a performance optimization. The `String` values it returns can be used in the same way as the strings from `String::new`, but they may perform better in certain instances. It is safe to grow a string past its capacity using `push`; the string will reallocate its buffer internally.

You may be wondering about converting between Rust's two different string types, so let's explore how to do that. Both conversions are easy for the developer to perform, but one direction is much costlier for the computer at run time. Converting a `String` to an `&str` is very cheap. Since `&str` values are simply a pointer and a length, we can copy the starting pointer of the `String`'s buffer and its length. That's just two 64-bit integers to copy on most machines, which is very inexpensive to do. The following listing demonstrates.

Listing 2.19 Converting a `String` to a string reference

```
fn print_admiration(name: &str) {
  println!("Wow, {} really makes you think.", name);
}

fn main() {
  let value = String::new();

  print_admiration(value.as_str());
}
```

Going the other way, converting an `&str` to a `String` is a bit more expensive for the computer. Since all `String` values have their own heap-allocated buffer, creating a `String` from an `&str` requires the computer to allocate a buffer that is at least large enough to hold all the data in the `&str` and then copy all of the data from the `&str` to the newly created buffer. If you're doing that in a tight loop, it can tank your performance. The upside is that it's easy to see where this conversion is happening and limit it in most cases. You've been doing this conversion in this chapter; it's accomplished by calling the `.to_string()` method on `&str` values.

Listing 2.20 Converting a string reference to a `String`

```
fn print_admiration(name: String) {
  println!("Wow, {} really makes you think.", name);
}

fn main() {
  let value = "Artwork";

  print_admiration(value.to_string());
}
```

It's a common idiom for Rust to provide similar methods with `as_` and `to_` prefixes. `as_` generally means that you're getting a cheap reference to something, and `to_` indicates that you're allocating and copying to an owned data structure.

Like most of the material in this chapter, these different string types will prove helpful in the long run but can be confusing in the short term. Knowing when to use the different string types comes with experience; for now, we can generalize. If you're storing data in a struct, which will live for a long time, you should probably use a `String`, and if you're just passing read-only data to a function, it should probably take an `&str`. If you're not sure which one to use, `String` is the more flexible option, and the extra allocations that come from creating `String`s from string references can be cleaned up later. Now let's move on to the final area where Rust differs significantly from other programming languages—error handling.

2.5 Enums and error handling

Many programming languages use exceptions for propagating errors up the stack from the place where they originated to some kind of handling code. Rust differs from these languages. Errors are normal values handled with normal control flow elements that are not specific to the errors. First, let's use an example to walk through a simple use case for enums outside of the error context. We'll introduce error handling after we have a solid understanding.

2.5.1 Enums

FizzBuzz is a popular programming challenge to test a candidate's ability to use basic control flow elements such as loops and `if` statements. It goes like this: write a program that counts from 1 to 100. Each time you reach a number that is divisible by 3, print the word `"fizz"`. Each time you reach a number divisible by 5, print the word `"buzz"`. If a number is divisible by both 3 and 5, print `"fizzbuzz"`. Otherwise, print the number itself. We're going to implement FizzBuzz using one outer function to do the looping and printing and a helper function to perform the divisible checking. The helper function should return an enum that tells the `main` function what to do.

Let's start by writing our `main` function, which will perform the looping and printing of the numbers.

Listing 2.21 Function that loops through the numbers 1 to 100

```
fn main() {
    for i in 1..101 {
        println!("{}", i);
    }
}
```

This for loop will iterate over the numbers 1 to 100. The range syntax of x..y has an inclusive lower bound and an exclusive upper bound.

Next, let's take a first pass at our helper function that performs divisibility checking on an input value.

Listing 2.22 FizzBuzz program with a helper function

```
fn main() {
    for i in 1..101 {
        print_fizzbuzz(i);
    }
}
```

```
fn print_fizzbuzz(x: i32) {
  println!("{}", fizzbuzz(x));
}

fn fizzbuzz(x: i32) -> String {
  if x % 3 == 0 && x % 5 == 0 {
    String::from("FizzBuzz")
  } else if x % 3 == 0 {
    String::from("Fizz")
  } else if x % 5 == 0 {
    String::from("Buzz")
  } else {
    format!("{}", x)
  }
}
```

⟵ The separate print_fizzbuzz and fizzbuzz functions separate the result computation from the presentation of that result to the user. The benefits will become more clear as we go on.

⟵ format! is a macro that uses the same syntax as println!, but instead of printing its result to stdout, it returns a String.

Although this code solves our FizzBuzz problem, it has some room for improvement. In a large system, we don't want to pass strings around to communicate state. Rust is a strongly typed language, and we should take advantage of that strong typing to ensure that the return values of `fizzbuzz` are always handled correctly. What if we wanted to use the same divisibility checking but display the results in a different way? For example, we may want to send the result over some kind of network stream in a compact way. We'd need to parse the "Fizz"/"Buzz"/"FizzBuzz" strings and parse the numbers from strings as well. We can do better.

The proper way to communicate between the `print_fizzbuzz` and `fizzbuzz` functions is with an enum. Enums are types that can have exactly one of a predetermined number of possible values. Since our `fizzbuzz` function has four possible return values ("fizz", "buzz", "fizzbuzz", or something to indicate indivisibility), it's the perfect use case. Enums exist in many programming languages, but they are at the core of Rust. Later in this section, we'll see how enums are used for error handling in Rust, but for now, we'll stick to FizzBuzz. Let's write an enum that allows our helper function to communicate the different results of the helper function back to the `print_fizbuzz` function. The following listing shows what this enum looks like.

Listing 2.23 The enum holding the results of the `fizzbuzz` function

```
enum FizzBuzzValue {
  Fizz,
  Buzz,
  FizzBuzz,
  NotDivisible,
}
```

Each entry in the list of possible states for the enum is called a *variant*. We can see that all of the possible return values are represented within the `FizzBuzzValue` enum. Now let's take a look at how we can use it from our `fizzbuzz` function.

2.5 Enums and error handling

Listing 2.24 Returning an enum from a function

```
enum FizzBuzzValue {
  Fizz,
  Buzz,
  FizzBuzz,
  NotDivisible,
}

fn fizzbuzz(x: i32) -> FizzBuzzValue {
  if x % 3 == 0 && x % 5 == 0 {
    FizzBuzzValue::FizzBuzz
  } else if x % 3 == 0 {
    FizzBuzzValue::Fizz
  } else if x % 5 == 0 {
    FizzBuzzValue::Buzz
  } else {
    FizzBuzzValue::NotDivisible
  }
}
```

Now, if we want to use the return value of `fizzbuzz` to print out a message, we can use a `match` expression. `match` is similar to `switch` statements in Java, C, C++, and Go, but it has some additional functionality that we'll explore in a moment.

Listing 2.25 Using `match` expressions with enums

```
enum FizzBuzzValue {
  Fizz,
  Buzz,
  FizzBuzz,
  NotDivisible,
}

fn main() {
  for i in 1..101 {
    print_fizzbuzz(i);
  }
}

fn print_fizzbuzz(x: i32) {
  match fizzbuzz(x) {
    FizzBuzzValue::FizzBuzz => {
      println!("FizzBuzz");
    }
    FizzBuzzValue::Fizz => {
      println!("Fizz");
    }
    FizzBuzzValue::Buzz => {
      println!("Buzz");
    }
    FizzBuzzValue::NotDivisible => {
      println!("{}", x);
```

⟵ Each branch, or arm, of the match expression has a condition, the "big arrow" symbol (=>) and then an expression that will be evaluated if that condition is true.

```rust
    }
  }
}

fn fizzbuzz(x: i32) -> FizzBuzzValue {
  if x % 3 == 0 && x % 5 == 0 {
    FizzBuzzValue::FizzBuzz
  } else if x % 3 == 0 {
    FizzBuzzValue::Fizz
  } else if x % 5 == 0 {
    FizzBuzzValue::Buzz
  } else {
    FizzBuzzValue::NotDivisible
  }
}
```

This approach seems to be working well. We have effectively separated the computation of results from the presentation of those results to the user. In an example this small, it may seem odd to have this separation when it would certainly be less code to remove it or even put the `println!` macro calls inside the `fizzbuzz` function, but in larger programs, it is very beneficial to use enums to create a single, standardized way to represent values that may have multiple variants at run time.

Our `FizzBuzzValue` enum works well enough for this small example, but it does have a flaw that would show up in larger programs. The final variant in the enum, `NotDivisible`, has an extra piece of data that should be associated with it, but our code doesn't capture it—namely, the input number that wasn't divisible by 3 or 5. If we want to print this result in the program somewhere else, we'd need to come up with a way to store the number and the `NotDivisible` information. Rust's enums make this extra storage extremely straightforward. Each enum variant can hold, in addition to the data on which variant it is, any number of extra data fields. Let's see an example of what that might look like.

Listing 2.26 **FizzBuzzValue enum holding a number not divisible by 3 or 5**

```rust
enum FizzBuzzValue {
  Fizz,
  Buzz,
  FizzBuzz,
  NotDivisible(i32),
}

fn main() {
  for i in 1..101 {
    print_fizzbuzz(i);
  }
}

fn print_fizzbuzz(x: i32) {
  match fizzbuzz(x) {
    FizzBuzzValue::FizzBuzz => {
```

This i32 argument indicates that the NotDivisible variant will always have an i32 value associated with it.

```
      println!("FizzBuzz");
    }
    FizzBuzzValue::Fizz => {
      println!("Fizz");
    }
    FizzBuzzValue::Buzz => {
      println!("Buzz");
    }
    FizzBuzzValue::NotDivisible(num) => {       ⟵  The num variable is assigned a value
      println!("{}", num);                            from the i32, which is stored in the
    }                                                 NotDivisible variant of the enum.
  }
}

fn fizzbuzz(x: i32) -> FizzBuzzValue {
  if x % 3 == 0 && x % 5 == 0 {
    FizzBuzzValue::FizzBuzz
  } else if x % 3 == 0 {
    FizzBuzzValue::Fizz
  } else if x % 5 == 0 {
    FizzBuzzValue::Buzz                             We put the value of the
  } else {                                          number x into the NotDivisible
    FizzBuzzValue::NotDivisible(x)         ⟵       variant of the enum here.
  }
}
```

Our final match arm has changed slightly. Now we add the num variable, which gets its value from the i32, which is stored in the NotDivisible variant. This removal of values from container types like enum variants is known as *destructuring*. We know that every NotDivisible variant will contain an i32 because the enum declaration requires it. With this enum declaration, it is not possible to construct a NotDivisible without providing an i32. Further, it is not possible to access the i32 within the NotDivisible variant without some kind of checking to ensure that the FizzBuzzValue value holds a NotDivisible.

Now that we have a bit of an understanding about how to use enums and match, let's take a look at how we can use them for error handling.

2.5.2 Error handling with enums

Many programming languages represent errors as exceptions, and they have methods for communicating exceptional conditions in programs. Exceptions "bubble up" the stack until they encounter some special error-handling code, like a try/except block. In Rust, errors are represented in the same way as normal values, and they use the same control flow elements as normal values. This section will demonstrate how to write functions that might fail at run time, and how to handle the errors from those functions.

Let's imagine that we received a new requirement for our fizzbuzz function. Now, in addition to its functionality determining divisibility, the function should return an error if the number provided is negative. In our program, the values that will be provided to fizzbuzz are known because they are, of course, typed directly into the source code. However, imagine for a moment that they're coming from some user input somewhere. We should be able to handle these errors differently from the normal enum return values that the function has, and the `FizzBuzzValue` enum should not be expanded to account for the possible error state.

Let's take a look at how we might represent this possible failure condition in our program. The Rust standard library contains a type called `Result` which holds either an indication of a successful computation and the output of that computation or an indication of an error and more detailed information on that error. The following listing shows the declaration of that enum.

Listing 2.27 The definition of the `Result` type

```rust
enum Result<T, E> {
    Ok(T),
    Err(E),
}
```

The `<T, E>` syntax creates two generic variables, or type variables, T and E.

The T refers to the type variable T created on the first line. It indicates that the Ok variant can hold a value of absolutely any type.

Like the Ok variant, the Err variant can hold a value of any type.

The `Result` is one of the most commonly used types in Rust code because any function that might possibly fail returns its value wrapped in a `Result`. Let's revisit our program to see how it needs to change if the `fizzbuzz` function might return an error.

Listing 2.28 `fizzbuzz` function that may return an error

```rust
enum FizzBuzzValue {
    Fizz,
    Buzz,
    FizzBuzz,
    NotDivisible(i32),
}

fn main() {
    for i in 1..101 {
        match print_fizzbuzz(i) {
            Ok(()) => {}
            Err(e) => {
                eprintln!("Error: {}", e);
                return;
            }
        }
    }
}

fn print_fizzbuzz(x: i32) -> Result<(), &'static str> {
    match fizzbuzz(x) {
        Ok(result) => {
            match result {
                FizzBuzzValue::FizzBuzz => {
                    println!("FizzBuzz");
                }
```

The eprintln! macro works the same as println!, but it prints its message to STDERR instead of STDOUT. It is commonly used for showing error messages, as the error messages will not interfere with the normal output of the program, still taking place on STDOUT.

The success type is (), which is the unit type (see the next section). The type that we've provided for the Err variant is &'static str. Strings and &'static str are sometimes used for simple error communication like this.

Just like with the NotDivisible variant, we're not able to access the FizzBuzzValue inside the Result unless we have a match expression that ensures the value returned from fizzbuzz was successful or Ok.

```
        FizzBuzzValue::Fizz => {
          println!("Fizz");
        }
        FizzBuzzValue::Buzz => {
          println!("Buzz");
        }
        FizzBuzzValue::NotDivisible(num) => {
          println!("{}", num);
        }
      }
      Ok(())
    }
    Err(e) => {
      Err(e)
    }
  }
}

fn fizzbuzz(x: i32) -> Result<FizzBuzzValue, &'static str> {
  if x < 0 {
    Err("Provided number must be positive!")
  } else if x % 3 == 0 && x % 5 == 0 {
    Ok(FizzBuzzValue::FizzBuzz)          ◁──┐  All of the code paths in this function no longer
  } else if x % 3 == 0 {                     │  return just a FizzBuzzValue; they must now
    Ok(FizzBuzzValue::Fizz)                  │  wrap the FizzBuzzValue values in an Ok to
  } else if x % 5 == 0 {                     │  indicate that the computation succeeded.
    Ok(FizzBuzzValue::Buzz)
  } else {
    Ok(FizzBuzzValue::NotDivisible(x))
  }
}
```

A few new important things are going on in this code. The first and most obvious is the introduction of the `Result` values in the return types of `print_fizzbuzz` and `fizzbuzz`. Both functions now return `Result` values with the same error type (`&'static str`), but they have different types for `Ok`. `fizzbuzz` returns the same `FizzBuzzValue` that it did before, but what is `()` in the return type of `print_fizzbuzz`? It is the *unit type*, and we're going to take a look at it right now.

2.5.3 The unit type

The unit type is a type whose only possible value is itself and can hold no information. It represents the concept of nothing. It is similar to `null` in other programming languages but with a very important difference. In most programming languages that have `null` values, `null` is a valid value for any reference type. For example, the following Java code compiles and runs, printing `null` to the console.

> Listing 2.29 `null` in Java

```
public class Main {
  public static void main(String[] args) {
```

```
    String x = null;
    System.out.println(x);
  }
}
```

This code works because Java and many other languages allow all reference types to be assigned the value `null`. This can cause a great many bugs at run time, when programmers forget to check whether a reference holds the value `null` or not. Let's try writing the same code in Rust.

Listing 2.30 Unit type in Rust

```
fn main() {
  let x: String = ();
  println!("{}", x);
}
```

If we try to run this code, we'll find that it doesn't compile. The Rust compiler provides us with an error message explaining that the actual type `()` does not match the expected type of `String`:

```
$ cargo run
error[E0308]: mismatched types
 --> src/main.rs:2:19
  |
2 |     let x: String = ();
  |            ------   ^^ expected struct `String`, found `()`
  |            |
  |            expected due to this

error: aborting due to previous error
```

It doesn't compile because the unit type is its own type, completely independent from all other types. A better analog for the unit type than `null` is `void`. You may have noticed that the main method in the Java code in listing 2.29 returns type `void`. `void` is Java's type-level representation of nothing. In contrast to Rust's unit type, a value of type `void` cannot be stored in Java. You may also have noticed when writing our Rust code that we do not annotate the return types of functions if they don't return a value, not because they don't return a value, but rather because unannotated functions all return the unit type. The three functions in the following listing are equivalent.

Listing 2.31 Three functions that all return the unit type

```
fn foo() {
  println!("Hello!");
}
```
⬅ This unannotated function is how we normally write functions that don't return values. Note that this function still returns the unit type, but it is implicit.

```
fn bar() -> () {
  println!("Hello!");
}
```
⬅ This function introduces the explicit annotation for the unit type as the return type of the function.

```
fn baz() -> () {
  println!("Hello!");
  ()
}
```

In addition to the return type annotation, this function includes this explicit return of the unit value.

All three of these functions print "Hello" and exit, returning a value of the unit type. The only difference is that the latter two are more explicit. The `bar` function is similar to how a `void` function might be written in another language—explicit annotation of the return type but implicit return of the value itself.

Let's go back to the `print_fizzbuzz` function in listing 2.28. The declaration is

```
fn print_fizzbuzz(x: i32) -> Result<(), &'static str>
```

The `Result` returned has a unit type in its `Ok` type position, which means that when the `Ok` variant is constructed, it will always hold a value that provides zero extra information. If you think about what the function is doing, it makes sense. If the function completes successfully, what value would it possibly have to provide to its caller, other than an indication that it succeeded? Because the success case for the function doesn't communicate any meaningful extra information, we return the unit type when the function succeeds. Values of the unit type are generally not useful by themselves; we just need to use it in this instance because the `Result` type requires us to provide a type for the `Ok` and `Err` variants and `()` is the most sensible type for the `Ok` variant of a function that doesn't need to send back any other values. Before we added the result, the return type of `print_fizzbuzz` was actually `()`; it was just implicit rather than explicit as it is now.

Let's return to our FizzBuzz code and finish our look at error handling by introducing a custom error type.

2.5.4 Error types

As developers, we know what types of errors our code may encounter when running; it might encounter I/O errors, network errors, precondition failures, missing data, etc. Most Rust programs will create custom types that enumerate the errors that might be returned so that they can each be handled in their own way. After encountering a network error, you may want to repeat a request, while an error like a missing file should probably be logged, and the program should continue if possible or abort if not. Since we want to represent different possibilities for errors in a single type, we will create an enum. Since our FizzBuzz program only has one possible error—returned when the `fizzbuzz` function receives a negative number—let's see what that might look like.

Listing 2.32 The error type for our FizzBuzz program

```
enum Error {
  GotNegative,
}
```

The name `Error` is conventional, but it really can be named anything we want; remember, it's just a normal type. A program that does more operations may have many different variants on its error type, or it may have variants that wrap error types from other libraries. Now that we have an Error type, let's add it to our code.

Listing 2.33 FizzBuzz with custom error type

```rust
enum FizzBuzzValue {
  Fizz,
  Buzz,
  FizzBuzz,
  NotDivisible(i32),
}

enum Error {
  GotNegative,
}

fn main() {
  for i in 1..101 {
    match print_fizzbuzz(i) {
      Ok(()) => {}
      Err(e) => {
        match e {
          Error::GotNegative => {
            eprintln!("Error: Fizz Buzz only
              supports positive numbers!");
            return;
          }
        }
      }
    }
  }
}

fn print_fizzbuzz(x: i32) -> Result<(), Error> {
  match fizzbuzz(x) {
    Ok(result) => {
      match result {
        FizzBuzzValue::FizzBuzz => {
          println!("FizzBuzz");
        }
        FizzBuzzValue::Fizz => {
          println!("Fizz");
        }
        FizzBuzzValue::Buzz => {
          println!("Buzz");
        }
        FizzBuzzValue::NotDivisible(num) => {
          println!("{}", num);
        }
      }

      Ok(())
    }
    Err(e) => {
```

2.5 Enums and error handling

```
      Err(e)
    }
  }
}

fn fizzbuzz(x: i32) -> Result<FizzBuzzValue, Error> {
  if x < 0 {
    Err(Error::GotNegative)
  } else if x % 3 == 0 && x % 5 == 0 {
    Ok(FizzBuzzValue::FizzBuzz)
  } else if x % 3 == 0 {
    Ok(FizzBuzzValue::Fizz)
  } else if x % 5 == 0 {
    Ok(FizzBuzzValue::Buzz)
  } else {
    Ok(FizzBuzzValue::NotDivisible(x))
  }
}
```

We can see that including a custom error type is not a big change from what the code looked like before. Some return types changed, and we had to update what we did with the error in the `print_fizzbuzz` function since it can't be printed directly anymore.

Now, let's look at how the error handling in the `print_fizzbuzz` function can be simplified. Right now, it's returning any error it sees directly to its caller. It's not doing any inspection of the error other than "Is it an error or not?" This error-handling pattern is very common in Rust functions. If some function returns an error, just forward it to this function's caller, which is similar to how exceptions bubble up the stack until they hit error-handling code. The difference is that this choice is deliberately made by the programmer and not something that can be forgotten.

Since this pattern is so common, language-level support for it can be found in the syntax. This syntax is the question mark operator (`?`). The `?` operator is most frequently used on `Result` types, and here's how it works when you inspect a `Result`:

- If it contains an `Ok` variant, the expression evaluates to the value inside the `Ok`.
- If it contains an `Err` variant, it returns this `Err` from the function immediately.

Let's look at some real Rust code. Imagine that we want to call `fizzbuzz` and print out a message if it succeeds or forward along the error if it fails. The two Rust functions in the following listing solve the problem in the same way, but one uses the question mark operator. Remember, our `fizzbuzz` function returns a `Result<FizzBuzzValue, Error>`.

Listing 2.34 Example use of the ? operator

```
fn foo(i: i32) -> Result<FizzBuzzValue, Error> {
  let result = match fizzbuzz(i) {     ⬅  Because match is an expression, not a
    Ok(x) => {                             statement, in Rust, we can use it in an
      x                                    expression position, like assigning a variable
    }                                      to the result of a match expression.
```

```
      Err(e) => {
        return Err(e);
      }
    };

    println!("{} is a valid number for fizzbuzz", i);

    Ok(result);
}

fn bar(i: i32) -> Result<FizzBuzzValue, Error> {
  let result = fizzbuzz(i)?;

  println!("{} is a valid number for fizzbuzz", i);

  Ok(result);
}
```

> Note the use of the ? operator. This line will early-return from the function if the call to fizzbuzz returns an Err.

> The only way for this line to be reached is if the call to fizzbuzz returns an Ok.

You may notice that in the first function, we use the result of our `match` expression as the assignment for the variable `result`. Because the `Err` arm of the match expression returns from the function when it runs, if the `Ok` arm runs, the whole match expression will evaluate to `FizzBuzzValue`, which is inside of the `Ok`. So, the type of `result` in this function is `FizzBuzzValue`, not `Result<FizzBuzzValue, Error>`.

The functionality of the second function is identical, as the `?` operator is basically a condensed form of the match and early return seen in the first function. Let's apply this `?` error handling to our existing FizzBuzz code.

Listing 2.35 FizzBuzz program with ? added

```
enum FizzBuzzValue {
  Fizz,
  Buzz,
  FizzBuzz,
  NotDivisible(i32),
}

enum Error {
  GotNegative,
}

fn main() {
  for i in 1..101 {
    match print_fizzbuzz(i) {
      Ok(()) => {}
      Err(e) => {
        match e {
          Error::GotNegative => {
            eprintln!("Error: Fizz Buzz only
              supports positive numbers!");
            return;
          }
```

```rust
              }
            }
          }
        }
    }

    fn print_fizzbuzz(x: i32) -> Result<(), Error> {
      match fizzbuzz(x)? {                          // ◁── We added the ? operator, which will
        FizzBuzzValue::FizzBuzz => {                //     early-return from the print_fizzbuzz
          println!("FizzBuzz");                     //     function if fizzbuzz(i) evaluates to an Err.
        }
        FizzBuzzValue::Fizz => {
          println!("Fizz");
        }
        FizzBuzzValue::Buzz => {
          println!("Buzz");
        }
        FizzBuzzValue::NotDivisible(num) => {
          println!("{}", num);
        }
      }

      Ok(())
    }

    fn fizzbuzz(x: i32) -> Result<FizzBuzzValue, Error> {
      if x < 0 {
        Err(Error::GotNegative)
      } else if x % 3 == 0 && x % 5 == 0 {
        Ok(FizzBuzzValue::FizzBuzz)
      } else if x % 3 == 0 {
        Ok(FizzBuzzValue::Fizz)
      } else if x % 5 == 0 {
        Ok(FizzBuzzValue::Buzz)
      } else {
        Ok(FizzBuzzValue::NotDivisible(x))
      }
    }
```

Many Rust libraries are designed with well-formed error types that can be used to determine the root cause of failures. However, sometimes we need to do a bit of extra work to wrap overly generic errors with more specific contexts. Let's briefly look at how we can transform errors.

2.5.5 Transforming errors

Functions that can fail in Rust return values of the `Result` type. Thus, we can cleanly separate the error case from the success case when inspecting the return value of a function. Usually the type in the error variant expresses the cause of the error so that we can determine why the function failed, but in some cases, we can't.

Imagine that you need to write a function to perform some simple validations in a user creation tool. You must write a function `validate_username` that accepts an `&str`

username as input and returns a result indicating whether the validation succeeded or failed, along with the nature of the failure if present. Two library functions are provided to perform the validation: `validate_lowercase` asserts that the username is all lowercase characters, and `validate_unique` validates that this username does not already exist in the system. You do not write either of these validation functions, and you cannot change their type signatures. Their function signatures look like this:

```
fn validate_lowercase(username: &str) -> Result<(), ()>

fn validate_unique(username: &str) -> Result<(), ()>
```

Your `validate_username` function needs to have this signature and use this error type:

```
enum UsernameError {
  NotLowercase,
  NotUnique,
}

fn validate_username(username: &str) -> Result<(), UsernameError>
```

If we took a simple initial pass at this problem, we might come up with something like this:

```
fn validate_username(username: &str) -> Result<(), UsernameError>
{
  validate_lowercase(username)?;
  validate_unique(username)?;

  Ok(())
}
```

If `validate_lowercase` and `validate_unique` are written with the `UsernameError` type in mind, then this code is exactly how we would write the validation function. However, these functions both return the exact same error type—the unit type. We need some sort of mechanism to convert this unit value into values of `UsernameError` that match the individual validation functions. If `validate_lowercase` fails, we should return `UsernameError::NotLowercase`; similarly, `NotUnique` should be returned for `validate_unique`. We can accomplish this with a standard `match` expression, but it would be nice if we did not need to write a lot of unnecessary code for doing nothing in the `Ok` case.

One tool that we can reach for to help us out is a function on the `Result` type called `map_err`. If you are familiar with the `map` function in functional programming, you may be able to guess the purpose of the `map_err` function. `map_err` is a function that accepts another function, which we will call F, as its input and calls F when the result holds an `Err` variant. F accepts the type in the original `Result`'s `Err` variant as its input and returns a new value, which is wrapped in the `Err` variant of a new `Result`. That may sound a bit daunting, but the implementation is really quite simple:

```
fn map_err<T, E1, E2>(
  r: Result<T, E1>,
  transform: fn(E1) -> E2,
) -> Result<T, E2> {
  match r {
    Ok(x) => Ok(x),
    Err(e) => Err(transform(e)),
  }
}
```

That's it—that's the whole function! This implementation is slightly simplified since we have not looked at how to write instance functions yet. In practice, this freestanding function works exactly the same as `Result::map_err` in the standard library. Let's look back at our username validation example.

You have `Result<(), ()>` and you want `Result<(), UsernameError>`. To get it, you can use `map_err` and pass it a function with this signature:

```
fn(err: ()) -> UsernameError
```

The `err` value is the value in the `Err` variant of the original `Result`. The `Username-Error` returned from this function will be placed in the `Err` variant of the `Result` returned from `map_err`. If the `Result` holds an `Ok` variant, the function passed to `map_err` will never be called. Let's see how we can apply `map_err` to our username validation function:

```
fn validate_username(username: &str) -> Result<(), UsernameError>
{
  validate_lowercase(username).map_err(lowercase_err)?;
  validate_unique(username).map_err(unique_err)?;

  Ok(())
}

fn lowercase_err(x: ()) -> UsernameError {
  UsernameError::NotLowercase
}

fn unique_err(x: ()) -> UsernameError {
  UsernameError::NotUnique
}
```

This code will successfully match the `UsernameError` variants to the functions they should be associated with. You may be wondering if this method uses less code than using some `match` statements. In fact, using `map_err` with named functions and explicit parameter/return types doesn't reduce the amount of code much. However, we can use a closure to express the same thing in less code.

Closures, sometimes called *lambdas* by other programming languages, are anonymous functions written inline. They are very helpful when using functions that accept other functions as parameters, like `map_err`. Closures in Rust can contain a single expression or a block with multiple expressions. For now, we will look at closures containing a single expression. To write a closure that accepts two parameters and returns the sum of these two parameters, we would write the following:

```
|x, y| x + y
```

Parameters appear between the *pipe* characters separated by commas, and the pipes are immediately followed by the expression to be returned from the closure. Closures may have their parameter types explicitly written out using syntax that mirrors the standard Rust syntax for functions. However, annotating return types requires wrapping the return expression in curly braces. The following two closures are functionally identical and can both be used like normal functions:

```
fn main() {
  let add1 = |x: i32, y: i32| -> i32 {x + y};

  let add2 = |x: i32, y: i32| x + y;

  println!("{}", add1(3, 4));
  println!("{}", add2(3, 4));
}
```

> We don't need to tell the compiler that this closure returns an i32 because adding an i32 with an i32 can only ever result in an i32.

Although you *can* annotate return types explicitly, due to the nature of closures being used as arguments to other functions, which themselves provide type hinting to the compiler, it is almost never necessary to write types for closure parameters or return types in practice.

Now, by combining what we learned about `map_err` with closures, we can get a much more compact implementation of `validate_username`:

```
fn validate_username(username: &str) -> Result<(), UsernameError>
{
  validate_lowercase(username).map_err(
    |x| UsernameError::NotLowercase)?;
  validate_unique(username).map_err(
    |x| UsernameError::NotUnique)?;

  Ok(())
}
```

If we try to compile this code, we get a warning that the parameter x is unused in our closures. We can silence this warning by replacing x with an underscore, which hints to the compiler that we know we are ignoring the value and not using it:

```
fn validate_username(username: &str) -> Result<(), UsernameError>
{
  validate_lowercase(username).map_err(
    |_| UsernameError::NotLowercase)?;
  validate_unique(username).map_err(
    |_| UsernameError::NotUnique)?;

  Ok(())
}
```

2.5 Enums and error handling

Let's put all of this code together into one program that does the validation and shows the result to the user.

Listing 2.36 Program that validates usernames

```
enum UsernameError {
  NotLowercase,
  NotUnique,
}

fn main() {
  match validate_username("user1") {
    Ok(()) => println!("Valid username"),
    Err(UsernameError::NotLowercase) => println!(
      "Username must be lowercase"),
    Err(UsernameError::NotUnique) => println!(
      "Username already exists"),
  }
}

fn validate_username(username: &str) -> Result<(), UsernameError>
{
  validate_lowercase(username).map_err(
    |_| UsernameError::NotLowercase)?;
  validate_unique(username).map_err(
    |_| UsernameError::NotUnique)?;

  Ok(())
}

fn validate_lowercase(username: &str) -> Result<(), ()> {
  Ok(())
}

fn validate_unique(username: &str) -> Result<(), ()> {
  Ok(())
}
```

⟵ We didn't implement validate_lowercase or validate_unique because we are assuming that these are library functions that already exist.

Sometimes, instead of passing an error back to the caller, we want to assert that an error did not occur and exit the whole program if it did. To do so, we need to take a look at panicking with errors.

2.5.6 Panicking with errors

In Rust, errors are values. They are normal values that live in variables just like numbers or strings or any other kind of data your program might interact with. They're not scary; they don't have their own kind of special control flow logic (aside from explicit early returns with ?). They are simply values that need to be dealt with. How to deal with them is usually delegated to a caller at some level. The caller may log the errors and continue, retry the operation until achieving a success, or totally give up and exit the program with an error.

Let's go back to our FizzBuzz program and imagine that we want to rewrite the `print_fizzbuzz` function so that it never returns an error value and ends the whole program if it encounters an error. We can do this by removing the ? syntax from our match statement, reintroducing the `Ok`/`Err` matching from listing 2.33, and replacing the code that passes an `err` variant back to the caller with one that calls the `panic!` macro.

Listing 2.37 Panicking when `print_fizzbuzz` sees an error

```rust
enum FizzBuzzValue {
  Fizz,
  Buzz,
  FizzBuzz,
  NotDivisible(i32),
}

enum Error {
  GotNegative,
}

fn main() {
  print_fizzbuzz(-1);           // The call site in the main function is changed to be sure that our error handler is exercised.
}

fn print_fizzbuzz(x: i32) {     // The function no longer returns a Result. The possibility that the function may fail is no longer visible in its type signature.
  match fizzbuzz(x) {
    Ok(result) => match result {
      FizzBuzzValue::FizzBuzz => {
        println!("FizzBuzz");
      }
      FizzBuzzValue::Fizz => {
        println!("Fizz");
      }
      FizzBuzzValue::Buzz => {
        println!("Buzz");
      }
      FizzBuzzValue::NotDivisible(num) => {   // We removed the trailing Ok(()) at the end of this match branch in previous listings because the function does not return a Result anymore.
        println!("{}", num);
      }
    },
    Err(Error::GotNegative) => {
      panic!("Got a negative number for fizzbuzz: {}", x);
    }
  }
}

fn fizzbuzz(x: i32) -> Result<FizzBuzzValue, Error> {
  if x < 0 {
    Err(Error::GotNegative)
  } else if x % 3 == 0 && x % 5 == 0 {
    Ok(FizzBuzzValue::FizzBuzz)
  } else if x % 3 == 0 {
```

```
      Ok(FizzBuzzValue::Fizz)
    } else if x % 5 == 0 {
      Ok(FizzBuzzValue::Buzz)
    } else {
      Ok(FizzBuzzValue::NotDivisible(x))
    }
}
```

panic! is a new macro for us, so let's briefly touch on what it means. Rust's panic! macro is similar to the panic function in Go: it panics the current thread and unwinds the stack until the top of the thread's stack is reached. Since our program has only a single main thread, panic! will exit the program with an error state. Calling panic! from a background thread will exit that particular thread. It may seem odd to exit the program if we encounter a single error, but panic! is most useful for performing runtime assertions that guarantee that the program is not in an invalid state or exiting if an unrecoverable error is seen. If we run our code, we can see the results of panicking the main thread:

```
$ cargo run
thread 'main' panicked at 'Got a negative
  number for fizzbuzz: -1', main.rs:35:7
note: run with `RUST_BACKTRACE=1` environment
  variable to display a backtrace
```

We do get some helpful output from Rust telling us that we can provide an environment variable to get backtrace information. Let's try that out:

```
$ env RUST_BACKTRACE=1 cargo run
thread 'main' panicked at 'Got a negative number
  for fizzbuzz: -1', main.rs:33:7
stack backtrace:
   0: rust_begin_unwind
          at /rustc/library/std/src/panicking.rs:475
   1: std::panicking::begin_panic_fmt
          at /rustc/library/std/src/panicking.rs:429
   2: chapter_02_listing_35::print_fizzbuzz
          at ./src/main.rs:33
   3: chapter_02_listing_35::main
          at ./src/main.rs:13
   4: core::ops::function::FnOnce::call_once
          at rustlib/src/rust/library/
            core/src/ops/function.rs:227
note: Some details are omitted, run with
  `RUST_BACKTRACE=full` for a verbose backtrace.
```

Although not immediately apparent, looking at items 2 and 3 in the stack trace shows that the main function calls print_fizzbuzz on line 13, and print_fizzbuzz panics on line 33. In a more complex Rust program, stack traces can be very helpful. Rust disables stack trace reporting for panics by default, but it can easily be enabled as we see here.

Adding panicking to our print_fizzbuzz function made the code a bit more annoying to read and write. What if we wanted to get the same panic behavior without rewriting our `match` statement blocks—something that works a bit more like the `?` operator? We can do this by using the `.unwrap()` or `.expect()` functions on the `Result` we get back from `fizzbuzz`. Let's take a look:

```
fn print_fizzbuzz(x: i32) {
  match fizzbuzz(x).unwrap() {
    FizzBuzzValue::FizzBuzz => {
      println!("FizzBuzz");
    }
    FizzBuzzValue::Fizz => {
      println!("Fizz");
    }
    FizzBuzzValue::Buzz => {
      println!("Buzz");
    }
    FizzBuzzValue::NotDivisible(num) => {
      println!("{}", num);
    }
  }
}
```

Our function got a lot shorter, but it still panics when an error is encountered. Let's try to run it now:

```
$ cargo run
error[E0599]: no method named `unwrap` found for enum
`std::result::Result<FizzBuzzValue, Error>` in the current scope
  --> src/main.rs:17:21
   |
8  | enum Error {
   | ---------- doesn't satisfy `Error: std::fmt::Debug`
...
17 |     match fizzbuzz(x).unwrap() {
   |                      ^^^^^^ method not found in
   |                      `std::result::Result<FizzBuzzValue, Error>`
   |
   = note: the method `unwrap` exists but
     the following trait bounds were
     not satisfied:
           `Error: std::fmt::Debug`
```

We have not seen this interesting compiler error before! The `note` near the bottom tells us that `.unwrap()` does exist, but our call to it is not valid because our `Error` type does not implement the `Debug` trait. Traits are discussed in more depth in chapter 3, but for now, let's just say that types that implement the `Debug` trait can be printed to the terminal in a representation that is useful for developers. We can easily add `Debug` to our `Error` type using a special compiler directive on it called a `derive`. Here is what that looks like:

```
#[derive(Debug)]
enum Error {
  GotNegative,
}
```

A few different traits can be derived like this, but `Debug` is one of the most common. Essentially, this code tells the Rust compiler to generate code that can turn an `Error` value into a string representation so that we can determine what type of error it is by looking at it. Rust enums are represented at run time by numbers, and printing out the numeric value of an enum is not generally useful. `Debug` is very similar to the `toString` method in Java, but it can be autogenerated by the compiler with `derive`. The following listing shows what the complete program should look like.

Listing 2.38 Using `.unwrap()` to panic when an error is encountered

```rust
enum FizzBuzzValue {
  Fizz,
  Buzz,
  FizzBuzz,
  NotDivisible(i32),
}

#[derive(Debug)]
enum Error {
  GotNegative,
}

fn main() {
  print_fizzbuzz(-1);
}

fn print_fizzbuzz(x: i32) {
  match fizzbuzz(x).unwrap() {
    FizzBuzzValue::FizzBuzz => {
      println!("FizzBuzz");
    }
    FizzBuzzValue::Fizz => {
      println!("Fizz");
    }
    FizzBuzzValue::Buzz => {
      println!("Buzz");
    }
    FizzBuzzValue::NotDivisible(num) => {
      println!("{}", num);
    }
  }
}

fn fizzbuzz(x: i32) -> Result<FizzBuzzValue, Error> {
  if x < 0 {
    Err(Error::GotNegative)
  } else if x % 3 == 0 && x % 5 == 0 {
    Ok(FizzBuzzValue::FizzBuzz)
  } else if x % 3 == 0 {
    Ok(FizzBuzzValue::Fizz)
  } else if x % 5 == 0 {
    Ok(FizzBuzzValue::Buzz)
  } else {
```

```
    Ok(FizzBuzzValue::NotDivisible(x))
  }
}
```

Now that our error type implements `Debug`, let's try running our program to see how the panic looks:

```
$ cargo run
thread 'main' panicked at 'called `Result::unwrap()` on an `Err`
  value: GotNegative', src/main.rs:18:21
note: run with `RUST_BACKTRACE=1` environment
  variable to display a backtrace
```

Notice that the error message includes the location of the panic (line 18 of `main.rs` from listing 2.38), and we get the value (the `Debug` representation of the `Error`, which is `GotNegative`). If you are just starting a Rust program, the simplest form of error handling is often adding `.unwrap()` after all of the functions that might fail because it can be easier than setting up the proper `Result` return types with higher-level error handling. In larger programs, it is very important to have proper error-handling code. You don't want a web server to panic and crash at run time because someone sent a request with invalid data. However, it may be valid to panic during the initialization phase in a web server if config files have syntactic or semantic errors because there is no valid path forward in that scenario.

Using `.unwrap()`, we can get some information in the console, but sometimes we want to provide just a little bit more. `expect`, a function very similar to `.unwrap()`, allows us to write a small message that prints out along with the panics, so we can provide the user with some additional context for the error. Let's edit `print_fizzbuzz` to use `expect` instead of `unwrap`:

```
fn print_fizzbuzz(x: i32) {
  match fizzbuzz(x).expect("Failed to run fizzbuzz") {
    FizzBuzzValue::FizzBuzz => {
      println!("FizzBuzz");
    }
    FizzBuzzValue::Fizz => {
      println!("Fizz");
    }
    FizzBuzzValue::Buzz => {
      println!("Buzz");
    }
    FizzBuzzValue::NotDivisible(num) => {
      println!("{}", num);
    }
  }
}
```

Running the code now, we get a slightly better error message:

```
$ cargo run
thread 'main' panicked at 'Failed to run fizzbuzz:
  GotNegative', main.rs:18:21
```

```
note: run with `RUST_BACKTRACE=1` environment variable
  to display a backtrace
```

Now, without looking at the code, we know that the error was tied directly to the `fizz-buzz` function. The source of errors in this small program is quite obvious, but `expect` can be much more helpful than `unwrap` in larger programs.

Summary

- Rust's ownership and borrowing system provides fast performance without the worries of errors coming from manual memory management.
- The ownership of a value allows the Rust compiler to determine when it will be created, valid for use, and dropped before the program ever runs.
- All values in all programming languages have lifetimes, but Rust's compiler explicitly enforces the rules.
- The lifetime system in Rust lets the compiler know that references are always valid and that you will never read from invalid memory.
- Rust has multiple string types that give the programmer strong control over allocations. Some types allow mutability after creation, while others are read-only views.
- Enums can be used to store things that have a predefined list of possible values.
- Functions that might fail at run time return a `Result`, which is an enum containing an indicator of success or failure, plus a value in the success case and an error value in the failure case.
- It is not possible to use the success value from a `Result` without dealing with the possibility of an error.
- The unit type, or `()`, is a type and value that represents nothing.
- Creating a custom error type is the best practice for Rust code.
- `?` can be used to early-return from a function if a `Result` holds an error.
- `map_err` can be used to transform a `Result` holding one error type into a `Result` holding another error type.
- Closures can be used as arguments to functions that accept other functions as parameters.
- `panic!` can be used to unwind the stack of a thread when a program is in an invalid state and should exit.
- `.unwrap()` and `.expect()` can be used to panic if a `Result` holds an error.

Introduction to C FFI and unsafe Rust

This chapter covers

- Understanding C Foreign Function Interface and its relation to unsafe Rust
- Performing normally forbidden operations with `unsafe` Rust
- Refactoring a component of a C program into Rust

The last chapter provided a high-level overview of Rust code and discussed some elements of Rust that may be surprising or difficult to understand for new developers. Now that we're able to write simple Rust programs, this chapter walks through an example of how to embed Rust code within an existing C program.

If we want to embed Rust code within an existing application, we need some very well-defined semantics for how the two languages communicate, how values are passed back and forth between them, and how memory may or may not be shared between them. Ideally, this interface between the two languages will be well supported across a number of different languages and platforms so we can avoid rewriting code to perform a specific integration.

One well-supported method is to write functions that behave identically to C functions at run time. They use the same calling conventions, pass parameters and return values in the same way, and use types that can be represented safely in either language. This method is referred to as the *C Foreign Function Interface* (FFI). This chapter discusses how to write such Rust functions and use FFI support in Rust to integrate Rust code into a C application. We'll also discuss how to use `unsafe` blocks and functions to perform some operations that normal Rust code doesn't allow and when and why these blocks are necessary when writing FFI code.

3.1 Unsafe Rust

One of Rust's main selling points is the memory safety it affords application developers. However, we may want to shed some of that memory safety to improve performance, increase simplicity, or, most interesting to us, deal with types that the Rust compiler can't reason about. As we know from our discussion of the lifetime and ownership system in chapter 2, the Rust compiler can reason about when memory is safe to use and discard based on the adherence to a few rules in Rust code. However, the Rust compiler is not able to make any assumptions about the ways in which memory is allocated, accessed, or deallocated in any code other than Rust code. If we want to deal with dynamic memory that was not created from within Rust code, we need to use *unsafe* code.

> **NOTE** "Unsafe" is a bit of a misnomer because it does not invalidate the safety concerns that we have in the rest of our Rust code. It simply means that the developer is responsible for upholding Rust's safety rules without the compiler strictly checking them. A more correct term might be *unchecked*. However, `unsafe` is the language keyword used to mark these blocks, so we will continue to refer to them as *unsafe*.

Unsafe code blocks allow a few operations that are forbidden in safe Rust code:

- Dereference raw pointers
- Call functions marked as `unsafe`
- Implement traits marked as `unsafe`
- Mutate static values
- Access fields of a `union`

There really isn't anything beyond these five items. There are no other secret magic or dangerous operations. Without a doubt, the most fundamental of all of these unsafe operations is the dereferencing of raw pointers.

3.1.1 Raw pointers

As discussed in chapter 2, pointers are values that tell us the memory locations of other values. If we imagine our computer's main memory as a giant array of bytes, pointers are indices into that array. The value of a pointer is a memory address, which varies in size depending on your computer's architecture. On most modern systems, memory is addressed at the byte level using 64-bit addresses, meaning that pointers are 64-bit numbers that point to individual bytes in computer memory.

To dereference a pointer is to access the value that the pointer points to. Figure 3.1 shows the stack memory while a simple C program is running. It includes a character variable x, a variable that points to the character variable y, and a character variable that is assigned the result of dereferencing y. Imagine running this C program on a theoretical computer that has single-byte pointer addresses. The arrow on the left represents the line in the program that has just been executed, and the diagram on the right represents the stack memory at that point in time.

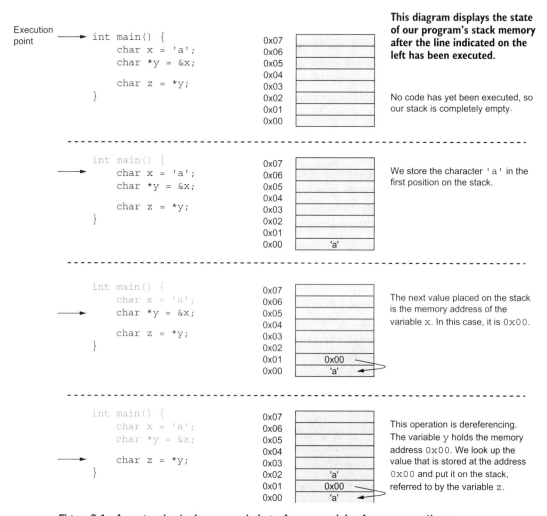

Figure 3.1 A program's stack memory during reference and dereference operations

The reason why this operation needs to be hidden behind `unsafe` blocks is very simple. Recall, from chapter 2, the second rule of Rust references: references must always be valid. At run time, a reference and a raw pointer are identical: they are both values that hold a memory address, which is used to look up a value in memory. The only difference is their behavior at compile time. Because Rust references have extra information about them known by the compiler, such as their lifetimes, the compiler knows that they are always valid and that dereferencing them is always safe. If a raw pointer is created, it is simply an address in memory; it has no lifetime or ownership information attached to it. The compiler has no way to validate that the memory it points to is valid, so it is up to the programmer to validate it.

One of the most common operations in Rust code operating between languages is reading through a buffer of data, such as a C-style array.

Listing 3.1 Reading the elements of a vector using pointer arithmetic

```
fn main() {
    let data: Vec<u8> = vec![5, 10, 15, 20];

    read_u8_slice(data.as_ptr(), data.len());
}

fn read_u8_slice(slice_p: *const u8, length: usize) {
    for index in 0..length {
        unsafe {
            println!("slice[{}] = {}", index,
                *slice_p.offset(index as isize));
        }
    }
}
```

- A Vec in Rust is a growable, contiguous block of memory, holding many values of the same type.
- The as_ptr method is perfectly safe.
- The two varieties of pointers in Rust are immutable pointers (*const) and mutable pointers (*mut).
- An unsafe block is required because we perform two unsafe operations: we call the unsafe offset function and then dereference the pointer that is returned.
- The offset function performs pointer arithmetic; it requires its input to be isize because it accepts negative offsets.

A `Vec` is analogous to a C++ `std::vector` or a Java `ArrayList` and similar to a `list` in Python, although `list`s may hold values of different types. A `u8` is an unsigned, 8-bit integer, a single byte. Combining these as a `Vec<u8>`, we get a growable block of memory containing individual byte values.

The `as_ptr` method is used to get a pointer to the data buffer inside of the `Vec`. Getting the pointer is a completely safe operation. We only need to introduce `unsafe` when we want to dereference the pointer.

Immutable pointers (`*const`) and mutable pointers (`*mut`) are very similar to immutable and mutable references, respectively. If a value is behind a `*const`, it cannot be mutated. If you need to mutate a value, you must use a `*mut`. One key difference between pointers and references in this respect is that an immutable pointer can be cast to a mutable pointer. It is the developer's responsibility to know when this action is safe or not safe.

3.2 C Foreign Function Interface

Now that we understand pointer dereferencing, we can write Rust code that communicates with C code. Reading from and writing to pointers that Rust code accepts from C requires us to apply our knowledge of pointer operations.

Imagine that we have an existing C application that solves simple arithmetic expressions in Reverse Polish Notation (RPN). Currently, this program accepts expressions containing a single operation. You have been tasked with extending the application to support multiple operations in a single expression. This extra functionality should be written in Rust; however, the current C code that performs user operations like text input and output should remain in C.

RPN is a way to write arithmetic expressions that negates the need for precedence rules for operations. It is essentially a simple programming language that operates on a stack machine. Elements are separated by spaces, and arithmetic operators work on the previous two items in the expression, instead of the preceding element and following element, as is the case with the more commonly used infix operations. Some example expressions written in infix notation and their counterparts in RPN are, respectively,

```
Infix: 3 + 4 * 12
RPN  : 4 12 * 3 +
     = 51

Infix: (3 + 4) * 12
RPN  : 3 4 + 12 *
     = 84
```

Figure 3.2 shows the stack that is used to calculate the result of the second RPN expression.

RPN avoids the ambiguity of infix notation by always operating in strictly left-to-right order. The orders of operations for the first and second RPN expressions is different because the operations are literally written in a different order. It is far easier to write a calculator that parses expressions in the RPN format because we can avoid the complications of ordering operations and just work from left to right.

Our C application currently takes newline-delimited integer arithmetic expressions from the user on STDIN, parses the expression, and then calculates and displays the result on STDOUT. We need to add support for multiple nested arithmetic expressions; right now, our calculator only does one operation at a time. We could keep all this code in C, or we could move the string-parsing code out of C and into Rust. Since we've heard some nice things about Rust, let's try using it to solve our problem. First, let's look at what the C code looks like.

3.2 C Foreign Function Interface

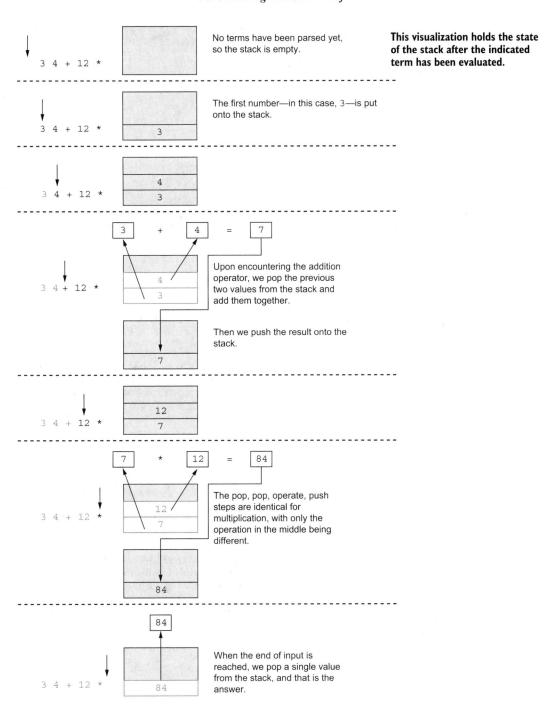

Figure 3.2   RPN stack used to calculate 3 4 + 12 *

Listing 3.2 Simple C arithmetic calculator program

```c
#include <stdio.h>
#include <string.h>

int solve(char *line, int *solution);

int main() {
  char line[100];            ◁─┐ Allocates space on the stack
  int solution;                 │ of the main function

  while (1) {
    printf("> ");
    if (fgets(line, 100, stdin) == NULL) {   ◁─┐ fgets reads data from
      return 0;                                 │ a file—in this case, STDIN.
    }

    if (solve(line, &solution)) {
      continue;
    }

    printf("%d\n", solution);
  }

  return 0;
}                                       ┌─ solve takes a pointer to the line of text read
                                        │  from STDIN and a pointer to an int, which
int solve(char *line, int *solution) {  ◁┘  solve writes the solution value to.
  int num1, num2;
  char operator;

  int values_read = sscanf(
    line, "%d %d %c", &num1, &num2, &operator);   ◁─┐ The format string here will
  if (values_read != 3) {                            │ look for an integer, followed
    return 1;                                        │ by a single character, followed
  }                                                  │ by another integer. These
                                                     │ values will be used to
  switch (operator) {                                │ compute the math expression.
  case '+':
    *solution = num1 + num2;    ◁─┐ In this switch statement, we calculate the
    return 0;                      │ result of the provided math expression
  case '-':                        │ and write the result to the integer
    *solution = num1 - num2;       │ pointed to by the solution pointer. Recall
    return 0;                      │ that solution points to an int variable on
  case '*':                        │ the stack of the main function.
    *solution = num1 * num2;
    return 0;
  case '/':
    *solution = num1 / num2;
    return 0;
  }

  return 1;
}
```

`char line[100];` allocates space on the stack of the main function to store up to 100 characters for the data we're going to read in from the user. Since we don't need to access multiple lines of text at once, we can keep reusing the same memory buffer over and over again. The `fgets` function will clear it when it reads data from STDIN.

`fgets` reads the data from STDIN and takes a `char` pointer as its first argument, which should point to the allocated memory where the data from the file will be read to. The memory must have allocated space for at least as many characters as the second argument. Because we allocated space for 100 characters, we give `100` as the second argument. C pointers and their associated memory don't contain data on where the allocated memory region ends, so for many functions, the developer needs to explicitly specify the size of memory regions, which ensures that `fgets` never writes past the end of our buffer.

`solve` returns an `int`, which is a status code. `0` means the function worked correctly, and `1` means that the string did not parse as expected.

If we put this code into a file named `calculator.c` and run it, it will solve simple arithmetic problems as expected:

```
$ gcc calculator.c -o calculator
$ ./calculator
> 3 40 *
120
> 120 3 /
40
> 40 1345 *
53800
> 53800 3 /
17933
```

It does great with these simple expressions, but what happens if we try to add extra operations?

```
> 3 40 * 2 -
120
> 10 10 * 10 *
100
> 10 10 * hello!
100
```

Anything after the first three items is ignored. Remember that we have been tasked with adding support for multiple operations in a single expression to this calculator. Let's see whether we can extract a key component from it and move it into Rust! The first step is to identify what we want to extract. Given that our program here only has two functions and one of them is the `main` function, we should start by moving the `solve` function into Rust.

Let's start a new Rust project with the Cargo command. In previous examples, we used `cargo new PROJECT_NAME`, but that creates a new project with a `main.rs` entry point—something that can run directly as an executable. We're not creating an executable; instead, we want to create a library. So, we need to provide an additional flag to `cargo new` to indicate this desire:

```
cargo new --lib calculate
```

Open the newly created `calculate/src/lib.rs` file, and we can begin. Recall that when creating an executable, newly created `main.rs` files include the "Hello world!" program by default. Similarly, when creating a library, Cargo will fill our `lib.rs` file with basic unit test scaffolding, which we can use to validate the functionality of our program. We go over cross-language testing in more detail in chapter 7; for now, just delete the contents of this file.

When we bring over the functionality of the `solve` function from C to Rust, we need to provide our C code with a function that has the same *signature* as the old `solve` function. The signature of a function refers to the types of all the values that a function accepts as parameters and returns, as well as the semantic meanings of those values. Recall the signature of our C function:

```
int solve(char *line, int *solution)
```

For our C code to call a Rust function, we need to write a Rust function that accepts a `char` pointer and an `int` pointer as parameters and returns an `int`. Here is what that same signature will look like in Rust:

```
fn solve(line: *const c_char, solution: *mut c_int) -> c_int
```

We can already glean more information from our Rust function's signature than from the signature of the C function. The Rust function tells us that the value of `solution` may be modified inside the function and the value of `line` will not be modified. The C code provides no indication, other than reading the code, that `solution` will be modified by the `solve` function. A developer can always add comments, of course, but comments may be inaccurate or become out of date.

The `c_char` and `c_int` types in the function signature are not built into the Rust standard library; they need to be imported from the `libc` crate. *Crates* are the Rust term for packages or libraries—collections of functions and types that can be used by others to perform certain tasks. The `libc` crate provides raw FFI bindings to the C standard library. The C standard does provide some relative sizing guarantees. For example, `int` is always at least as large as `short int`, but beyond that, a C `int` is platform specific. `libc` abstracts over some of this platform-specific nature by providing Rust types for the C primitives, whose sizing is determined by the platform on which they were compiled. Since many Rust programs don't need to interact with C libraries, this functionality is not included in the standard library and is instead in an external library.

3.2.1 Including a crate

When we've used Cargo in the past, it's been to create new Rust packages or to compile and run a Rust program. However, Cargo can do so much more than that. Cargo can also download, compile, and link dependencies and perform many other functions that would normally require lots of configuration in C or C++ programs. It is an all-in-one program for interacting with Rust. For now, we're going to ask Cargo to include `libc` when compiling our `calculate` crate.

Cargo's configuration file is `Cargo.toml`. All the information that Cargo needs about how to compile a crate is contained herein. It contains compiler feature sets to activate, third-party crates to download/compile and their versions, conditional compilation flags, and information that you need to include if you're creating a crate you want others to be able to use (e.g., your contact information, readme, version information, and more).

Open `calculate/Cargo.toml` in your editor. The content should be prepopulated by `cargo new` and should look something like the following listing.

Listing 3.3 Default Cargo configuration file

```
[package]
name = "calculate"
version = "0.1.0"
authors = ["You <you@you.com>"]
edition = "2018"

# See more keys and their definitions at
# https://doc.rust-lang.org/cargo/reference/manifest.html

[dependencies]
```

The `[dependencies]` section is the most commonly used section of the file for most Rust developers. Under this line, we type the name and version number of the crate we wish to include. Subsequently, when we use Cargo commands that compile our Rust program, Cargo will download the appropriate version of the crates we requested, compile them, and link them with our crate. We don't need to worry about setting compiler flags. There is no separate step; just write the crates you want, and Cargo will get them. To search for available crates, see crates.io. When Cargo is used to build and publish packages, they go (by default) to crates.io. Here you can see all of the publicly available crates that you can use when building Rust applications and crates of your own.

To include `libc` in our `calculate` crate, let's add a line under the `[dependencies]` section. Dependencies are specified with the name of the package, an equals sign (=), and the version of the package you'd like to use. At the time of this writing, the latest release of `libc` was `0.2.80`, so let's use that version. The `Cargo.toml` file after this addition should look like the following:

```
[package]
name = "calculate"
version = "0.1.0"
authors = ["You <you@you.com>"]
edition = "2018"

# See more keys and their definitions at
# https://doc.rust-lang.org/cargo/reference/manifest.html
```

```
[dependencies]
libc = "0.2.80"
```

We can include as many dependencies as we want here, but for now, we only need `libc`.

After making this addition, open the `calculate/src/lib.rs` file once again, and let's try writing a basic `solve` function.

> **Listing 3.4 The most basic `solve` function in Rust that compiles**

```
use libc::{c_char, c_int};

fn solve(line: *const c_char, solution: *mut c_int) -> c_int {
    0
}
```

The use statement includes types/functions/variables from other Rust crates or modules.

The last expression in a function is treated as a return value if it has no semicolon after it, so this line is equivalent to return 0;.

We discuss the modules system in chapter 5, but for now, just know that `use` includes items from other crates. A `use` statement isn't necessary for each item that we want to include, but if we left `c_char` out from this statement, we would need to refer to it as `libc::c_char` in our functions signature. The implicit return without a semicolon rule may seem odd at first, but when it is combined with some of Rust's other expressions, it becomes invaluable.

If we compile this code, we will see that Cargo includes the `libc` crate. Since we're not creating an executable that can be run directly, we can use the `cargo build` command to compile our crate, without trying to run it. The `cargo run` command, which we used in earlier examples, does the same thing as `cargo build`, but it will run the resulting executable if the crate is an executable:

```
$ cargo build
    Updating crates.io index
   Compiling libc v0.2.80
   Compiling calculate v0.1.0 (/home/you/calculate)
    Finished dev [unoptimized + debuginfo] target(s) in 5.81s
```

Now that we've compiled our `solve` function, let's see if we can call it from our C code!

3.2.2 Creating a dynamic library with Rust

If you've done much programming beyond "Hello world!" you've interacted with libraries before. Libraries are collections of functions, types, variables, or other things depending on what your programming language supports, which are packaged up together to accomplish some functionality so you won't need to reimplement it each time you want to use it. For example, if you want to perform HTTP requests in Python, you might use the `requests` library, or in C, you could use `libcurl`. It's much easier to import a library to make HTTP requests than it is to use raw sockets and `read`/`write` system calls.

Different programming languages have different formats for libraries. For example, Python libraries are simply collections of Python source code files, which the Python interpreter reads when imported. In C, there are a few different types of libraries, but the most commonly used on Unix-like operating systems, and the type that we'll be focusing on here, is the dynamic library.

We need to take several steps before our Rust `solve` function can be called from our C program:

1. Tell Cargo to compile our crate as a dynamic library that the C linker understands.
2. Add our newly created dynamic library to the linker search path.
3. Mark our Rust `solve` function so that the Rust compiler knows to compile it with C calling conventions.
4. Recompile our C program using the `solve` function from our Rust dynamic library.

Let's walk through these steps.

CREATING THE DYNAMIC LIBRARY

When Cargo compiles a Rust crate, by default, it doesn't produce something that a C compiler knows how to use. It generates something called an `rlib` file, which is a type of file specific to the Rust compiler and only used as an intermediate artifact that will be later used in some other Rust compilation. Instead of an `rlib`, we want Cargo to generate a dynamic library that the C linker knows how to use. We need to make another edit to our `Cargo.toml` file. This time we will tell it to output something compatible with C. Add these lines to your `Cargo.toml` file above the `[dependencies]` section:

```
[lib]
crate-type = ["cdylib"]
```

Cargo can generate many different types of crates, but the most common are the default `rlib` and the `cdylib`, which will cause Cargo to build a dynamic library compatible with native C programs. After making this addition to the `Cargo.toml` file, rerun `cargo build`.

ADDING THE DYNAMIC LIBRARY TO THE LINKER SEARCH PATH

When Cargo compiles anything, it goes into a directory called `target`. Inside of `target`, Cargo will create subdirectories for different build profiles. For now, this is just to `debug`, since by default Cargo produces binaries with debugging information and no optimizations, but we will look at how to create optimized builds later. You should see a few files and folders if you look in the `target/debug` directory, but the most important one is our new dynamic library, `libcalculate.so`. We need to put our dynamic library file in a location that the C compiler and linker will search for when running our calculator program. We can do so by creating a link in the `/lib` directory that points to our library file. The /lib directory stores dynamic library files, and it is searched by the C compiler, linker, and the operating system when starting our program:

```
$ ln -s $(pwd)/target/debug/libcalculate.so /lib/libcalculate.so
```

Now that we have our library file in a proper location, let's try to compile our C program against it. First, remove the existing `solve` function, shown in listing 3.2, from our `calculator.c` file. The new contents of the file are shown in the following listing.

Listing 3.5 C calculator program without the `solve` function

```c
#include <stdio.h>
#include <string.h>

int solve(char *line, int *solution);

int main() {
  char line[100];
  int solution;

  while (1) {
    printf("> ");
    if (fgets(line, 100, stdin) == NULL) {
      return 0;
    }

    if (solve(line, &solution)) {
      continue;
    }

    printf("%d\n", solution);
  }
  return 0;
}
```

It's important to keep the forward declaration of `solve` before the main function. This tells the C compiler that we're eventually going to define a function that matches the signature. We provide this definition by linking our Rust `solve` function.

Now we should be able to compile our C program and link it against our Rust library. We can tell the compiler that we want to link against the `libcalculate` library by providing the `-lcalculate` argument:

```
$ gcc calculator.c -o bin -lcalculate
/usr/bin/ld: /tmp/ccwBuRCw.o: in function `main':
calculator.c:(.text+0x13f): undefined reference to `solve'
collect2: error: ld returned 1 exit status
```

Hmm, it doesn't look like that worked. The error says that we're calling the `solve` function in our `main` function, but it doesn't see where a function called `solve` is defined. Consequently, the C linker can't find our Rust `solve` function. Let's look at how to fix that.

MARKING THE SOLVE FUNCTION AS C-LINKABLE

Even though we asked Rust to compile the `calculate` crate as a `cdylib`, it doesn't export every function and type in a C-compatible format. It only exports the specific functions and types that we ask it to. Three steps are required to make a Rust function callable from C. We need to

- Disable name mangling.
- Mark the function as public.
- Tell the Rust compiler to use C calling conventions for the function.

The following listing shows a properly annotated function.

Listing 3.6 Rust `solve` function that can be exported as compatible with C

```
#[no_mangle]
pub extern "C" fn solve(
  line: *const c_char, solution: *mut c_int) -> c_int {
  0
}
```

A number of new elements appear here, and they all have a slightly different purpose; let's look at them one at a time.

The first one, `#[no_mangle]`, is a function attribute macro, which instructs the compiler to not perform name mangling on this function. If you've done much C++ development, you may be familiar with the concept of name mangling. If not, name mangling refers to a process that the compiler uses to ensure that function and type names are unique inside of a system library or executable. On Unix-like systems, executables and system libraries do not have namespaces. Thus, if we define a `solve` function in our executable, there can only ever be a single `solve` function across all libraries that we're using and across all files. If any library has an internal function called `solve`, it will conflict with the one we're trying to create.

To overcome this problem, the Rust compiler puts extra information into the name of the symbols within it, which ensures that no symbol names overlap. If we leave name mangling enabled, our Rust `solve` function will be given a name like `_ZN9calculate5solve17h6ed798464632de3fE`. The method that the compiler uses to create these unique names is unimportant for our purposes here. Just know that predicting these mangled names is very difficult and unwieldy. Therefore, if we expect to call any Rust functions from C, which has no understanding of Rust's name-mangling scheme, we must use `no_mangle` to disable it for those specific functions.

The next new bit of code, `pub`, is a very common Rust keyword. It tells the Rust compiler that the symbol should be exported outside of the module in which it is defined. By default, all symbols in Rust are private and unexported. The way to export a function or type is to add the `pub` keyword before its definition, as we have done here.

Finally, we have `extern "C"`, which tells Rust to generate the `solve` function using C-compatible calling conventions. By default, the Rust compiler's calling conventions are not strictly compatible with C's. Rust supports a number of different calling conventions, but the most commonly used is the default Rust convention, followed by `"C"`.

Figure 3.3 breaks down what each of these new pieces of syntax is responsible for.

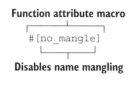

Figure 3.3 Anatomy of a C-compatible function declaration

Now that we're generating a function that can be called by C, let's make our Rust library and our C application work together.

RECOMPILING THE C PROGRAM AGAINST OUR RUST DYNAMIC LIBRARY
We can start by rebuilding our Rust library and recompiling our C program:

```
$ cargo build
$ gcc calculator.c -o bin -lcalculate
```

It works! Now let's see if we can run our new dynamically linked calculator program:

```
$ ./calculator
> 3 4 +
32686                ← Because we are reading memory that we never
> 4 10 +                wrote a value into, this number may be
32686                different each time this program is run.
> 10 1000000 *
32686
> hello
32686
```

So, our program runs, but it seems that we've lost the ability to do math. Our calculator always outputs an unpredictable number because we never assign a value to our `solution` variable. Since we've replaced our `solve` function with a no-op `return 0`, that makes sense. Let's write `solve` in Rust! Before we do any string parsing, we should make sure that we can communicate values as expected between Rust and C. Since `solve` takes a pointer to a `solution` out parameter, let's try writing a value to that. Because we're dereferencing a pointer to do this write, we'll need to wrap the operation in an `unsafe` block:

```
#[no_mangle]
pub extern "C" fn solve(
    line: *const c_char, solution: *mut c_int) -> c_int {    ← The is_null
    if solution.is_null() {                                     method
```

```
        return 1;
    }
    unsafe {
        *solution = 1024;
    }
    0
}
```

> Inside of the unsafe block, Rust's syntax for pointer dereferencing is the same as C's.

Recall that one of the reasons Rust requires pointer dereferences to happen within `unsafe` blocks is due to the possibility of `null` pointers. Before dereferencing untrusted pointers, we should check for null pointers. Dereferencing a null pointer in Rust is undefined behavior. The `is_null` method is built into the pointer primitive type. It cannot fail or cause an exception, like calling a method on a null object in Python or Java might.

Now, if we recompile our Rust code and rerun our executable, we should see the expected results:

```
$ cargo build
$ ./calculator
> 3 10 *
1024
> 1000 52 /
1024
> 1024 1 *
1024
```

Not that they're necessarily all *correct* results, but they are results. Notice that we did not need to recompile the C program to get the new results to show up in our executable. Because `libcalculate.so` is a *dynamic* library, it's loaded by the operating system each time we run `calculator`. So we can update our Rust code without needing to rerun the C compiler.

Now that we can write *to* C, we should try to read the string value that we're getting *from* C. C strings are contiguous blocks of platform-specific character types, terminated by a null character. Since we're only reading from our C string and not changing it at all, we can create an `&str` read-only string slice that points to the same memory created in our C `main` function. By doing this, we can avoid double-allocating the string. This is one of the great flexibilities of the multiple string types in Rust. If we only had the one `String` type, it could only be constructed by performing heap allocations in Rust code. This means that any time we want to use a string from C or any other language, we'd need to reallocate it, which would waste program memory and time.

There is a small overhead to creating string slices from untrusted input; we need to validate that they are valid UTF-8 before they can be constructed. All Rust strings are UTF-8, given that all string constructors either perform this validation or are `unsafe` and expect the developer to have done some other method of validation. Since our C strings may not contain UTF-8, we're going to perform that validation when we construct our strings.

We need to include another `use` statement to bring in a Rust type called `CStr`. `CStr` represents a C string that is borrowed memory from C. Recall the memory layout of `line`: it is a stack-allocated `char` array. Rust can never take ownership of this value, because if it tried to deallocate it, the memory would be deallocated from the stack of our C program. This is not possible and would probably result in a segmentation fault. Instead, our Rust program is just borrowing the C string, read-only, and all references to it will be dropped when `solve` returns. So, `CStr` is being used as a temporary value to facilitate the creation of an `&str`:

```rust
use libc::{c_char, c_int};
use std::ffi::CStr;

#[no_mangle]
pub extern "C" fn solve(
    line: *const c_char, solution: *mut c_int) -> c_int {
  if line.is_null() || solution.is_null() {
    return 1;
  }

  let c_str = unsafe { CStr::from_ptr(line) };
  let r_str = match c_str.to_str() {
    Ok(s) => s,
    Err(e) => {
      eprintln!("UTF-8 Error: {}", e);
      return 1;
    },
  };

  println!("line: {}", r_str);

  unsafe {
    *solution = 1024;
  }

  0
}
```

The `from_ptr` function is unsafe because it is the caller's responsibility to ensure that the pointer given is nonnull and the data it points to adheres to the expected structure of a C string.

The match expression in Rust is like an extremely powerful sibling of switch. In addition to matching on values, it can perform destructuring operations as it's doing here. The `to_str` function returns a Result value, which is either a successful Ok value or an Err value. To extract the success case, we need to use match, as is done here.

If we run our calculator program now, we can see that the line string is making its way into Rust:

```
$ cargo build
$ ./calculator
> 3 40 *
line: 3 40 *

1024
```

We can even validate that we're not reallocating the string, by comparing the line pointer we're given from C to the data pointer in `r_str`. Add the following line after `r_str` is created:

```rust
println!("r_str.as_ptr(): {:p}, line: {:p}", r_str.as_ptr(), line);
```

The `{:p}` placeholder in the format string tells `println!` to format these values as memory addresses:

```
$ cargo build
$ ./calculator
> 3 40 *
r_str.as_ptr(): 0x7fff78acb9b0, line: 0x7fff78acb9b0
line: 3 40 *

1024
```

We can see that they both have the same memory address, meaning that `r_str` wasn't reallocated on the heap; it's completely using borrowed memory from our C code. This won't make a huge difference in our simple program, but in larger programs with larger data being passed back and forth, it's important to know that we can effectively share memory between C and Rust.

Now that we have the boilerplate for communication between our C and Rust code, we can move on to solving the problem in Rust!

3.2.3 Solving arithmetic expressions in Rust

We currently have a `solve` function in Rust that does a lot of work with our C types that a normal Rust function doesn't do. It turns the C string into a Rust string, it writes to an `int` pointer as an out parameter, and it communicates an error state by returning an `int`. Ideally, we want to separate the code that does this FFI work between C and Rust from the code that contains our business logic. If we write a normal Rust function that has zero unsafe or FFI concerns, we could use it for other purposes later on down the line. We could call it from normal Rust code or from other languages, but if we tie it directly to our `solve` function, which is written especially for talking to C, we can't do any of that. Let's start a new function in the same file called `evaluate`, which will take in a string reference and return a result. The result communicates the success or failure of an expression's evaluation. We'll also create an `Error` enum for it, which we'll leave empty for now.

Listing 3.7 Basic evaluate function

```rust
enum Error {
}

fn evaluate(problem: &str) -> Result<i32, Error> {
  Ok(1)
}
```

We can update our `solve` function to use the new `evaluate` function to get the result that it will send back to our C code. This is also a good time to convert the Rust `Result` type into our `int` return code.

Listing 3.8 Updated solve function that calls evaluate

```rust
#[no_mangle]
pub extern "C" fn solve(
    line: *const c_char, solution: *mut c_int) -> c_int {
  if line.is_null() || solution.is_null() {
    return 1;
  }

  let c_str = unsafe { CStr::from_ptr(line) };
  let r_str = match c_str.to_str() {
    Ok(s) => s,
    Err(e) => {
      eprintln!("UTF-8 Error: {}", e);
      return 1;
    }
  };

  match evaluate(r_str) {
    Ok(value) => {
      unsafe {
        *solution = value as c_int;
      }
      0
    }
    Err(e) => {
      eprintln!("Error");

      1
    }
  }
}
```

We should also make sure that our program is still functioning as expected. So, go ahead and recompile the Rust library and rerun the calculator. We should see all expressions evaluate to 1 since that's what's being returned from `evaluate`:

```
$ cargo build
$ ./calculator
> 3 10 *
1
> 1000 52 /
1
> 1024 1 *
1
> hello
1
```

Now that we have that sorted, we shouldn't need to touch our `solve` function for a while. We can focus our attention on implementing `evaluate`. The first thing we need to do is split up the input on space characters and examine each piece separately. This is easily accomplished using the `.split` function available on `&str` values in Rust:

```rust
fn evaluate(problem: &str) -> Result<i32, Error> {
  for term in problem.split(' ') {
```

```
        println!("{}", term);
    }
    Ok(1)
}
```

If we run this code, we should be able to verify that we're splitting up the input on spaces:

```
$ cargo build
$ ./calculator
> 3 4 *
3
4
*

1
```

Next, we need to determine if the term that we're looking at is an operator, in which case we need to do some math with it, or a number, in which case we should store it somewhere for future math. We'll defer that "store somewhere" for just a moment until we get the parsing correct. We can use the `match` expression in a way very similar to the `switch` statement in C to determine if the string in the loop is an operator. We can add some simple prints to ensure that we're parsing the terms as expected:

```
fn evaluate(problem: &str) -> Result<i32, Error> {
    for term in problem.split(' ') {
        match term {
            "+" => println!("ADD"),
            "-" => println!("SUB"),
            "*" => println!("MUL"),
            "/" => println!("DIV"),
            other => println!("OTHER {}", other),
        }
    }
    Ok(1)
}
```

⊲ By using a variable name here instead of a string literal, we create a variable called `other`.

The `other` variable is valid inside of the block to the right of the "big arrow" (=>) on this line. `other` is not a keyword; it's just the name of a variable that we're creating. `other`'s block of the `match` expression will only run if no other blocks match the value provided. In our case, we only run the `other` block if the `term` does not equal any of +-*/.

If we run this code, we will get some surprising results:

```
$ cargo build
$ ./calculator
> 3 4 *
OTHER 3
OTHER 4
OTHER *

1
```

If our `evaluate` function was working correctly, we should expect the output to look like this:

```
> 3 4 *
OTHER 3
OTHER 4
MUL
1
```

But it seems that our program is not parsing the final term correctly, it's only parsing the * operator when it is not the final term in the expression. Let's add another `println!`, this one before our `match` expression. Up until this point, we've been using the `{}` placeholder for printing all values. It uses the `Display` formatter, which is intended to display data in an end user–appropriate form. We're going to change it up slightly by using the `Debug` formatter, which provides more detailed output. You can get the `Debug` representation of a value by using the `{:?}` placeholder:

```
fn evaluate(problem: &str) -> Result<i32, Error> {
  for term in problem.split(' ') {
    println!("Term - {:?}", term);
    match term {
       "+" => println!("ADD"),
       "-" => println!("SUB"),
       "*" => println!("MUL"),
       "/" => println!("DIV"),
       other => println!("OTHER {}", other),
    }
  }

  Ok(1)
}
```

If we run our program again, the problem becomes clear:

```
$ cargo build
$ ./calculator
> 3 4 *
Term - "3"
OTHER 3
Term - "4"
OTHER 4
Term - "*\n"
OTHER *

1
```

There is a trailing newline character in the final term of our expression. We can remove this from the `problem` string by using the `.trim` method, which removes leading and trailing whitespace. Let's see if adding `.trim` gives us the expected output. The `evaluate` function should now look like the following:

```
fn evaluate(problem: &str) -> Result<i32, Error> {
  for term in problem.trim().split(' ') {
```

```
    match term {
      "+" => println!("ADD"),
      "-" => println!("SUB"),
      "*" => println!("MUL"),
      "/" => println!("DIV"),
      other => println!("OTHER {}", other),
    }
  }

  Ok(1)
}
```

And here is the output:

```
$ cargo build
$ ./calculator
> 3 4 *
OTHER 3
OTHER 4
MUL
1
```

Since we're using a few nested methods on our input string, let's quickly check to see whether we're still using borrowed memory from the C stack. Remember that we verified that the &str that we pass to the evaluate function is shared memory from the C stack and not reallocated within Rust. We can use the {:p} formatter and the .as_ptr method to get the memory address of problem and term:

```
fn evaluate(problem: &str) -> Result<i32, Error> {
  println!("problem: {:p}", problem.as_ptr());

  for term in problem.trim().split(' ') {
    println!("term: {:p} - {:?}", term.as_ptr(), term);
    match term {
      "+" => println!("ADD"),
      "-" => println!("SUB"),
      "*" => println!("MUL"),
      "/" => println!("DIV"),
      other => println!("OTHER {}", other),
    }
  }

  Ok(1)
}
```

If the memory is still being shared from the C stack, problem and the first value of term should point to the same location in memory, and subsequent values should be offset by the number of characters in the substring. Running this validates our hypothesis that the memory is still shared from C:

```
$ cargo build
$ ./calculator
> 3 4 *
problem: 0x7ffc117917b0
```

The exact addresses shown in the output will be different on your computer and may be different each time the program is run.

```
term    : 0x7ffc117917b0
OTHER 3
term    : 0x7ffc117917b2
OTHER 4
term    : 0x7ffc117917b4
MUL
1
```

◁── The memory location of term and problem is the same, so the memory is still being shared for our string buffers.

The memory location has changed by 2 bytes, a single byte for the 3 character and another byte for the space character.

Our memory is still shared! We've never reallocated our string from C's stack. Since we don't need to change the value inside the string buffer, only the part of the string buffer we're viewing, we never need to reallocate it. With Rust's &str type, we can perform as many substring operations as we want, and we never need to reallocate. This ability is a huge boon for memory and time efficiency. It's inefficient to have many copies of the same data sitting around, and it takes time to reallocate and copy string buffers that will only be used once.

Next, we need to take the terms that are not operators and try to parse them as integers. We can do this using the .parse method, available on strings. .parse is generic over its return type, meaning it could return an int of varying sizes, a floating-point number, or a great deal of other types. We need to tell the parse method the return type we want, which will determine the parsing logic it will use. We'll also need to add a variant to our Error enum to account for the possible failure of .parse:

```
enum Error {
  InvalidNumber,
}

fn evaluate(problem: &str) -> Result<i32, Error> {
  for term in problem.trim().split(' ') {
    match term {
      "+" => println!("ADD"),
      "-" => println!("SUB"),
      "*" => println!("MUL"),
      "/" => println!("DIV"),
      other => match other.parse::<i32>() {
        Ok(value) => println!("NUM {}", value),
        Err(_) => return Err(Error::InvalidNumber),
      }
    }
  }

  Ok(1)
}
```

Running this yields no surprises:

```
$ cargo build
$ ./calculator
> 3 4 *
NUM 3
NUM 4
MUL
1
> 3 4 hello
```

```
NUM 3
NUM 4
Error
```

At this stage, we want to begin exploring how we might start doing math. Since our calculator is parsing RPN expressions, we need a simple stack data structure, implemented on top of a double-ended queue. Rust's standard library provides a double-ended queue in the form of the `VecDeque` type. A `VecDeque` is a double-ended queue backed by a standard `Vec` growable array. The main difference between the more general `Vec` and `VecDeque` is that `VecDeque` provides double-ended operations, like `push_front`, `push_back`, `pop_front`, and `pop_back`. By comparison, `Vec` only provides `push` and `pop` methods, which provide first in, first out (FIFO) ordering. Since we're implementing a stack, we need to use the `push_front` and `pop_front` methods from `VecDeque` to provide last in, first out (LIFO) ordering. We're going to create a wrapper type around `VecDeque` to provide some functionality that is specific to the needs of our RPN solver. This type is called `RpnStack`. Also, since `VecDeque` is not used quite as commonly as `Vec`, we'll need to import it explicitly from the standard library:

```
use std::collections::VecDeque;

#[derive(Debug)] //
struct RpnStack {
  stack: VecDeque<i32>,
}
```

`#[derive]` is a macro that instructs the compiler to generate code for a struct or enum. In this case, it's an implementation of the `Debug` trait, which allows us to print out our `RpnStack` using the `Debug` formatter that we introduced earlier. Although it's possible to manually write this code, it's easier (especially for types with many fields) to allow the compiler to generate it automatically.

Let's add some methods to perform the standard stack operations of `push` and `pop`: they add a new number to the top of the stack and remove the top number from the stack, respectively. We'll also add an `Error` variant to mark the error of popping from an empty stack:

```
enum Error {
  InvalidNumber,
  PopFromEmptyStack,
}

impl RpnStack {        ⟵ Methods for a struct or
                          enum go into impl blocks.
  fn new() -> RpnStack {      ⟵ It is convention to write a new method that accepts all
    RpnStack {                   required parameters for constructing an instance of a
      stack: VecDeque::new(),    type. Rust does not have language-level support for
    }                            constructor functions like C++ or Java; a constructor
  }                              function is just a normal function.

  fn push(&mut self, value: i32) {   ⟵ Methods that take in a parameter
    self.stack.push_front(value);       called self operate on an individual
  }                                     instance of the type.
```

```rust
    fn pop(&mut self) -> Result<i32, Error> {
      match self.stack.pop_front() {
        Some(value) => Ok(value),
        None => Err(Error::PopFromEmptyStack),
      }
    }
  }
```

`impl` blocks contain the methods that can be called on a given type. If you're coming from a language like Python or Java, where function definitions live within the same block as the class definition, this may seem odd, but the flexibility that comes from having separate `impl` blocks is very worthwhile.

Note that `push` and `pop` have an `&mut self` parameter on them, and `new` does not. `push` and `pop` are *methods* that operate on a specific instance of `RpnStack`, whereas `new` is a *function* that does not take an instance as its input. Functions within `impl` blocks are similar to static methods in Java or class methods in Python. `impl` blocks can contain both methods and functions; the only difference is the presence or absence of the leading `self` parameter, similar to Python methods, which have a leading `self` parameter. In languages like Java, JavaScript, Ruby, and C++, a `self` or `this` variable may be available within methods, but it is not marked as an explicit parameter. It is required in Rust because of Rust's explicit rules around mutability and ownership control. `self` parameters can take many forms: they can be owned `self` values, immutable references (`&self`), or, as we see here, mutable `self` references (`&mut self`). The `&mut self` is required for both methods because they both mutate the `stack` field of our `RpnStack` value. You can only call `push` or `pop` if you have a mutable reference to the `RpnStack`.

With these methods, we should be able to implement our `evaluate` function. We can start by pushing integer values onto the stack and printing them out afterward. Also, instead of always returning 1, we can start returning the top value on the stack:

```rust
fn evaluate(problem: &str) -> Result<i32, Error> {
  let mut stack = RpnStack::new();           // We use the Type::function() syntax to
                                             // call a function associated with a type.
  for term in problem.trim().split(' ') {
    match term {
      "+" => println!("ADD"),
      "-" => println!("SUB"),
      "*" => println!("MUL"),                // Explicitly hinting that
      "/" => println!("DIV"),                // parse should return an i32
      other => match other.parse() {         // is no longer necessary.
        Ok(value) => {
          stack.push(value);                 // We use the instance.method()
          println!("STACK: {:?}", stack);    // syntax to a method on a
        },                                   // specific instance of a type.
        Err(_) => return Err(Error::InvalidNumber),
      }
    }
  }
                                             // Recall that the ? operator returns an error early from a
                                             // function if the expression it's applied to is an Err variant. pop
                                             // returns an error when the stack is empty, so this ? operator
  let value = stack.pop()?;                  // is necessary to forward that possible error to the caller.
  Ok(value)
}
```

Note that we no longer need to explicitly hint that `parse` should return an `i32`. We take the returned `value` variable and immediately pass it into the `push` method. This method only accepts an `i32` as its input, so the compiler will reason that `parse` must return an `i32` to be valid. The Rust compiler works very hard to try to save you from writing types over and over again.

Let's see if our stack is working as expected:

```
$ cargo build
$ ./calculator
> 3 4 *
STACk: RpnStack { stack: [3] }
STACk: RpnStack { stack: [4, 3] }
MUL
4
> *
MUL
Error
```

Now that we have numerical storage, we should be able to implement addition. Remember that, in RPN math, we need to pop two values off of the stack, add them together, and put the result back onto the stack:

```
fn evaluate(problem: &str) -> Result<i32, Error> {
  let mut stack = RpnStack::new();

  for term in problem.trim().split(' ') {
    match term {
      "+" => {
        let y = stack.pop()?;
        let x = stack.pop()?;

        stack.push(x + y);
      }
      "-" => println!("SUB"),
      "*" => println!("MUL"),
      "/" => println!("DIV"),
      other => match other.parse() {
        Ok(value) => stack.push(value),
        Err(_) => return Err(Error::InvalidNumber),
      }
    }
  }

  let value = stack.pop()?;
  Ok(value)
}
```

⬅ **Our stack is in LIFO order, so the top item on the stack is the second element in the expression. Thus, we need to pop them from the stack in "backward" order of y and then x. The results are the same for addition but try swapping these lines for subtraction or division.**

If we run this program now, we can compute arbitrarily nested addition expressions:

```
$ cargo build
$ ./calculator
> 3 4 +
7
> 100 300 + 200 +
600
```

It should be easy enough to provide similar implementations for the other operators.

Listing 3.9 Using `evaluate` for all four arithmetic operations

```rust
fn evaluate(problem: &str) -> Result<i32, Error> {
  let mut stack = RpnStack::new();

  for term in problem.trim().split(' ') {
    match term {
      "+" => {
        let y = stack.pop()?;
        let x = stack.pop()?;

        stack.push(x + y);
      }
      "-" => {
        let y = stack.pop()?;
        let x = stack.pop()?;

        stack.push(x - y);
      }
      "*" => {
        let y = stack.pop()?;
        let x = stack.pop()?;

        stack.push(x * y);
      }
      "/" => {
        let y = stack.pop()?;
        let x = stack.pop()?;

        stack.push(x / y);
      }
      other => match other.parse() {
        Ok(value) => stack.push(value),
        Err(_) => return Err(Error::InvalidNumber),
      }
    }
  }

  let value = stack.pop()?;
  Ok(value)
}
```

And it seems to work as expected:

```
$ cargo build
$ ./calculator
> 3 4 * 10 + 20 -
2
> 3 4 *
12
> 3 4 + 10 * 20 -
50
> 100 2 /
50
```

```
> 100 5 /
20
> /
Error
```

The program is so close to completion. The largest gap in functionality right now is due to error messages not surfacing to the user outside of `Error`. This is less than helpful; we should try printing out a message with specific information about the error. We could add another `match` to the `solve` function to inspect the variant of our `Error`, but this method is less than ideal. It may seem okay for our small program, but what if `evaluate` is called in multiple places, and they all want to log the same error message when an error occurs? We need to centralize the error messages that our `Error` struct can generate. The standard way to do this is by using the `Display` trait.

3.2.4 The Display trait

Traits in Rust are very similar to interfaces in Java or Go or abstract classes in C++. They are definitions of functionality that any type might implement so that those types can be handled in similar ways. For example, numeric types all implement the `Add` trait in the standard library, indicating that addition can be performed on them. We're going to look at the `Display` trait, which we've been using this whole time without realizing it! Every time we used the `println!` macro and the {} placeholder to print a value, we were using the `Display` implementation for that value.

Let's see how we might write the "Hello world!" program using the `Display` trait.

Listing 3.10 "Hello World!" with `Display`

```rust
use std::fmt::{Display, Formatter};

struct Hello {}

impl Display for Hello {
    fn fmt(&self, f: &mut Formatter) -> std::fmt::Result {
        write!(f, "Hello world!")
    }
}

fn main() {
    let x = Hello {};
    println!("{}", x);
}
```

Trait implementations are always written as impl Trait for Type.

The write! macro uses the same format string with placeholder syntax as println!/format! and friends. The macro returns a std::fmt::Result, so we omit the semicolon on this line to ensure the result is returned from our fmt function.

Whenever you implement the Display trait, you must implement the fmt function with this exact signature. We could import Result from the fmt package as well to shorten the return type, but it often conflicts with the normal Result type, so it's generally not imported. We use the full path instead.

We use the same {} placeholder that we've been using throughout the book. The only difference is that we can now use it on our own type instead of just on standard library types.

Implementing the `Display` trait for custom types is very straightforward. Outside of the type signature for the `fmt` function, it's basically just replacing `println!` with `write!` and adding a leading `f` argument. `f` is a `Formatter` struct, which may contain a handle to stdout (for `println!`), stderr (for `eprintln!`), or a string (for `format!`).

Now, let's implement the Display trait for our Error type.

Listing 3.11 Display implementation for the Error type

```
use std::fmt::{Display, Formatter};

enum Error {
  InvalidNumber,
  PopFromEmptyStack,
}

impl Display for Error {
  fn fmt(&self, f: &mut Formatter) -> std::fmt::Result {
    match self {
      Error::InvalidNumber => write!(
        f, "Not a valid number or operator"),
      Error::PopFromEmptyStack => write!(
        f, "Tried to operate on empty stack"),
    }
  }
}
```

NOTE It is highly recommended that you provide a Display implementation for error types.

Next, we can update our solve function to take advantage of this new Display implementation.

Listing 3.12 solve function updated to print out error messages

```
#[no_mangle]
pub extern "C" fn solve(
    line: *const c_char, solution: *mut c_int) -> c_int {
  if line.is_null() || solution.is_null() {
    return 1;
  }

  let c_str = unsafe { CStr::from_ptr(line) };
  let r_str = match c_str.to_str() {
    Ok(s) => s,
    Err(e) => {
      eprintln!("UTF-8 Error: {}", e);
      return 1;
    }
  };

  match evaluate(r_str) {
    Ok(value) => {
      unsafe {
        *solution = value as c_int;
      }
      0
    }
    Err(e) => {
      eprintln!("Error: {}", e);          ◁── This line is the only one that needs to change. We print out our error value with the {} placeholder.
```

```
          1
      }
    }
}
```

We've done it! We now have a calculator program that is communicating with the user in C, solving the equation in Rust, and sending the result back to C. For reference, the following listing shows the full contents of the `lib.rs` file of the `calculate` crate when you are finished. The calculator library can be used from C FFI or normal Rust code.

Listing 3.13 Calculator library

```rust
use libc::{c_char, c_int};
use std::collections::VecDeque;
use std::ffi::CStr;
use std::fmt::{Display, Formatter};

#[no_mangle]
pub extern "C" fn solve(
    line: *const c_char, solution: *mut c_int) -> c_int {
  if line.is_null() || solution.is_null() {
    return 1;
  }

  let c_str = unsafe { CStr::from_ptr(line) };
  let r_str = match c_str.to_str() {
    Ok(s) => s,
    Err(e) => {
      eprintln!("UTF-8 Error: {}", e);
      return 1;
    }
  };

  match evaluate(r_str) {
    Ok(value) => {
      unsafe {
        *solution = value as c_int;
      }
      0
    }
    Err(e) => {
      eprintln!("Error: {}", e);
      1
    }
  }
}

enum Error {
  InvalidNumber,
  PopFromEmptyStack,
}

impl Display for Error {
  fn fmt(&self, f: &mut Formatter) -> std::fmt::Result {
    match self {
      Error::InvalidNumber => write!(
```

```rust
            f, "Not a valid number or operator"),
        Error::PopFromEmptyStack => write!(
            f, "Tried to operate on empty stack"),
      }
    }
}

#[derive(Debug)]
struct RpnStack {
  stack: VecDeque<i32>,
}

impl RpnStack {
  fn new() -> RpnStack {
    RpnStack {
      stack: VecDeque::new(),
    }
  }

  fn push(&mut self, value: i32) {
    self.stack.push_front(value);
  }

  fn pop(&mut self) -> Result<i32, Error> {
    match self.stack.pop_front() {
      Some(value) => Ok(value),
      None => Err(Error::PopFromEmptyStack),
    }
  }
}

fn evaluate(problem: &str) -> Result<i32, Error> {
  let mut stack = RpnStack::new();

  for term in problem.trim().split(' ') {
    match term {
      "+" => {
        let y = stack.pop()?;
        let x = stack.pop()?;
        stack.push(x + y);
      }
      "-" => {
        let y = stack.pop()?;
        let x = stack.pop()?;
        stack.push(x - y);
      }
      "*" => {
        let y = stack.pop()?;
        let x = stack.pop()?;
        stack.push(x * y);
      }
      "/" => {
        let y = stack.pop()?;
        let x = stack.pop()?;
        stack.push(x / y);
      }
      other => match other.parse() {
        Ok(value) => stack.push(value),
```

```
            Err(_) => return Err(Error::InvalidNumber),
        },
      }
    }

    let value = stack.pop()?;
    Ok(value)
}
```

Let's try running it to verify that it all works together with our new error-handling code:

```
$ cargo build
$ ./calculator
> 3 4 *
12
> 19 8 /
2
> hello
Error: Not a valid number or operator
> 4 *
Error: Tried to operate on empty stack
> 30 2 -
28
> 30 4 +
34
> 4
4
```

It works exactly as intended.

Figure 3.4 shows the lifetime graph for this calculator FFI program.

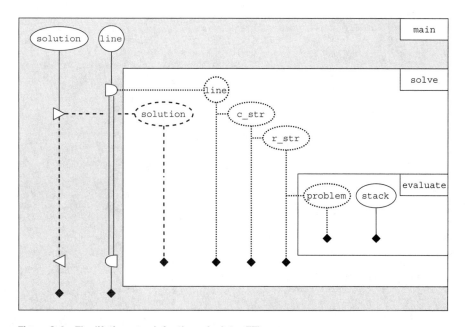

Figure 3.4 The lifetime graph for the calculator FFI program

Summary

- `unsafe` functions and blocks can be used to perform some operations that normal Rust code forbids, like dereferencing raw pointers.
- `unsafe` means that a few rules are unchecked by the compiler, and it is the developer's responsibility to ensure that Rust's memory safety rules are enforced.
- You can write a normal Rust function with your business logic in it and a wrapper function that handles communicating with C over FFI boundaries.
- A `cdylib` Rust crate can be linked with a normal C program, and Rust functions annotated for FFI can be called from C.
- `CStr` can be used to turn a null-terminated C-style string into a Rust `&str`.
- Normal Rust types like `&str` can provide safe and easy-to-use abstractions over shared memory with C code.
- `&str` doesn't need to reallocate memory to perform substring operations.
- `match` expressions can be used like C `switch` statements to perform multiple comparison operations on a single value.
- `Debug` formatting can provide information like hidden escape codes within a string or the internals of a data structure.
- The `Display` trait is used for printing values with the `{}` placeholder.
- Implementing the `Display` trait for error types is considered best practice.

Advanced FFI

This chapter covers
- Creating an NGINX extension module with Rust
- Generating Rust bindings for an existing C codebase
- Using a C memory allocator from Rust
- Sharing functions between Rust crates

The previous chapter centered around a simple example of calling a Rust function from C code. We used a single C stack–allocated string value from our Rust code, but the Rust code did not send any heap-allocated values to the C code, nor did it call any C functions. The API surface of our C calculator program was very small, and thus it was quite straightforward to add Rust to it. This chapter is an extension of the previous chapter's calculator example. Instead of adding our calculator function to a simple CLI application, we're going to write an NGINX extension module that responds to HTTP requests with calculation results. This chapter is not intended as a general guide on writing NGINX extensions; NGINX is simply a stand-in for a sufficiently complex C codebase to which we want to add some Rust code.

Our goal is to create a module for NGINX that solves Reverse Polish Notation (RPN) math expressions using the `calculate` library that we created in chapter 3.

It should read the expressions from the request POST body. So, assuming that the NGINX server is running on port 8080, it should be usable like this:

```
$ curl -X POST -d '3 4 +' http://localhost:8080/calculate
7
$ curl -X POST -d '3 4 * 2 -' http://localhost:8080/calculate
10
```

NGINX is a popular HTTP load balancer and reverse proxy written in C. It's currently used in over 400 million websites across the internet. NGINX has a module system that allows developers to write C code that can control its behavior or add totally new functionality. We will use this C API from both C and Rust to create an HTTP handler that uses the same RPN calculator we created in chapter 3. Chapter 3 provided a STDIN/STDOUT interface for using the calculator, but in this chapter, we will create an HTTP interface. As NGINX is far more complicated than our STDIN/STDOUT program in chapter 3, we must take a number of steps to accomplish this task:

1 Download the NGINX source code.
2 Write some C glue code between NGINX and Rust.
3 Link the C module code to a Rust HTTP handler function.
4 Extract request details from the NGINX request struct.
5 Invoke the calculator library we wrote in chapter 3.
6 Return the calculation result on the HTTP response.

4.1 Downloading the NGINX source code

Downloading the NGINX source code is the most straightforward of all the steps. We will use version 1.19.3 of NGINX, which can be downloaded freely from the NGINX website (https://nginx.org). It is provided as a gzipped tarball, and we can easily extract it once it's been downloaded. Let's also create a new crate directory with Cargo to put all these files into:

```
$ cargo new --lib ngx_http_calculator_rs
$ cd ngx_http_calculator_rs
$ wget https://nginx.org/download/nginx-1.19.3.tar.gz
$ tar -xfz nginx-1.19.3.tar.gz
```

We're now ready to start writing some code!

> **NOTE** The following sections have a large number of file paths and commands in them. Assume that all file paths are relative to the ngx_http_calculator_rs crate directory that we just created. Assume all command-line sessions begin in this directory, and, if required, the command-line session will contain a cd line at the beginning to indicate which subdirectory commands should be run within.

4.2 Creating the NGINX module

NGINX has a large and complicated C API surface, and this chapter is not intended to be a guide on how to write an NGINX plugin. This section provides some starter code for a C NGINX module that calls out to a Rust function to provide an HTTP handler.

NGINX allows developers to write dynamic modules, which are loaded into memory by the NGINX binary after it's started up. We're going to create a dynamic module for this example, which should allow us to update the module by recompiling our Rust code, without needing to recompile the whole NGINX binary each time. To create a new dynamic module, we begin by creating a directory called `module` and placing two new files in it. The first file is `module/config`, and it should look like this:

```
ngx_module_type=HTTP
ngx_module_name=ngx_http_calculator
ngx_module_srcs="$ngx_addon_dir/ngx_http_calculator.c"
ngx_module_libs=""

. auto/module

ngx_addon_name=$ngx_module_name
```

This file is a shell script that sets some environment variables that NGINX uses in its custom build steps for modules. The variables this file is expected to set are documented on the NGINX webpage (https://mng.bz/oKWp).

By reading the variables set in the shell script, you may have been able to guess the path of the second file we're going to create. Go ahead and create `module/ngx_http_calculator.c`. This C source code file sets some global variables and provides some functions required for initializing our NGINX module. It is possible to write these variables and functions in Rust, which would enable you to write zero C code. However, these initialization functions are simple, and they rely a bit heavily on preprocessor macros, which are not easily translatable to Rust. This chapter does not discuss moving them into Rust, but it could be a good exercise to try on your own!

Add the following contents to your `module/ngx_http_calculator.c` file:

Listing 4.1 NGINX module starter code

```
#include <ngx_config.h>
#include <ngx_core.h>
#include <ngx_http.h>

typedef struct {
  ngx_flag_t enable_calculation;
} ngx_http_calculator_loc_conf_t;

ngx_int_t ngx_http_calculator_handler(ngx_http_request_t *r);

static void *ngx_http_calculator_create_loc_conf(ngx_conf_t *cf);
static char *ngx_http_calculator_merge_loc_conf(
    ngx_conf_t *cf, void *parent, void *child);

static ngx_command_t ngx_http_calculator_commands[] = {
    {ngx_string("calculate"),
     NGX_HTTP_LOC_CONF | NGX_CONF_FLAG,
     ngx_conf_set_flag_slot, NGX_HTTP_LOC_CONF_OFFSET,
```

The forward declaration for the function that we're going to define in our Rust library

This block allows us to write calculate on; in our NGINX config file to tell NGINX that this library should handle specific HTTP requests.

Chapter 4 Advanced FFI

```
        offsetof(ngx_http_calculator_loc_conf_t,
          enable_calculation), NULL},
    ngx_null_command};
```

> The variable ngx_http_calculator matches the name of the module in the module/config file. It lets NGINX know which symbol to load from our dynamic library when it opens the module.

```
static ngx_http_module_t ngx_http_calculator_module_ctx = {
    NULL, NULL, NULL, NULL, NULL, NULL,
        ngx_http_calculator_create_loc_conf,
        ngx_http_calculator_merge_loc_conf};

ngx_module_t ngx_http_calculator = {
    NGX_MODULE_V1,
    &ngx_http_calculator_module_ctx,
    ngx_http_calculator_commands,
    NGX_HTTP_MODULE,
    NULL, NULL, NULL, NULL,
    NULL, NULL, NULL, NGX_MODULE_V1_PADDING};
```

> This V1 macro allows NGINX to version its C API a bit. There is currently only a V1 to this API, and for now, we need to include the V1 constant at the top of the module, and the V1 padding macro at the end of it.

> This macro tells NGINX that our module will control the HTTP subsystem. NGINX has a number of subsystems, and many of them have hooks for modules.

```
static void *ngx_http_calculator_create_loc_conf(ngx_conf_t *cf)
{
  ngx_http_calculator_loc_conf_t *conf;

  conf = ngx_pcalloc(cf->pool, sizeof(
    ngx_http_calculator_loc_conf_t));
  if (conf == NULL) {
    return NULL;
  }

  conf->enable_calculation = NGX_CONF_UNSET;

  return conf;
}

static char *ngx_http_calculator_merge_loc_conf(
  ngx_conf_t *cf, void *parent, void *child)
{
  ngx_http_calculator_loc_conf_t *prev = parent;
  ngx_http_calculator_loc_conf_t *conf = child;

  ngx_conf_merge_value(conf->enable_calculation,
    prev->enable_calculation, 0);

  if (conf->enable_calculation) {
    ngx_http_core_loc_conf_t *clcf;

    clcf = ngx_http_conf_get_module_loc_conf(
      cf, ngx_http_core_module);
    clcf->handler = ngx_http_calculator_handler;
  }

  return NGX_CONF_OK;
}
```

> Tells NGINX to call our Rust function when the HTTP handler is invoked. If the calculate on argument is provided in the NGINX configuration, we set the HTTP handler function to our Rust handler function.

Don't let the large number of NULL values scare you! The NGINX module system has a large number of hooks, and many of them are not required to solve the problem we're trying to solve.

4.2 Creating the NGINX module

Now that we have the C code required for our NGINX module, let's try compiling it! Move into the NGINX source directory that we created earlier and run the `configure` script with the `module` directory we previously created:

```
$ cd nginx-1.19.3
$ ./configure --add-dynamic-module=../module
```

Given the `../module` path, the `configure` script will run the `../module/config` file to tell the build process some metadata about how it should build our module. Next, we can compile NGINX and our module with a single `make` command:

```
$ cd nginx-1.19.3
$ make -j16 build modules
```

The `build` target is the main `nginx` executable, and `modules` represents all the configured plugin modules (such as ours). These modules produce lots of output and may take a bit of time. We recommend using the `-j` (which stands for jobs) option on make to parallelize the build. We used `-j16` on our machine as our CPU has 16 cores.

Once `make` has finished compiling our module and the NGINX binary, a few new files should appear in the output directory `objs`, where NGINX's build process places binaries and libraries once they are built. Searching for executables in this directory reveals two important-looking files:

```
$ cd nginx-1.19.3
$ find objs -executable -type f
objs/ngx_http_calculator.so     ◁── The dynamic library file for our module. It contains the
objs/nginx                            definition for the ngx_http_calculator variable, which
         ◁── The NGINX server      tells NGINX what to do when it loads our module.
             binary itself
```

Now that we have a compiled NGINX and a compiled module, let's try starting NGINX with our module loaded! However, first, NGINX needs a working directory to put its temp files, config files, and logs into. We will create these now. Let's call it `ngx-run`. In addition to the top-level folder, it must have a `logs` subdirectory:

```
$ mkdir ngx-run
$ mkdir ngx-run/logs
```

> **NOTE** NGINX will use this `ngx-run` directory as a scratch space while running. Other than the `logs` directory and the configuration file, don't worry too much about the structure of this directory.

Now, create the file `ngx-run/nginx.conf` and add the following to it:

```
load_module ../nginx-1.19.3/objs/ngx_http_calculator.so;   ◁── Instructs NGINX to load our dynamic
                                                              module at the given file path
worker_processes 1;
daemon off;
error_log /dev/stderr info;    ◁── Directs err information directly to the console.
                                   Normally NGINX swallows this line and adds it to
events {                           log files. While ideal for production workloads,
  worker_connections 1024;         it makes live debugging much more challenging.
}
```

```
http {
  access_log /dev/stdout;            ◁─┐ Similarly, directs request logs
                                       │ to STDOUT instead of a file
  server {
    listen       8080;

    location /calculate {
      calculate on;                  ◁─┐ Tells NGINX that requests
    }                                  │ routed to /calculate should be
  }                                    │ handled by our calculate library
}
```

Now that we have a configuration file for NGINX, let's start it up! We'll be using the following command many times throughout the chapter to run our NGINX instance:

```
$ ./nginx-1.19.3/objs/nginx -c nginx.conf -p ngx-run
nginx: [emerg] dlopen() "ngx_http_calculator.so" failed
(ngx_http_calculator.so: undefined symbol:
  ngx_http_calculator_handler)
in nginx.conf:1
```

NGINX doesn't start! But why? After all that work, don't we deserve *something*? Well, we lied to NGINX a bit. We have a forward declaration in our C file that tells NGINX, "We're going to define the function ngx_http_calculator_handler at some point," but we have not provided that definition anywhere yet. The next section walks through creating this function in Rust and exposing it to our existing C code.

4.3 Linking C to Rust

In the previous section, we wrote a forward declaration for an HTTP handler that looks like this:

```
ngx_int_t ngx_http_calculator_handler(ngx_http_request_t *r);
```

And we understood that we'd later provide this function in our Rust library. Translating that C function declaration to a Rust function declaration is straightforward. Let's take a look:

```
#[no_mangle]
pub unsafe extern "C" fn ngx_http_calculator_handler(
  r: *mut ngx_http_request_t
) -> ngx_int_t {
  0
}
```

This function needs to exist to be callable from NGINX, but a few things need to happen first. You may have noticed that some types in that function signature start with the prefix ngx_. These types are exposed by the NGINX module API in its header files. Normally, when writing a module in C, you can simply include these header files in your C code, and the types would be available to you. Since we're not writing our handler function in C, we need to do some work to get these types into Rust.

We're going to need to generate Rust *bindings* for the C types in NGINX. A binding is essentially metadata about an API that exists for a library implemented in a different programming language. It's the metadata about all the functions, types, and global variables that exist in that library—without the implementation of any of those things. In chapter 3, we created C bindings for the Rust calculate library with a C-compatible solve function as a part of that library. Bindings don't always exist as a part of a library itself; they are often provided by separate libraries. For example, the openssl library is written in C; to directly interact with the C functions from Rust, you can use the openssl-sys Rust crate. This crate provides Rust bindings for the openssl C library. Figure 4.1 shows the way the high-level Rust bindings in the openssl crate call down to direct bindings in the openssl-sys crate, which then cross the FFI boundary into the openssl C library (figure 4.1).

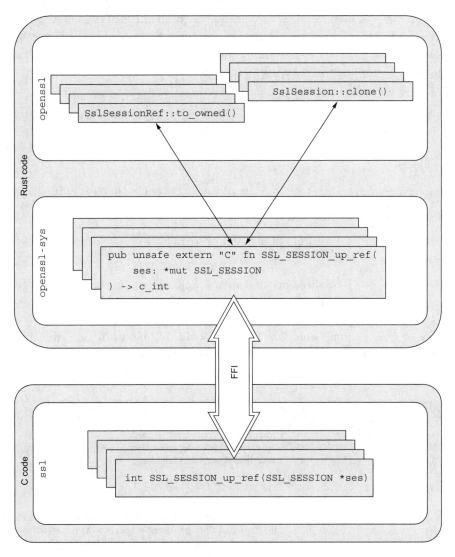

Figure 4.1 High- and low-level Rust bindings for the openssl C library

To generate these C bindings, we're going to need to introduce a new Rust concept—the *build script*.

4.3.1 Build scripts

A build script is a small Rust program that Cargo compiles and runs just before our larger library or executable is compiled. It can do anything that a normal Rust program would do. It's useful to us because it can *generate* Rust code dynamically at build time, which is fed back into the compiler. Let's table the NGINX discussion for a moment to consider a simplified example.

Imagine that you are building a greeting application, and you want to provide the ability for your program to greet people in multiple languages. However, you do not want to ship a single massive application with all the world's languages in it. You decide you would like to accomplish your task by using an environment variable passed to the compiler to determine which language the greeting application should support. You will provide appropriately compiled versions to different regions. Let's get started!

> **NOTE** This example is contrived to teach you about build scripts; it is not a good way to accomplish internationalization. Far better internationalization mechanisms are available for Rust. So, please don't follow this method in real life.

Create a new crate directory (outside of the NGINX crate directory) with Cargo:

```
$ cargo new build-script-test
```

> **NOTE** In this subsection, all paths are relative to the root of the new `build-script-test` crate directory.

Move into your new directory and create and open the file `build.rs`. By default, Cargo will look for a file at the root of a crate directory called `build.rs` and treat it as a build script if present. Since build scripts are run like normal Rust programs, we need to give it a main function. We can fill out this main function with the two most important jobs that this build script will do: read an environment variable and write out a file.

Listing 4.2 Basic build script that writes to a file

```
use std::fs::File;         ◁── Imports the Write trait so that
use std::io::Write;            we can call file.write_all on the
                               final line of our main function
fn main() {
  let language = std::env::var("GREET_LANG").unwrap();   ◁──
```

std::env::var looks up the value of environment variables at run time. It returns an Option<String> because the requested variable may not be set. So, we need to unwrap the Option before we can use it.

```
    let mut file = File::create("src/greet.rs").unwrap();
    file.write_all(language.as_bytes()).unwrap();
}
```

Creates (or recreates if already existing) a file on disk

Writes out the contents of the language variable. write_all expects to receive bytes as its input since files may not always contain text data, so we use .as_bytes on our string to get the underlying byte data.

Let's try running our build script now with Cargo:

```
$ cargo run
   Compiling build-script-test v0.1.0
error: failed to run custom build command for
  `build-script-test v0.1.0`

Caused by:
  process didn't exit successfully:
  --- stderr
  thread 'main' panicked at 'called `Result::unwrap()` on an `Err`
    value: NotPresent'
  note: run with `RUST_BACKTRACE=1` environment variable to
    display a backtrace
```

It looks like our build script panicked because we did not provide it with a value for the newly expected GREET_LANG environment variable. Let's try that again:

```
$ env GREET_LANG=en cargo run
   Compiling build-script-test v0.1.0
    Finished dev [unoptimized + debuginfo] target(s) in 0.25s
     Running `build-script-test`
Hello, world!
```

We managed to run our build script successfully! Let's see whether it created the expected output. We should now see a file called `src/greet.rs` containing whatever we passed to the compiler as the GREET_LANG environment variable:

```
$ ls src
main.rs greet.rs

$ cat src/greet.rs
en
```

We can write a string into a file, but `en` is certainly not a valid Rust file. We need to edit our build script a bit to write out different Rust code, depending on the value of GREET_LANG it sees.

Listing 4.3 Build script writing code with environment variables

```
use std::fs::File;
use std::io::Write;

fn main() {
    let language = std::env::var("GREET_LANG").unwrap();
```

```
    let greeting = match language.as_ref() {
      "en" => "Hello!",
      "es" => "¡Hola!",
      "el" => "?ε?α σα?",
      "de" => "Hallo!",
      x => panic!("Unsupported language code {}", x),
    };

    let rust_code = format!("fn greet() {{
      println!(\"{}\"); }}", greeting);

    let mut file = File::create("src/greet.rs").unwrap();
    file.write_all(rust_code.as_bytes()).unwrap();
}
```

> We use .as_ref because std::env::var returns a String. To use a match expression with string literals (which are &strs), we must convert the String into an &str. using .as_ref.

> {{ is necessary because the format! macro uses curly braces as placeholders for formatting. To get the literal curly brace character necessary to create a function body, we use {{. Similarly, we need to escape the quotes within the println! macro so that we do not prematurely end the rust_code string literal.

Now, if we rerun our build script by compiling our library a few times with different language options, we should see the text in `src/greet.rs` change:

```
$ env GREET_LANG=en cargo run
hello!

$ cat src/greet.rs
fn greet() { println!("hello!"); }

$ env GREET_LANG=el cargo run
?ε?α σα?

$ cat src/greet.rs
fn greet() { println!("?ε?α σα?"); }
```

So, we have managed to write out some Rust code, but we need to update our executable to take advantage of it. Currently, the executable just has the basic "Hello world!" code provided by Cargo.

Listing 4.4 Greeting program using the generated `greet.rs` file

```
include!("greet.rs");

fn main() {
  greet();
}
```

> Includes (include!) the text contents of our src/greet.rs file, parses it as Rust code, and adds it to the src/main.rs file. We do not need the src/ prefix on the path because include! relative paths are relative to the source file in which they are used.

> We can call the greet function here because we defined it in src/greet.rs and then used include! to add the text from src/greet.rs into src/main.rs.

We introduced a new macro here—`include!`. It works similarly to the C/C++ `#include` directive. It takes the text contents of a file, parses it as Rust code, and inserts it where `include!` is called. Figure 4.2 diagrams how our program works between the build script and the `src/main.rs` file.

NOTE include! should *not* be used for importing Rust files in the general sense. See chapter 5 for a discussion on the Rust module system. include! should generally only be used with code files generated dynamically at build time.

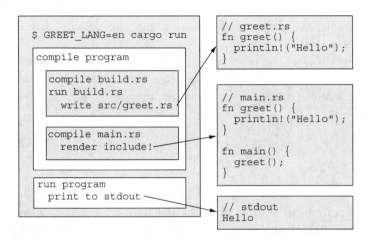

Figure 4.2 Compilation and execution of a program with a build script

Now that we understand a bit about how build scripts can be used to generate Rust code, let's move back to our NGINX code. Recall that we want to generate Rust bindings for the NGINX C API. To generate these bindings, we can write out a bunch of Rust code ourselves, or we can use a build script to do it for us. We're going to do the latter. We will create a build script that uses a Rust library called (appropriately) bindgen.

4.3.2 bindgen

bindgen is a Rust library that parses C/C++ code and outputs Rust bindings automatically. In its simplest form, bindgen generates Rust-compatible definitions for C/C++ types and functions loaded from a single header file. Let's begin by adding bindgen to our Cargo.toml file:

```
[package]
name = "ngx_http_calculator_rs"
version = "0.1.0"
authors = ["You <you@you.com>"]
edition = "2018"

[dependencies]

[build-dependencies]
bindgen = "0.56.0"
```

Notice that we did not include bindgen under the dependencies section but rather the new-to-us build-dependencies section. Since bindgen will only be used from the build script to generate Rust code, it does not need to be included in our finished binary as a normal dependency; we only need it to be included in the dependencies of our build script.

We need our build script to generate Rust bindings for NGINX using the `bindgen` crate. `bindgen` works by parsing a C/C++ header file (and following all `include` directives) for type, variable, and function declarations, and outputting Rust code that is compatible with those declarations.

Before we can use `bindgen`, we need to create this header file. It needs to `#include` all of the headers that our Rust module might need access to. Let's start by adding the headers that we're using from inside our C module. Put the following contents into a file called `wrapper.h`:

```
#include <ngx_config.h>
#include <ngx_core.h>
#include <ngx_http.h>
```

This code is just a normal C header file, but instead of being used to compile C code, we will use it to generate Rust code. So, now that we have our header ready, let's create `build.rs` and open it to look at how we can use `bindgen` to create our bindings.

Listing 4.5 Build script creating NGINX bindings for Rust

```
fn main() {
  let nginx_dir = "nginx-1.19.3";

  let bindings = bindgen::builder()
    .header("wrapper.h")
    .clang_args(vec![
      format!("-I{}/src/core", nginx_dir),
      format!("-I{}/src/event", nginx_dir),
      format!("-I{}/src/event/modules", nginx_dir),
      format!("-I{}/src/os/unix", nginx_dir),
      format!("-I{}/objs", nginx_dir),
      format!("-I{}/src/http", nginx_dir),
      format!("-I{}/src/http/v2", nginx_dir),
      format!("-I{}/src/http/modules", nginx_dir),
    ])
    .generate()
    .unwrap();

  bindings
    .write_to_file("nginx.rs")
    .unwrap();
}
```

wrapper.h is the header file we just created. bindgen only accepts a single header file as its input, and because we need the types from three different NGINX header files, we need to write our own header file that includes (#include) all of them.

This list represents command-line arguments fed to the clang C/C++ compiler when it's used to parse the wrapper.h header file. We provide it with the directories required to resolve all the #include directives down to the dependency tree of header files within NGINX.

Specifies the output location for bindgen. Our bindings will be written to nginx.rs.

Let's run our build script by recompiling our library. It may take a bit longer this time, as the compiler is now doing a lot of work inspecting NGINX header files when it runs. After the build step finishes, you should see a new file placed into the root of the crate directory `nginx.rs`. Open this file and take a look around. After getting past some of the generated Rust code for dealing with bit fields, you may notice that a lot of the types and functions laid out in this file have little to do with NGINX itself. To start, the entire C standard library is described here! This API surface is probably far more than we're going to need for our integration, and keeping it included will only bloat our compile times. This file appears to contain over 51,000 lines, and any efforts to reduce that size would be well spent. We can constrain this file using the `whitelist` functionality of `bindgen`.

> **NOTE** If you get an error about missing `libclang.so` files, you need to install `libclang` from your operating system's package manager. `bindgen` uses `libclang` to parse the C and C++ files passed to it.

Eagle-eyed readers may have noticed that the types and functions in the NGINX module API begin with the `ngx_` prefix. We can use a regular expression to only include types, functions, and global variables that begin with this prefix, ignoring all others. Let's go back to our `build.rs` file and add those rules.

Listing 4.6 bindgen build script only accepting `ngx_` prefixed items

```
fn main() {
  let nginx_dir = "nginx-1.19.3";

  let bindings = bindgen::builder()
    .header("wrapper.h")
    .whitelist_type("ngx_.*")
    .whitelist_function("ngx_.*")
    .whitelist_var("ngx_.*")
    .clang_args(vec![
      format!("-I{}/src/core", nginx_dir),
      format!("-I{}/src/event", nginx_dir),
      format!("-I{}/src/event/modules", nginx_dir),
      format!("-I{}/src/os/unix", nginx_dir),
      format!("-I{}/objs", nginx_dir),
      format!("-I{}/src/http", nginx_dir),
      format!("-I{}/src/http/v2", nginx_dir),
      format!("-I{}/src/http/modules", nginx_dir),
    ])
    .generate()
    .unwrap();

  bindings
    .write_to_file("nginx.rs")
    .unwrap();
}
```

These `whitelist_` methods accept strings formatted as regular expressions.

Rerunning the build, we now have an `nginx.rs` file containing 30,000 lines of code. It's not ideal, but it's certainly an improvement over the previous step. A sufficiently motivated developer could go through and explicitly allow every individual type required to make their FFI integration work, but it's not necessary at this stage.

We need to change on more thing about our build script: up until now, we've been placing the nginx.rs file in the root of our crate directory. However, it doesn't really belong there. When we generate files as a part of a build script that are meant to be included in later compilation steps, they should be placed in the out directory. Cargo manages the out directory, which is unique to each run of the compiler. It is where all generated files should be placed, as we probably do not want to be committing 30,000 lines of generated code into our version control system!

The location of the out directory is only knowable by inspecting environment variables that Cargo sets. For build scripts, Cargo sets a number of environment variables when the script is being executed, and these same environment variables are provided to our main crate at compile time. Let's see how we can reference this environment variable to place our nginx.rs file inside the out directory. Replace the last three lines of the bottom of the main function of our build.rs file with the following lines:

```
let out_dir = std::env::var("OUT_DIR").unwrap();

bindings
    .write_to_file(format!("{}/nginx.rs", out_dir))
    .expect("unable to write bindings");
```

← **Cargo automatically sets the OUT_VAR variable for build scripts.**

Now that our generated code is going to the correct place, we need to add it to our Rust library using the include! macro that we discussed earlier in the chapter. Since the source file is in $OUT_DIR/nginx.rs, we need a way to look up variables at compile time. We could use std::env::var like we did in the build script, but it is used for *runtime* lookups. We need to check the value of this variable at compile time. Instead, we can use the env! macro. This macro expands to a string containing the value of the environment variable at the time the program was compiled. It is a compiler error if the variable is not provided. For our example, we can look up the OUT_DIR environment variable using

```
env!("OUT_DIR")
```

So, we have our out directory, and we know that we need nginx.rs inside of that directory, but how can we combine these two things? At run time, we could just use format! to smash them together with a path separator in the middle, but how can we do this same thing at compile time? The concat! macro is the answer. This macro performs simple string concatenation operations for strings known at compile time. Because we want to generate a path that looks like $OUT_DIR/nginx.rs, we can use concat! as follows:

```
concat!(env!("OUT_DIR"), "/nginx.rs")
```

This method is a bit different from how we built up this same path in our build script, but remember that run time for the build script is essentially the same as compile time for our application code. We need slightly different semantics to accomplish the same task, unfortunately. Now that we have all the pieces, let's put them together.

4.3 Linking C to Rust

Open up `src/lib.rs` and add the following to the top of the file:

```
include!(concat!(env!("OUT_DIR"), "/nginx.rs"));
```

That's a lot of macros! Let's revisit them one at a time:

- `include!` is a source-include operation similar to `#include` in C/C++.
- `concat!` performs string concatenation at compile time.
- `env!` looks up the value of the `OUT_DIR` environment variable at compile time.

Figure 4.3 shows a visual look at each of these pieces.

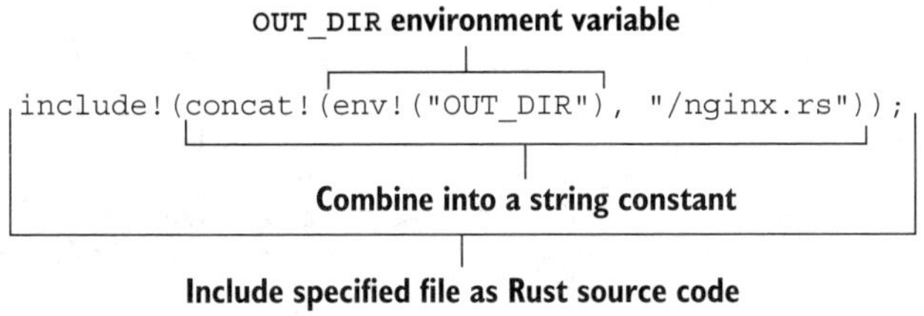

Figure 4.3 Diagram of our new syntax

Now that we understand how to include the generated NGINX code, we can finally revisit that HTTP handler function we declared so long ago. If we include it in `src/lib.rs`, along with the `include!` macro we just wrote and an extra "Hello world!" message, it should look like the following listing.

Listing 4.7 Fully formed minimum NGINX handler function in Rust

```rust
include!(concat!(env!("OUT_DIR"), "/nginx.rs"));

#[no_mangle]
pub unsafe extern "C" fn ngx_http_calculator_handler(
    r: *mut ngx_http_request_t
) -> ngx_int_t {
    eprintln!("Hello from Rust!");
    0
}
```

If we try to compile this code now, it works! We do get a large number of warnings due to the C-style names that `bindgen` generates that don't align with the Rust style guidelines. We can silence these warnings with some compiler directives, but for now let's continue.

Recall from chapter 3 that, when linking to Rust code from C code, we need to instruct Cargo to generate a C-compatible dynamic library instead of the usual Rust-compatible library format it generates. Open `cargo.toml` and add the following lines:

```
[lib]
crate-type = ["cdylib"]
```

Now, when we build our crate, we should find a dynamic library inside our `build` directory:

```
$ cargo build
$ ls target/debug/*.so
target/debug/libngx_http_calculator_rs.so
```

Because this dynamic library contains our HTTP handler function, we need to link to it from our NGINX C module by adding an additional configuration variable to our `module/config` file:

```
ngx_module_type=HTTP
ngx_module_name=ngx_http_calculator
ngx_module_srcs="$ngx_addon_dir/ngx_http_calculator.c"
ngx_module_libs="/path/to/your/libngx_http_calculator_rs.so"   ⟵

. auto/module

ngx_addon_name=$ngx_module_name
```

> The newly added line. An absolute path is used to ensure that no differences in relative path resolution will cause problems when we try to load the module at NGINX run time.

Since we've updated the module configuration, we need to recompile it. Unfortunately, the NGINX build process requires us to rerun the configure script and rebuild the binary after we update the module configuration files. This is the last time this will be required:

```
$ cd nginx-1.19.3
$ ./configure --add-dynamic-module=../module
$ make -j16 build modules
```

Now, after all these steps, we are finally ready to run NGINX, and we should expect our "Hello world!" message to show up!

First, let's start NGINX using the same command from earlier. It should print out some "notice"-level messages and then do nothing as it waits to receive HTTP requests. Use a separate terminal to send an HTTP request to the `/calculate` endpoint that we enabled our module for in the `nginx.conf` file. The HTTP request itself should fail, but the more interesting thing is what shows up in the NGINX logs:

```
$ ./nginx-1.19.3/objs/nginx -c nginx.conf -p ngx-run
....
Hello from Rust!

# Concurrently, in a separate window after NGINX is started
$ curl -X POST -d '3 4 * 2 -' http://localhost:8080/calculate
<html>
<head><title>400 Bad Request</title></head>
<body>
<center><h1>400 Bad Request</h1></center>
<hr><center>nginx/1.19.3</center>
</body>
</html>
```

4.4 Reading the NGINX request

We've done it! We've successfully routed an HTTP request from NGINX's C code to our Rust HTTP handler function. Now that we have some level of communication between the two systems, we need to move on to implementing the business logic of the HTTP handler.

4.4 Reading the NGINX request

Getting the request body data off our NGINX POST request is not too difficult. It's quite similar to the method we used to read data off the stack-allocated STDIN buffer in chapter 3. However, instead of accessing the buffer as a simple *const u8 function argument, NGINX provides us with mut ngx_http_request_t, which has a lot of different fields on it. We'll need to turn this value into something that our Rust code can understand.

The NGINX HTTP stack has many different modules for handling requests built in, and not all of them require the contents of the HTTP request body to be read in. Therefore, the request struct passed to HTTP handler functions does not actually have the request body loaded yet. We need to call the HTTP library's body-parsing method to get this data out. The function we need is ngx_http_read_client_request_body. It takes a pointer to a request and a function pointer to be called when the request body has been read into memory. Let's see how we can use it to load in the request body.

Listing 4.8 Request handler that can read off the request body

```
include!(concat!(env!("OUT_DIR"), "/nginx.rs"));

#[no_mangle]
pub unsafe extern "C" fn ngx_http_calculator_handler(
  r: *mut ngx_http_request_t,
) -> ngx_int_t {
  let rc = ngx_http_read_client_request_body(
    r, Some(read_body_handler));
  if rc != 0 {
    return rc;
  }
  0
}

unsafe extern "C" fn read_body_handler(
    r: *mut ngx_http_request_t) {
  if r.is_null() {
    eprintln!("got null request in body handler");
    return;
  }

  let request = &*r;

  let body = match request_body_as_str(request) {
```

ngx_http_calculator_handler is the entry point that NGINX calls when it receives a request.

ngx_http_read_client_request_body reads the body off of the network and adds it to a buffer on the request struct. Since reading from the network may take some time, we must provide a callback function for NGINX to call when it is finished.

read_body_handler is the callback function that NGINX calls when it has read the request body into memory from the network.

```
    Ok(body) => body,
    Err(e) => {
      eprintln!("failed to parse body: {}", e);
      return;
    }
  };

  eprintln!("Read request body: {:?}", body);   ◁──┐
}                                                  │  Prints out the request body
                                                      after we've parsed it off of
                                                      the NGINX request struct

unsafe fn request_body_as_str<'a>(              ◁──┐
  request: &'a ngx_http_request_t,                  │  request_body_as_str reads the
) -> Result<&'a str, &'static str> {                   request body off of the NGINX
  if request.request_body.is_null()                    request struct and tries to
    || (*request.request_body).bufs.is_null()          interpret it as a Rust string
    || (*(*request.request_body).bufs).buf.is_null()   slice. It does not allocate any
  {                                                    additional memory; it simply
    return Err("Request body buffers                   reinterprets the existing bytes.
      were not initialized as expected");
  }

  let buf = (*(*request.request_body).bufs).buf;

  let start = (*buf).pos;
  let len = (*buf).last.offset_from(start) as usize;

  let body_bytes = std::slice::from_raw_parts(start, len);

  let body_str = std::str::from_utf8(body_bytes)
    .map_err(|_| "Body contains invalid UTF-8")?;

  Ok(body_str)
}
```

Now, several things can be highlighted in this code example, but let's start with the three functions defined in it. First, notice the various levels of annotations that appear on these functions. Let's look at the signatures of the functions without any parameters or body code. All three of these functions include some additional annotations on them in addition to the standard `fn` keyword, but none have exactly the same annotations:

```
#[no_mangle]
pub unsafe extern "C" fn ngx_http_calculator_handler

unsafe extern "C" fn read_body_handler

unsafe fn request_body_as_str
```

Figure 4.4 points out all these parts visually.

4.4 Reading the NGINX request

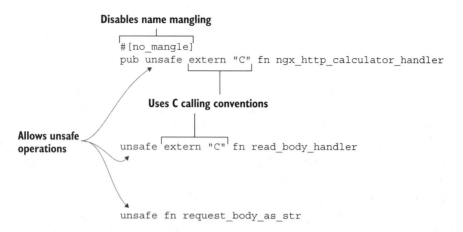

Figure 4.4 Breakdown of the different elements of the function signatures

The first function is `ngx_http_calculator_handler`. This function needs to be called by name from the C code, and it needs to perform unsafe operations within it. It needs `#[no_mangle]` and `pub` to expose its name across the FFI boundary to the C code, and it needs `extern "C"` to be safely callable by the C code. In addition, because name mangling is disabled, we need to use C-style namespacing on the function, hence the `ngx_http_calculator` prefix to avoid clashing with other C functions.

Next, we have `read_body_handler`. This callback function needs to be callable from C code, but the C code does not need to know its name, just its memory location. Consequently, we provide `extern "C"` so that C calling conventions will be used and the function can be used over the FFI boundary. Because the name of the function will only ever be used from Rust code, we do not need to disable name mangling or publicly expose this function. We do perform unsafe operations within this function, so the `unsafe` keyword is added to the signature also.

Finally, `request_body_as_str`: this function is only called from normal Rust code; it will never be called from C. This is obvious because of its lack of an `extern "C"` annotation. So, Rust calling conventions will be used, and it is not safe to call this function from C code.

Now that we have an understanding of the signatures of these three functions, let's dive a little deeper into their implementations. We'll start with `ngx_http_calculator_handler`:

```rust
#[no_mangle]
pub unsafe extern "C" fn ngx_http_calculator_handler(
  r: *mut ngx_http_request_t,
) -> ngx_int_t {
  let rc = ngx_http_read_client_request_body(
    r, Some(read_body_handler));
  if rc != 0 {
    return rc;
```

```
    }
    0
}
```

This function only does three things: it calls `ngx_http_read_client_request_body` to set up the event chain to read in the HTTP POST request body, checks the return code of that, and returns a zero to tell NGINX that there are no errors. Because this function is only called by NGINX itself, it needs to adhere to the quite rigid definition of what an NGINX HTTP handler function does. It needs to take in a single request struct as its parameter and return an `int` status code. Many functions in NGINX return `int` status codes, with zero representing a success status.

Let's look a little closer at `ngx_http_read_client_request_body`. If we open the autogenerated `$OUT_DIR/nginx.rs`, we can see the Rust definition for this function, and if we look at `nginx-1.19.3/src/http/ngx_http_request_body.c`, we can compare it with the C signature:

```
pub fn ngx_http_read_client_request_body(            ◁─┐ Rust function signature
    r: *mut ngx_http_request_t,                         │ autogenerated by bindgen
    post_handler: ngx_http_client_body_handler_pt,
) -> ngx_int_t;

ngx_int_t ngx_http_read_client_request_body(         ◁─┐ C function
    ngx_http_request_t *r,                              │ signature
    ngx_http_client_body_handler_pt post_handler,
)
```

The two function signatures are essentially identical. We also include the definitions for the `post_handler` type, which both functions require:

```
                                                        │ Rust type autogenerated
pub type ngx_http_client_body_handler_pt =           ◁──┘ by bindgen
    Option<unsafe extern "C" fn(r: *mut ngx_http_request_t)>;                    ◁──┐

typedef void (*ngx_http_client_body_handler_pt)      ◁──┤ C type
    (ngx_http_request_t *r);
                                                        The Rust ngx_http_client_body_handler_pt type
                                                        wraps the function handle in an Option so we can
                                                        cleanly deal with the case of a null function pointer.
```

We can see that `bindgen` has made the nullability of the function parameter a bit more obvious by wrapping it in an `Option`. So, we need to wrap the `read_body_handler` in a `Some` when passing it as a callback to `ngx_http_read_client_request_body`. This is simply how `bindgen` generates function pointer types in Rust code coming from C code. You may also notice from looking at the Rust type definition that the function signature within the `Option` matches the signature of the callback function that we defined. Here they both are:

```
pub type ngx_http_client_body_handler_pt =
    Option<unsafe extern "C" fn(r: *mut ngx_http_request_t)>;
```

4.4 Reading the NGINX request

```
unsafe extern "C" fn read_body_handler(
  r: *mut ngx_http_request_t)
```

The type indicates that we must provide a callback that accepts a request pointer and returns nothing. We provided this callback with `read_body_handler`. Now that we have an understanding of our handler entry point, let's look at how this callback is implemented:

```
unsafe extern "C" fn read_body_handler(r: *mut ngx_http_request_t)
{
  if r.is_null() {
    eprintln!("got null request in body handler");
    return;
  }

  let request = &*r;

  let body = match request_body_as_str(request) {
    Ok(body) => body,
    Err(e) => {
      eprintln!("failed to parse body: {}", e);
      return;
    }
  };

  eprintln!("Read request body: {:?}", body);
}
```

Most of the code in this function is quite predictable. Only one thing is new to us here. Just before calling `request_body_at_str`, we have this line:

```
let request = &*r;
```

We already know that `&` is used for taking a reference to something, but what does `*` mean? This symbol is called the *dereference* operator in Rust. As the name implies, dereference means to use a reference to get the thing that the reference points to. It is very similar to the dereference operator in languages like C, C++, and Go.

Using these two operators together on a raw pointer is an operation called *reborrowing*. Essentially, reborrowing is converting a raw pointer into a Rust reference. The difference between the two things may be a bit unclear, but that is because, at run time, they are exactly the same!

A Rust reference is simply a pointer that the compiler has a bit of extra information about. If you think about a pointer in C or C++, the compiler has absolutely no information about where the memory underlying the pointer comes from, how long it will be valid, or if the underlying value is initialized. A Rust reference allows the compiler to know all of this information. Since all references are associated with a lifetime, we know how long a reference will be valid. All references are assumed by the compiler to be aligned, not null, and point to initialized values.

We may want to convert a pointer to a reference for a few reasons:

- Most Rust code is written to work with references and not pointers, so using references over pointers makes code reuse much easier.
- We can perform the null check one time before the conversion and then never worry about it again because Rust references *must always* be nonnull.
- We don't need to use `unsafe` to access data behind a reference. While all the functions in this example are `unsafe`, as we will see in chapter 5, the majority of our code base does not have to be.
- Accessing fields on a struct pointer is awkward because Rust does not have a pointer field access operator like C or C++.
- Having a reference allows us to tie related lifetimes together, as we will see in the declaration of `request_body_as_str` in a moment.

That being said, we need to adhere to a few guidelines when converting from a pointer to a reference:

- Since Rust references are assumed by all code to be nonnull, we must verify this before doing the conversion. You can see that this null check is the first thing we do in `read_body_handler`.
- The thing stored at the pointer must be a valid instance of the type. For example, many C memory allocation functions return uninitialized memory; it is not safe to reborrow this memory as an `&mut T` and then initialize the memory using the reference. It must be initialized using pointer operations.
- Once something is a reference, it must follow Rust's borrowing rules. Because we're creating an immutable reference here, the Rust compiler will assume that no other code will mutate the contents of our pointer. If a background thread writes to this pointer while Rust holds an immutable reference to it, an undefined behavior is created.

After we have completed the null checks, it is important to consider the lifetime. We are taking a pointer that has no lifetime information and turning it into a reference that does have lifetime information. Where does this lifetime come from? The short answer is that it was always there; the compiler just didn't know about it!

Since we know that the NGINX executable doesn't modify this request in the background, we have a null check, and we can reasonably believe that the memory is initialized. Thus, it is safe to turn this pointer into a reference.

Let's look at one more function in our handler—`request_body_as_str`. This function takes a reference to the NGINX request struct and returns a string slice containing the HTTP request body or an error if it could not be read. This function has a number of new elements in it, and we will investigate all of them:

```
unsafe fn request_body_as_str<'a>(
  request: &'a ngx_http_request_t,
) -> Result<&'a str, &'static str> {
  if request.request_body.is_null()
    || (*request.request_body).bufs.is_null()
```

```
    || (*(*request.request_body).bufs).buf.is_null()
  {
    return Err("Request body buffers
      were not initialized as expected");
  }

  let buf = (*(*request.request_body).bufs).buf;

  let start = (*buf).pos;
  let len = (*buf).last.offset_from(start) as usize;

  let body_bytes = std::slice::from_raw_parts(start, len);

  let body_str = std::str::from_utf8(body_bytes)
    .map_err(|_| "Body contains invalid UTF-8")?;

  Ok(body_str)
}
```

The first thing that stands out as new is very close to the start of the function signature. We have a new kind of function argument here—a generic lifetime argument! What is the purpose of this?

```
unsafe fn request_body_as_str<'a>(
  request: &'a ngx_http_request_t,
) -> Result<&'a str, &'static str>
```

It's a bit tricky to wrap our heads around, so let's briefly step away from our NGINX example and its complexity to consider a far simpler program.

4.4.1 Lifetime annotations

To effectively share memory in Rust programs, we sometimes need to help the compiler understand how multiple references relate to one another. The compiler is often smart enough to figure out these relationships implicitly, but sometimes it needs a helping hand. We can provide this help in the form of *lifetime annotations*.

Listing 4.9 Simple Rust program

```
fn main() {
  let numbers = vec![1, 2, 3, 4, 5];

  let value = &numbers[0];

  println!("value: {}", value);
}
```

This program creates a `Vec` containing five numbers, borrows the first number, and prints it out. Let's imagine that we need to move the core functionality of this program, the piece that gets the number from the list, into a separate function. We can do this in a very straightforward way.

Listing 4.10 Rust program using helper function

```
fn main() {
  let numbers = vec![1, 2, 3, 4, 5];

  let value = get_value(&numbers);

  println!("value: {}", value);
}
fn get_value(numbers: &Vec<i32>) -> &i32 {
  &numbers[0]
}
```

This code compiles, but why does it compile? How does the compiler know from the signature of get_value that the lifetimes here are valid? Remember what happens when we try to return a reference to a local variable? The function certainly doesn't compile.

Listing 4.11 Function trying to return reference to local variable

```
fn get_value() -> &i32 {
  let x = 4;
  &x
}
```

The reason the code in listing 4.10 compiles and in the code in listing 4.11 does not is that the compiler is able to infer that the output lifetime in listing 4.10 matches the input lifetime. Figure 4.5 illustrates the lifetime graph for this program.

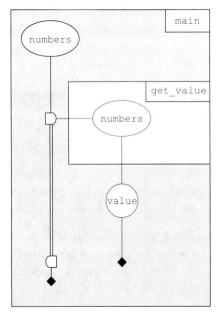

Figure 4.5
Lifetime graph for listing 4.10

4.4 Reading the NGINX request

This lifetime graph shows that the reference coming out of get_value is directly descended from the reference that goes into it. Both references have the same lifetime. We can see the effects if we attempt to use the reference returned from get_value after invalidating it:

```
fn main() {
  let mut numbers = vec![1, 2, 3, 4, 5];

  let value = get_value(&numbers);

  numbers.push(6);

  println!("value: {}", value);
}

fn get_value(numbers: &Vec<i32>) -> &i32 {
  &numbers[0]
}
```

The Rust compiler will not accept this program. We get the following error message:

```
$ cargo run
error[E0502]: cannot borrow `numbers` as mutable
  because it is also borrowed as immutable
 --> src/main.rs:6:3
  |
4 |     let value = get_value(&numbers);
  |                            -------- immutable borrow occurs here
5 |
6 |     numbers.push(6);
  |     ^^^^^^^^^^^^^^^ mutable borrow occurs here
7 |
8 |     println!("value: {}", value);
  |                           ----- immutable borrow later used here
```

The compiler complains that we cannot mutate numbers because the variable value holds an immutable borrow of numbers. Because the compiler knows that value references memory within numbers, it will not allow us to mutate numbers. Experienced C and C++ developers may have encountered pointer invalidation due to buffer reallocation, which is not possible in safe Rust due to this rule preventing mutating memory that is already borrowed.

Now, in this case, the Rust compiler is smart enough to figure out how the input and output lifetimes of references match up, but we can make a very small change to our function that will prevent the compiler from being able to effectively reason about this.

Listing 4.12 Returning a reference to an argument

```
fn main() {
  let numbers = vec![1, 2, 3, 4, 5];

  let value = get_value(&numbers, "Getting the number");

  println!("value: {}", value);
}
```

```
fn get_value(numbers: &Vec<i32>, s: &str) -> &i32 {
  println!("{}", s);
  &numbers[0]
}
```

If we attempt to run the code in listing 4.12, we will get a new compiler error:

```
$ cargo run
error[E0106]: missing lifetime specifier
 --> src/main.rs:9:46
  |
9 | fn get_value(numbers: &Vec<i32>, s: &str) -> &i32 {
  |                       ---------     ----     ^ expected named
  |                                                 lifetime parameter
  |
  = help: this function's return type contains a borrowed value,
          but the signature does not say whether it is borrowed
          from `numbers` or `s`
help: consider introducing a named lifetime parameter
  |
9 | fn get_value<'a>(numbers: &'a Vec<i32>, s: &'a str) -> &'a i32 {
  |             ^^^^          ^^^^^^^^^^^^     ^^^^^^^     ^^^
```

The compiler error here gives us a great hint as to what the problem is and how we can fix it. The new get_value function has two references as its input parameters. However, the output parameter can only have a single lifetime, so the compiler needs to know which lifetime to assign to the output parameter. Is the number that get_value returns borrowed from numbers or from s? In this instance, we are borrowing from numbers, but the compiler needs to know before it can determine whether the program is valid. We tell the compiler using *lifetime annotations*. We have a little preview of them in the compiler error, but we do need to make one small change.

Listing 4.13 Returning a reference to an argument

```
fn main() {
  let numbers = vec![1, 2, 3, 4, 5];

  let value = get_value(&numbers, "Getting the number");

  println!("value: {}", value);
}
fn get_value<'a>(numbers: &'a Vec<i32>, s: &str) -> &'a i32 {
  println!("{}", s);
  &numbers[0]
}
```

The only line that changes: we add the explicit lifetime ('a) annotation.

A new syntax (<'a>) appears before the list of value parameters. These angle brackets are where Rust puts generic type arguments to functions, similar to how Java and Typescript format generic type arguments. But what is the 'a within the angle brackets? It is a lifetime annotation. Recall that when we first looked at lifetimes, we saw that the 'static lifetime was used for references that were valid for the whole run time of the program and would never be deallocated. Now we see that we can create other named lifetimes to refer to individual non-`'static` lifetimes. Figure 4.6 provides a closer look at how this syntax works in this example.

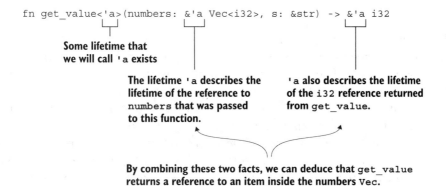

Figure 4.6 A closer look at the lifetime annotation syntax

Let's also look at the lifetime graph of this new program to see how the lifetime annotations help the compiler decide how the different borrows interact, as shown in figure 4.7.

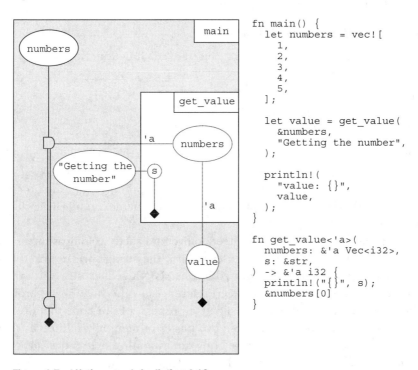

Figure 4.7 Lifetime graph for listing 4.13

You can always provide these lifetime annotations any time there is a reference argument to a function, but most of the time they are not necessary because the compiler can safely infer them. Just as correctly, we can write the signature to `get_value` like this:

```
fn get_value<'a, 'b>(numbers: &'a Vec<i32>, s: &'b str) -> &'a i32
```

This signature is explicit in naming the lifetime of the `s` reference as `'b`, but the compiler does not need to know this information because `'b` does not interact with any values other than `s`. The compiler automatically inserts these additional unnecessary lifetime rules into our code when we do not provide them, but it is technically correct (if stylistically undesirable) to name all lifetimes in function parameters explicitly.

In cases where the compiler cannot infer the lifetime information from the type signature alone, such as functions with multiple reference parameters and a reference return value, it needs to get this information from us. It cannot deduce it from the inside of the function because the output lifetime is effectively part of the public API contract of a function. If the compiler were to determine the output lifetime by looking at the code in the function body, you could have breaking API changes without changing function signatures. It is far less dangerous to ask the developer to write the annotations themselves to ensure that functions with complex lifetimes in their public APIs do not experience breaking changes.

Now that we understand a bit about the purpose and use of lifetime annotations, let's jump back to our NGINX plugin code.

4.4.2 Lifetime annotations in our NGINX plugin

We will specifically look at the `request_body_as_str` function. Recall that we're looking at the following function signature:

```
unsafe fn request_body_as_str<'a>(
  request: &'a ngx_http_request_t,
) -> Result<&'a str, &'static str>
```

Now that we understand how lifetime annotations work, we know that this signature indicates that the string returned from this function is, in fact, borrowed from the same memory as the `request` variable. We can therefore infer that the function does not reallocate any strings and simply reinterprets the memory underlying the NGINX request struct.

The returned string slice is guaranteed to live for exactly as long as the request reference passed into it. This makes sense because the string slice returned from the function points to memory that is owned by the NGINX request struct. It wouldn't be valid to deallocate the request and keep references to the body string around. The Rust lifetime system is used here to validate a property of our code that would otherwise be difficult to express—how these two pieces of memory are directly related to each other in a hierarchy. The request body cannot outlive the request struct, and we are protected from assuming that it will.

4.4 Reading the NGINX request

Now, let's look at the body of our function. We will first look at the function call `std::slice::from_raw_parts` in the middle of our function because it informs everything else that's going on. Before we can explore how this function works, we must talk about *slices*.

A slice is a contiguous block of memory containing elements of the same type, similar to an array or vector. However, a slice's representation is just a pointer and a length, so it can act as a cheap "view" of many underlying storages. This is essentially the same as the difference between a `String` (owned, growable, mutable) and an `&str` (read-only, view, may be from `String` or from `&'static str`). Figure 4.8 illustrates a `String` and multiple `&str` slices that point to substrings of it.

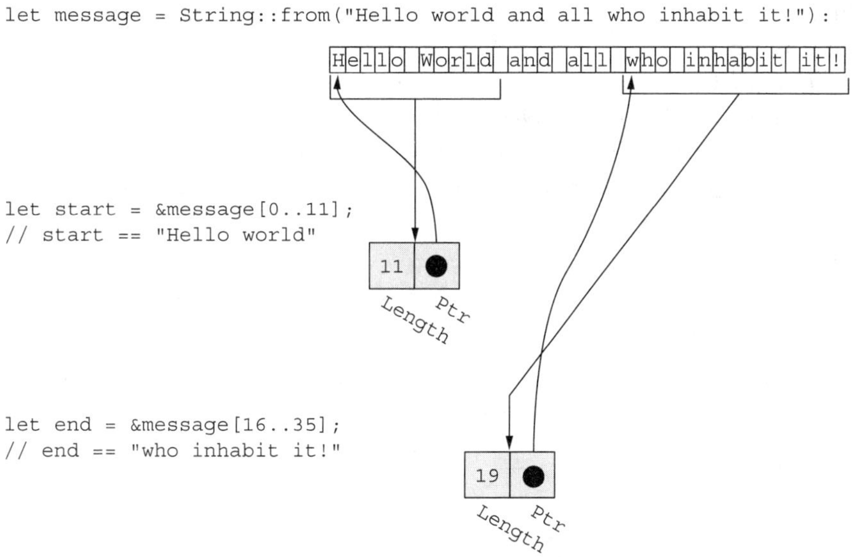

```
let message = String::from("Hello world and all who inhabit it!"):
```

```
let start = &message[0..11];
// start == "Hello world"
```

```
let end = &message[16..35];
// end == "who inhabit it!"
```

Figure 4.8 Taking multiple slices of the same string

Recall from chapter 3 that we were able to create a string reference (more correctly called a *string slice*) from a null-terminated C string. This string slice was not reallocated by Rust; we simply took a read-only view of the bytes that were passed to us by C. Since NGINX is passing us pointers into the request body buffers, we can similarly create a string slice that holds the request body. To do this, we must first create a slice of raw bytes (the type for this is written `&[u8]`). Then, we can turn this byte slice into a string slice after verifying that it is valid UTF-8 (required for all Rust strings).

To construct the slice, we use a slightly different method than the string slice construction code that we wrote in chapter 3. That code assumed we would be passed a null-terminated string and used the `CStr` helper struct. However, NGINX does not use null-terminated strings; instead, it passes around start and end pointers. Consequently, we need to use the slightly lower-level function `std::slice::from_raw_parts`. This function takes a start pointer and a length and converts them into a Rust slice.

Now, starting from the top of the function, the first thing we have is a group of null checks. You may notice something odd about these null checks, however. Let's take a look:

```
if request.request_body.is_null()
   || (*request.request_body).bufs.is_null()
   || (*(*request.request_body).bufs).buf.is_null()
{
  return Err("Request body buffers were
    not initialized as expected");
}
```

The first check seems normal enough, but subsequent checks have some odd syntax. The parenthesis and asterisk are how we access struct fields behind a pointer in Rust. It is equivalent to the -> operator in C or C++; Rust just lacks a dedicated operator for it.

It may be helpful to take a look at the structure of these types. This is a simplified look at the structure because the real types involved have a huge number of fields. `ngx_http_request_t` alone has up to (depending on compiler flags) 144 fields!

```
struct ngx_http_request_t {
  request_body: *mut ngx_http_request_body_t,
  ...
}

struct ngx_http_request_body_t {
  bufs: *mut ngx_chain_t,
  ...
}

struct ngx_chain_t {
  buf: *mut ngx_buf_t,
  ...
}

struct ngx_buf_t {
  last: *mut u_char,
  ...
}
```

This example shows equivalent operations for creating a stack-allocated struct and printing out a member based on a pointer in both C and Rust:

```
typedef struct {          ◁—│ C code
  x int
} foo_t;
foo_t foo = { 1 };
foo_t *foo_p = &foo;
printf("%d\n", foo_p->x);

struct Foo {              ◁—│ Rust code
  x: i32,
```

```
}
let foo = Foo { x: 1 };
let foo_p: *const Foo = &foo;
unsafe {
  println!("{}", (*foo_p).bar);
}
```

This code is reasonable enough for a single field access, but it can get a bit unwieldy when dealing with a larger C struct that has many nested pointer fields. The final null check in our body-getter function has only two nested pointer field accesses, and it's already a bit difficult to parse:

```
(*(*request.request_body).bufs).buf.is_null()
```

After the null checks, we find a new method call that we have not seen before:

```
let len = (*buf).last.offset_from(start) as usize;
```

When constructing string slices from raw pointers, we must first create a slice of bytes using the Rust function `std::slice::from_raw_parts`. This function takes two arguments, a pointer for the start of the slice and the length of the slice. NGINX provides a start and end pointer for its string types. To get the length of the string memory region, we can use the `offset_from` method on any pointer to get the memory offset between the end pointer and the start pointer. If we needed this information in C, we could use simple pointer arithmetic, but the pointer functions that Rust provides are a bit more descriptive. The following C and Rust functions accomplish the same goal of finding the size of a memory block between two pointers:

```
ptrdiff_t offset(char *start, char *end) {          ◁——| C code
  end - start
}

fn offset(start: *const u8, end: *const u8) -> usize {    ◁——| Rust code
  end.offset_from(start) as usize
}
```

You may notice that the Rust code also has a cast to the `usize` type because the `offset_from` method can return a negative number if `start` is greater than `end`, so it returns an `isize`. `usize` is the unsigned pointer size type, and `isize` is its signed equivalent. The `std::slice::from_raw_parts` function requires the length argument to be a `usize`, as constructing a slice of memory with a negative length doesn't make much sense. Therefore, we must convert `isize` to `usize` using an `as usize` cast expression. Because `isize` is guaranteed to be the same size as `usize`, this casting is a no-op and will never fail.

We already discussed the `std::slice::from_raw_parts` function; the only thing left is the code that turns the byte slice into a string slice. `std::str::from_utf8` performs a UTF-8 validity check on a slice of bytes and, if it passes, returns a Rust string slice.

After all this code runs and assuming no errors are raised, we have a string slice containing the request body that our NGINX HTTP handler received. Now that we understand how our handler function works, let's verify that we can extract the details we expect:

```
$ cargo build
$ ./nginx-1.19.3/objs/nginx -c nginx.conf -p ngx-run
....
Read request body: "3 4 * 2 -"

# Concurrently, in a separate window after NGINX is started
$ curl -X POST -d '3 4 * 2 -' http://localhost:8080/calculate
# this command will block forever
```

We've done it! Rust is reading the HTTP request body from NGINX. We haven't yet added the code to write out the HTTP response so curl will block until you exit it, but we are getting close to solving math from NGINX.

4.5 Using our calculator library

The calculator library we wrote for chapter 3 is already written, and we can use it to solve the same kind of RPN math problems that we expect this endpoint to receive. Let's try to add it to our NGINX handler project and do some math! First, we'll need to add the `calculate` crate as a dependency for our handler crate. Open the `Cargo.toml` in the handler project and add a new line to the [dependencies] section:

```
[dependencies]
calculate = { path = "../calculate" }
```

Normally, when we manage a dependency with Cargo, it pulls the dependency from crates.io. Since we don't want to publish our `calculate` library just yet, we can set up the `calculate` crate as a path dependency. So, the Cargo will look at the specified path as the location to search for the crate instead of crates.io. The path specified here assumes that you have a folder structure that looks like this:

```
some_directory/
  calculate/
    Cargo.toml
    src/
      lib.rs
  ngx_http_calculator_rs/
    Cargo.toml
    src/
      lib.rs
```

If not, you can set the path in quotes to the relative or absolute path of the crate directory for your `calculate` crate as appropriate.

Next, we can call the `evaluate` function from our `calculate` crate from inside of our NGINX HTTP handler function. Let's see what that would look like:

```
unsafe extern "C" fn read_body_handler(r: *mut ngx_http_request_t)
{
```

4.5 Using our calculator library

```
  if r.is_null() {
    eprintln!("got null request in body handler");
    return;
  }

  let request = &*r;

  let body = match request_body_as_str(request) {
    Ok(body) => body,
    Err(e) => {
      eprintln!("failed to parse body: {}", e);
      return;
    }
  };

  match calculate::evaluate(body) {
    Ok(result) => eprintln!("{} = {}", body, result),
    Err(e) => eprintln!("{} => error: {}", body, e),
  }
}
```

Now let's compile our handler function and try to run it:

```
$ cargo build
warning: The package `calculate` provides no linkable target.
The compiler might raise an error while compiling
`ngx_http_calculator_rs`. Consider adding 'dylib' or 'rlib' to
key `crate-type` in `calculate`'s Cargo.toml. This warning
might turn into a hard error in the future.

   Compiling ngx_http_calculator_rs v0.1.0
error[E0433]: failed to resolve: use of undeclared type or
  module `calculate`
  --> src/lib.rs:35:9
   |
35 |     match calculate::evaluate(body) {
   |           ^^^^^^^^^ use of undeclared type or module `calculate`
```

Our code does not compile! Why? If you recall from chapter 3, we told Cargo to compile our `calculate` crate as a C-compatible dynamic library. This works great for linking against C code, but it turns out that it doesn't work so well for linking against Rust code. We can resolve this error by telling Cargo to generate a Rust-compatible `rlib` in addition to a `cdylib`. The default for Cargo is to only generate `rlib` files, but if you override this setting, you lose the default. Open the `Cargo.toml` file in the `calculate` package and edit the `crate-type` field under the `[lib]` heading:

```
[lib]
crate-type = ["rlib", "cdylib"]
```

Cargo will generate both types of library files when it is configured like this, so we don't need to worry about losing any functionality. Let's try running that compile again:

```
$ cargo build
   Compiling ngx_http_calculator_rs v0.1.0
```

```
error[E0603]: function `evaluate` is private
  --> src/lib.rs:35:20
   |
35 |     match calculate::evaluate(body) {
   |                      ^^^^^^^^ private function
   |
note: the function `evaluate` is defined here
  --> calculate/src/lib.rs:73:1
   |
73 | fn evaluate(problem: &str) -> Result<i32, Error> {
   | ^^^^^^^^^^^^^^^^^^^^^^^^^^^^^^^^^^^^^^^^^^^^^^^^
```

Now we can't compile because evaluate is a private function. Remember that, when we exposed the solve function from Rust to C, we needed to add the pub keyword to the function declaration to tell the compiler that it should be visible outside of the crate. We need to do the same here with the evaluate function. The definition should change to look like this:

```
pub fn evaluate(problem: &str) -> Result<i32, Error> {
```

Rerunning the compiler gives us yet another new error:

```
$ cargo build
   Compiling calculate v0.1.0
error[E0446]: private type `Error` in public interface
  --> calculate/src/lib.rs:73:1
   |
35 | enum Error {
   | - `Error` declared as private
...
73 | pub fn evaluate(problem: &str) -> Result<i32, Error> {
   | ^^^^^^^^^^^^^^^^^^^^^^^^^^^^^^^^^^^^^^^^^^^^^^^^^^^^
   | can't leak private type
```

When an item (function, struct, or enum) is exposed publicly, the compiler tries to prevent the creation of an unusable API. In this function, for example, we mark a function as public, but part of its return type is private. If someone wanted to use this function and an error occurred, they would not be able to determine what kind of error it was. This outcome would not be good, so it is a good thing that the compiler prevented it.

As you may have already guessed, to resolve this error we need to also mark our Error enum as public. The definition of our error enum now becomes

```
pub enum Error {
  InvalidNumber,
  PopFromEmptyStack,
}
```

After we make this edit, we should be able to recompile our code with no errors:

```
$ cargo build
   Compiling calculate v0.1.0
   Compiling ngx_http_calculator_rs v0.1.0
    Finished dev [unoptimized + debuginfo] target(s) in 6.75s
```

The bulk of the `lib.rs` file in the `calculate` crate remains unchanged from chapter 3; the changed lines are shown in the following listing.

> **Listing 4.14 Changes required in the `calculate` crate**

```
...

pub enum Error {
  InvalidNumber,
  PopFromEmptyStack,
}

...

pub fn evaluate(problem: &str) -> Result<i32, Error> {
  ...
}
```

The next listing shows what our `read_body_handler` function should look like after we're done.

> **Listing 4.15 HTTP handler printing the result of a math expression**

```
unsafe extern "C" fn read_body_handler(r: *mut ngx_http_request_t)
{
  if r.is_null() {
    eprintln!("got null request in body handler");
    return;
  }

  let request = &*r;

  let body = match request_body_as_str(request) {
    Ok(body) => body,
    Err(e) => {
      eprintln!("failed to parse body: {}", e);
      return;
    }
  };

  match calculate::evaluate(body) {
    Ok(result) => eprintln!("{} = {}", body, result),
    Err(e) => eprintln!("{} => error: {}", body, e),
  }
}
```

Now that we can build our HTTP handler along with the `calculate` library, we can run NGINX with the new version of our module:

```
$ cargo build
$ ./nginx-1.19.3/objs/nginx -c nginx.conf -p ngx-run
....
3 4 * 2 - = 10
```

```
# Concurrently, in a separate window after NGINX is started
$ curl -X POST -d '3 4 * 2 -' http://localhost:8080/calculate
# this command will block forever
```

We are so close! We have linked C to Rust, read out the request body from the NGINX HTTP request struct, reused our existing `calculate` library, and solved a math problem. The only thing left is to write the result of our calculation into the HTTP response.

4.6 Writing the HTTP response

Our HTTP response is going to contain the result of our math expression in text form. It's easy enough to go from an `i32` to a `String` in Rust using the `format!` macro:

```
match calculate::evaluate(body) {
    Ok(result) => {
      eprintln!("{} = {}", body, result)

      let response_body = format!("{}", result);
    },
    Err(e) => eprintln!("{} => error: {}", body, e),
}
```

Going from this string to the NGINX response body is a bit more complicated. We're going to need to write another function that creates a number of intermediate structs and copies the memory from our `String` into an NGINX type. The full contents of this function are as follows:

```
unsafe fn write_response(
  request: &mut ngx_http_request_t,
  response_body: &str,
  status_code: ngx_uint_t,
) -> Result<(), &'static str> {
  let headers = &mut request.headers_out;

  headers.status = status_code;

  let response_bytes = response_body.as_bytes();
  headers.content_length_n = response_bytes.len() as off_t;

  let rc = ngx_http_send_header(request);     ◁─┐ Writes out the
  if rc != 0 {                                  │ HTTP status code
    return Err("failed to send headers");
  }

  let buf_p =
    ngx_pcalloc(request.pool, std::mem::size_of::<
      ngx_buf_t>() as size_t)                   ◁─┐ Creates an
      as *mut ngx_buf_t;                          │ NGINX "buffer"
  if buf_p.is_null() {
    return Err("Failed to allocate buffer");
  }
```

```rust
    let buf = &mut (*buf_p);

    buf.set_last_buf(1);           // ◀── Configures the
    buf.set_last_in_chain(1);      //     buffer for cleanup
    buf.set_memory(1);

    let response_buffer =
      ngx_pcalloc(request.pool, response_bytes.len() as size_t);  // ◀── Allocates a
    if response_buffer.is_null() {                                //     string buffer
      return Err("Failed to allocate response buffer");           //     to store the
    }                                                             //     response

    std::ptr::copy_nonoverlapping(     // ◀── Copies response body
      response_bytes.as_ptr(),         //     into a string buffer
      response_buffer as *mut u8,
      response_bytes.len(),
    );

    buf.pos = response_buffer as *mut u8;
    buf.last = response_buffer.offset(
      response_bytes.len() as isize) as *mut u8;

    let mut out_chain = ngx_chain_t {
      buf,
      next: std::ptr::null_mut(),
    };

    if ngx_http_output_filter(request, &mut out_chain) != 0 {     // ◀── Passes the
      return Err("Failed to perform http output filter chain");   //     response into
    }                                                             //     the NGINX
                                                                  //     output
    Ok(())                                                        //     handlers
}
```

Now this function is doing a lot of different things, so let's at a look at all of them. Our function performs the following high-level steps:

1. Writes out the HTTP status code and content length header
2. Creates an NGINX "buffer" object
3. Configures the NGINX buffer so that it will be correctly deallocated by NGINX
4. Allocates a string buffer to store the response body
5. Copies the response body bytes from the Rust string slice into the NGINX buffer
6. Passes our response body buffer into the NGINX HTTP output handlers

The order of operations is fairly standard for HTTP response operations. First, we must write out the response headers:

```rust
let headers = &mut request.headers_out;   // ◀── headers_out is a field of the request
                                          //     variable that holds information on the
headers.status = status_code;             //     headers that will be output to the
                                          //     client with the HTTP response.
```

```
    let response_bytes = response_body.as_bytes();
    headers.content_length_n = response_bytes.len() as off_t;

    let rc = ngx_http_send_header(request);
    if rc != 0 {
      return Err("failed to send headers");
    }
```

off_t is the pointer offset type, and it comes from the autogenerated NGINX bindings; it is not a standard Rust type.

Every Rust string (and string slice) is a collection of bytes that forms a valid UTF-8 text. We can go from the string representation to a slice of bytes using the as_bytes method.

Every HTTP response begins with a line containing the protocol version and the status code, followed by a number of lines containing the header data. The Content-Length header must *always* be set when a response body is provided that does not use the chunked response encoding. Therefore, before we can do anything with the response body text, we must write out the status code and the content length. The status code is provided to this function as an argument, and the content length can be calculated based on the number of bytes in the response body string. Once we have these two values set, we call the ngx_http_send_header function, which writes out the header data on the connection.

Next, we allocate ngx_buf_t to hold information about our response buffer. Let's see that part of the code:

```
let buf_p =
    ngx_pcalloc(request.pool, std::mem::size_of::<
      ngx_buf_t>() as size_t)
      as *mut ngx_buf_t;
  if buf_p.is_null() {
    return Err("Failed to allocate buffer");
  }

  let buf = &mut (*buf_p);

  buf.set_last_buf(1);
  buf.set_last_in_chain(1);
  buf.set_memory(1);
```

First, we use the ngx_pcalloc function. This is an allocation function that NGINX provides, similar to the C standard malloc function. It uses a pool of memory that is local to each request object to allocate the requested amount of memory.

These memory pools provide a mechanism very similar to Rust's ownership system, but they are specific to NGINX and require more run-time work. Each pool will deallocate its contents when the pool is deallocated, so when we finish handling the request, all the temporary buffers that were created in its pool will be deallocated. This deallocation allows plugin authors to allocate memory with the same lifetime as the request itself, without too much worry about setting up extra cleanup code.

A few new Rust concepts are found here; the first is the function std::mem::size_of<T>. This function returns the size in bytes of whatever type is passed to it in the type argument position. This allows us to tell the NGINX allocator how many bytes it should allocate to safely store our buffer. After a null check, we perform a mutable reborrow of the newly allocated pointer, so that we don't need to dereference it each time we want to use it.

Finally, we use some `set_` functions to initialize some settings that tell NGINX how our buffer should be handled. The exact meaning of these functions is quite specific to NGINX, but there is something interesting about these functions for our purposes. To see that, we will need to look at the definition of these fields on the `ngx_buf_t` type:

```
struct ngx_buf_t {
  ... (some fields omitted)
  unsigned       memory:1;
  unsigned       last_buf:1;
  unsigned       last_in_chain:1;
};
```

The three `set_` functions that we call (`set_last_buf`, `set_memory`, and `set_last_in_chain`) correspond with the bitfields (`last_buf`, `memory`, and `last_in_chain`) at the end of the `ngx_buf_s` type. Rust's `bindgen` tool generates `set` and `get` functions for these bitfields because Rust does not natively support them. Other than these functions, there is no good way to interact with these bitfields.

The next part of the function is quite straightforward: we allocate a block of memory to store the response body in, and we copy the data from our Rust string slice into this block. It is technically possible to simply pass NGINX a pointer to our Rust string slice, but Rust will deallocate the string when it goes out of scope, and the pointer will become invalid. We need to reallocate this string into a buffer owned by NGINX, as this is more straightforward than attempting to coordinate Rust's ownership system with NGINX (this may be possible but it will not be explored here):

```
let response_buffer =
    ngx_pcalloc(request.pool, response_bytes.len() as size_t);
if response_buffer.is_null() {
  return Err("Failed to allocate response buffer");
}

std::ptr::copy_nonoverlapping(
  response_bytes.as_ptr(),         ◁──┐ Uses as_ptr method to
  response_buffer as *mut u8,          │ get a pointer to the
  response_bytes.len(),                │ first element in a slice
);
```

We use the same `ngx_pcalloc` function as before, but this time we do not need to use `std::mem::size_of` because we are allocating a known number of bytes, rather than instances of a complex type. The function `std::ptr::copy_nonoverlapping` works the same as the C standard library `memcpy` function, with the order of the source and destination pointers flipped. It copies each byte from the Rust string slice into the newly allocated buffer.

After copying the data, we perform the final setup before passing our completed request back to NGINX so that it can perform the required IO operations to send our data across the network:

```
buf.pos = response_buffer as *mut u8;
  buf.last = response_buffer.offset(
    response_bytes.len() as isize) as *mut u8;

  let mut out_chain = ngx_chain_t {
    buf,
    next: std::ptr::null_mut(),
  };
```

We set the appropriate fields of our `ngx_buf_t` to the start and end pointers of the block of memory we just allocated. To get the end pointer for our block of memory, we need a new method, `.offset`. `.offset` is basically the opposite of `offset_from`, which returns the difference between two pointers. `.offset` takes a pointer and a number N, and returns a new pointer, which is N pointers away from the base pointer. Figure 4.9 shows a decision tree you can use to pick which method is appropriate for your use case.

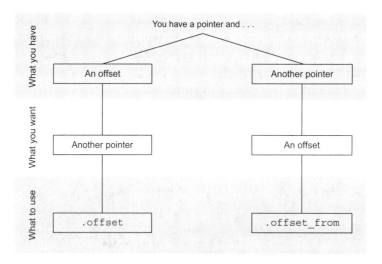

Figure 4.9 Decision between pointer/offset conversion methods

We put the buffer into an `ngx_chain_t`. This type is essentially a linked list of blocks of memory. Since we just have a single block, we initialize the chain with our single buffer, and a null pointer in the slot that would otherwise point to the next item in the chain.

Finally, with all of the configuration done and our buffers full of data, we can tell NGINX to start writing out the response data to the client:

4.6 Writing the HTTP response

```
    if ngx_http_output_filter(request, &mut out_chain) != 0 {
        return Err("Failed to perform http output filter chain");
    }

    Ok(())
```

The `ngx_http_output_filter` function takes a pointer to a request and a pointer to an `ngx_chain_t` and handles writing out the response data to the client. After calling this, we return an `Ok(())` to let the caller know that everything went as expected.

Now we can call it from our `read_body_handler` function:

```
unsafe extern "C" fn read_body_handler(r: *mut ngx_http_request_t)
{
    if r.is_null() {
        eprintln!("got null request in body handler");
        return;
    }
    let request = &mut *r;                      // The reborrow of our request pointer needs to
                                                // turn into a mutable reborrow, which allows
                                                // us to later mutate the fields of our request.
    let body = match request_body_as_str(request) {
        Ok(body) => body,
        Err(e) => {
            eprintln!("failed to parse body: {}", e);
            return;
        }
    };

    match calculate::evaluate(body) {
        Ok(result) => {
            let response_body = format!("{}", result);

            match write_response(request, &response_body, 200) {
                Ok(()) => {}
                Err(e) => {
                    eprintln!("failed to write HTTP response: {}", e);
                }
            }
        }
        Err(e) => eprintln!("{} => error: {}", body, e),
    }
}
```

Let's recompile the code and try using our HTTP handler:

```
$ cargo build
$ ./nginx-1.19.3/objs/nginx -c nginx.conf -p ngx-run
....

# Concurrently, in a separate window after NGINX is started
$ curl -X POST -d '3 4 * 2 -' http://localhost:8080/calculate; echo
10
```

The extra echo command here is because there is no newline at the end of the HTTP response, so it may be difficult to see the output of curl without this echo command adding a newline.

We did it! We have successfully created a Rust crate that provides an NGINX HTTP handler that performs math. It required a lot of steps and a lot of changes to the code files. The following listing provides the final version of what the lib.rs file should look like in your project.

Listing 4.16 Full calculator HTTP handler

```rust
include!(concat!(env!("OUT_DIR"), "/nginx.rs"));

#[no_mangle]
pub unsafe extern "C" fn ngx_http_calculator_handler(
  r: *mut ngx_http_request_t,
) -> ngx_int_t {
  let rc = ngx_http_read_client_request_body(
    r, Some(read_body_handler));
  if rc != 0 {
    return rc;
  }

  0
}

unsafe extern "C" fn read_body_handler(r: *mut ngx_http_request_t)
{
  if r.is_null() {
    eprintln!("got null request in body handler");
    return;
  }

  let request = &mut *r;

  let body = match request_body_as_str(request) {
    Ok(body) => body,
    Err(e) => {
      eprintln!("failed to parse body: {}", e);
      return;
    }
  };

  match calculate::evaluate(body) {
    Ok(result) => {
      let response_body = format!("{}", result);

      match write_response(request, &response_body, 200) {
        Ok(()) => {}
        Err(e) => {
          eprintln!("failed to write HTTP response: {}", e);
        }
      }
    }
    Err(e) => eprintln!("{} => error: {}", body, e),
  }
}
```

4.6 Writing the HTTP response

```rust
unsafe fn request_body_as_str<'a>(
  request: &'a ngx_http_request_t,
) -> Result<&'a str, &'static str> {
  if request.request_body.is_null()
    || (*request.request_body).bufs.is_null()
    || (*(*request.request_body).bufs).buf.is_null()
  {
    return Err("Request body buffers were not
      initialized as expected");
  }

  let buf = (*(*request.request_body).bufs).buf;

  let start = (*buf).pos;
  let len = (*buf).last.offset_from(start) as usize;

  let body_bytes = std::slice::from_raw_parts(start, len);

  let body_str = std::str::from_utf8(body_bytes)
    .map_err(|_| "Body contains invalid UTF-8")?;

  Ok(body_str)
}

unsafe fn write_response(
  request: &mut ngx_http_request_t,
  response_body: &str,
  status_code: ngx_uint_t,
) -> Result<(), &'static str> {
  let headers = &mut request.headers_out;

  headers.status = status_code;

  let response_bytes = response_body.as_bytes();
  headers.content_length_n = response_bytes.len() as off_t;

  let rc = ngx_http_send_header(request);
  if rc != 0 {
    return Err("failed to send headers");
  }

  let buf_p =
    ngx_pcalloc(request.pool, std::mem::size_of::<
      ngx_buf_t>() as size_t)
      as *mut ngx_buf_t;
  if buf_p.is_null() {
    return Err("Failed to allocate buffer");
  }

  let buf = &mut (*buf_p);

  buf.set_last_buf(1);
  buf.set_last_in_chain(1);
  buf.set_memory(1);
```

```rust
    let response_buffer =
      ngx_pcalloc(request.pool, response_bytes.len() as size_t);
    if response_buffer.is_null() {
      return Err("Failed to allocate response buffer");
    }

    std::ptr::copy_nonoverlapping(
      response_bytes.as_ptr(),
      response_buffer as *mut u8,
      response_bytes.len(),
    );

    buf.pos = response_buffer as *mut u8;
    buf.last = response_buffer.offset(
      response_bytes.len() as isize) as *mut u8;

    let mut out_chain = ngx_chain_t {
      buf,
      next: std::ptr::null_mut(),
    };

    if ngx_http_output_filter(request, &mut out_chain) != 0 {
      return Err("Failed to perform http output filter chain");
    }

    Ok(())
}
```

These 127 lines of Rust code have a lot of new ideas in them, but a lot of holdover C idioms can also be found in this code. Temporary buffers, unsafe function calls, and a number of other things that wouldn't appear in normal Rust code are built directly into our handler functions. The next chapter covers techniques that we can use to organize larger Rust code files into separate modules.

Summary

- `bindgen` can be used to generate Rust bindings for C and C++ code.
- Build scripts allow developers to write Rust code that runs at compile time.
- `include!` inserts a text file into our Rust source code files at compile time and compiles it as Rust code.
- Not all `extern "C"` functions need to be `#[no_mangle]`.
- Reborrowing lets us treat raw pointers as standard Rust references.
- `.offset_from` gets the difference in bytes between two pointers.
- `std::slice::from_raw_parts` constructs a view onto a contiguous block of memory from a pointer and a length.
- Path dependencies are used by Cargo to include crates that are on your machine, rather than uploaded to crates.io.
- Crates can be compiled as both `rlib` (for Rust) and `cdylib` (for C).
- When marking an item as `pub`, the compiler expects that all types that are part of its public API are also `pub`.

- `bindgen` creates `get_` and `set_` functions for C bitfields automatically.
- Slices are contiguous borrowed views of a region of memory.
- `.as_ptr` returns a pointer to the first element in a slice.
- `.offset` returns a pointer that is N elements away from the base pointer in a contiguous block.
- `std::mem::size_of` is the Rust equivalent of `sizeof`.
- `std::ptr::copy_nonoverlapping` is the Rust equivalent of `memcpy`.

Structuring Rust libraries

This chapter covers
- Organizing Rust code using modules
- Understand how paths work in relation to Rust modules
- Working with visibility rules

Virtually all programming languages have features that allow code to be divided into groups of items. So far, all the code examples that we have seen have used a flat namespace. In this chapter we will look at Rust's powerful module system and how you can use it to structure your crates.

5.1 Modules

In Rust, a *module* is a container for holding items. An *item* is a component of a crate such as a function, struct, enum, or type (there are others, but let's just worry about these for now). We have already used modules from the standard library when we imported the `Display` trait from the `fmt` module of the `std` crate. The `std` crate is the Rust standard library, and the `fmt` module contains items that help with text formatting, such as the `Display` and `Debug` traits.

5.1 Modules

Let's imagine that we wanted to organize a small program that gets a user's name and then says hello and goodbye to the user. Create a new Cargo project called `greetings` and add the following code listing to the `src/main.rs` file.

Listing 5.1 Code to get a user's name and greet them

```
use std::io::stdin;

fn main() {
  let name = get_name();

  hello(&name);
  goodbye(&name);
}

fn get_name() -> String {
  let mut name = String::new();

  println!("Please enter your name");
  stdin().read_line(&mut name).unwrap();    ⬅ The read_line function reads
                                              a line of text from stdin and
  name                                        copies it to a String buffer.
}

fn goodbye(name: &str) {
  println!("Goodbye, {}", name);
}

fn hello(name: &str) {
  println!("Hello, {}", name);
}
```

If we run it, we see that we have created a very polite program:

```
$ cargo run
Please enter your name
Thalia
Hello, Thalia

Goodbye, Thalia
```

We may want to organize these functions into two modules—one for input functions like `get_name` and one for output functions like `hello` and `goodbye`. Modules can be created in Rust code using the `mod` keyword followed by a module name and then the contents of the module inside of curly braces (`{}`).

Let's create the `input` and `output` modules now.

Listing 5.2 User greeting program with modules added

```
fn main() {
  let name = get_name();
```

```
    hello(&name);
    goodbye(&name);
}

mod input {
  use std::io::stdin;

  fn get_name() -> String {
    let mut name = String::new();

    println!("Please enter your name");
    std::io::stdin().read_line(&mut name).unwrap();

    name
  }
}

mod output {
  fn goodbye(name: &str) {
    println!("Goodbye, {}", name);
  }

  fn hello(name: &str) {
    println!("Hello, {}", name);
  }
}
```

If we try to run this now, we'll be hit with a trio of compiler errors:

```
$ cargo run
error[E0425]: cannot find function `get_name` in this scope
 --> src/main.rs:2:14
  |
2 |     let name = get_name();
  |                ^^^^^^^^ not found in this scope
  |
help: consider importing this function
  |
1 | use input::get_name;
  |

... (same error for `hello` and `goodbye`)
```

Thankfully, these error messages come with hints on how to resolve them. Because we put all our functions within the input and output modules, they're no longer in the same namespace as the main function. We can resolve this problem in a few different ways—one of which is highlighted in the help text the compiler provides us. We can add a use statement above our main function to import the get_name, hello, and goodbye functions from their modules.

For now, let's include the use statements that the compiler indicated to us. We can even combine the two statements for the output module into one.

Listing 5.3 Greeting program with use statements added

```
use input::get_name;
use output::{goodbye, hello};

fn main() {
  let name = get_name();

  hello(&name);
  goodbye(&name);
}

...
```

Let's try running our code again:

```
$ cargo run
error[E0603]: function `get_name` is private
  --> src/main.rs:1:19
   |
1  | use input::get_name;
   |                   ^^^^^^^^ private function
   |
note: the function `get_name` is defined here
  --> src/main.rs:14:3
   |
14 |   fn get_name() -> String {
   |   ^^^^^^^^^^^^^^^^^^^^^^^

... (same error for `hello` and `goodbye`)
```

The compiler can resolve the names now, but our `use` statements are causing errors because we're attempting to import private functions. Recall from chapter 3 that all functions in Rust are private by default and must be explicitly marked as public. To do that, we need to add the `pub` keyword before the definitions of our functions. Let's do this now.

Listing 5.4 Greeting program with public functions in its modules

```
...

mod input {
  use std::io::stdin;

  pub fn get_name() -> String {
    let mut name = String::new();

    println!("Please enter your name");
    stdin().read_line(&mut name).unwrap();

    name
  }
}
```

```
mod output {
  pub fn goodbye(name: &str) {
    println!("Goodbye, {}", name);
  }

  pub fn hello(name: &str) {
    println!("Hello, {}", name);
  }
}
```

Now we can run our program, and it will work as it did originally:

```
$ cargo run
Please enter your name
Pyramus
Hello, Pyramus

Goodbye, Pyramus
```

5.1.1 Who cares?

We have succeeded in repeating the functionality of our original program by adding a lot more syntax. So what? Why would someone want to go through the trouble of adding `mod`, `use`, and `pub` all over their code instead of putting everything in one large module? For many people, thinking about a few related functions in a single module is easier than thinking about every function in the program at once. If you're dealing with a bug in the database interaction of a program, it may be easier to track down if all the database code is in the same spot instead of being mixed around with HTTP, logging, timing, or threading code in a single global namespace. People generally like sorting related items into groups and categorizing them; modules are simply how we sort in Rust. Figure 5.1 shows a graph of the modules in this greeting program.

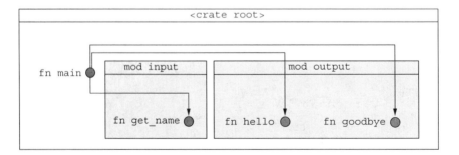

Figure 5.1 Graph of greeting program

We can also create modules that live in their own files. Let's look at how we can do that.

5.1.2 Multiple files

Right now, the input and output modules are in the same main.rs file as the rest of the code. Unless your modules are very small, it is generally considered best practice to place modules within their own files. To do so, we create a new file named module.rs, replacing module with the name of the module that we're creating. For our purposes, we will create input.rs and output.rs.

Listing 5.5 Greeter program `main.rs`

```rust
use input::get_name;
use output::{goodbye, hello};

mod input;
mod output;

fn main() {
    let name = get_name();

    hello(&name);
    goodbye(&name);
}
```

> The mod statements change in subtle ways. We move them to the top of the file, which is a style choice, and we remove the curly braces for the contents in favor of a semicolon, which indicates that we are using a file for this module instead of a block.

Listing 5.6 Greeter program `input.rs`

```rust
use std::io::stdin;

pub fn get_name() -> String {
    let mut name = String::new();

    println!("Please enter your name");
    stdin().read_line(&mut name).unwrap();

    name
}
```

Listing 5.7 Greeter program `output.rs`

```rust
pub fn goodbye(name: &str) {
    println!("Goodbye, {}", name);
}

pub fn hello(name: &str) {
    println!("Hello, {}", name);
}
```

The program still functions as intended after these changes:

```
$ cargo run
Please enter your name
world
Hello, world

Goodbye, world
```

NOTE Many programming languages use the implicit structure of the filesystem to construct a module hierarchy. Rust requires the `mod` statement in the source code to tell the compiler which files to look in. To tell the Rust compiler about the file `src/bananas.rs`, you must include `mod bananas` at the root of the crate. If you wanted to put `bananas.rs` within a `forest` module, you would need to place it in `src/forest/bananas.rs`; `src/forest.rs` would need to contain `mod bananas`; and `mod forest` would need to be at the crate root.

It is important to point out that, as far as the compiler knows, there are *no differences* between modules that use the block syntax (`mod my_mod { ... }`) and modules that use separate files for code (`mod my_mod;`). Both provide exactly the same amount of isolation; the only differences are the style differences that the programmer sees from them.

One helpful stylistic reason to place modules within their own files is that some developers find it helpful to be able to jump to specific files with known contents. It is easier in most text editors, for example, to open a file called `http.rs` than it is to search a 10,000-line-long `lib.rs` file for a module named `http`.

Now that we have divided our code into modules, let's look at how it might change when some new features are added. Imagine that we need to update our program to ask the user whether they had a good day and respond appropriately. At a high level, we may want to create items that look like this:

```
enum DayKind {
  Good,
  Bad,
}

fn get_day_kind() -> DayKind {
  ...
}

fn print_day_kind_message(day_kind: DayKind) {
  ...
}
```

With the current setup of our code, where do these items belong? `get_day_kind` probably belongs in the `input` module since it is taking input from the user, and `print_day_kind_message` similarly belongs in `output` since it writes a message to the user. Where, then, does the `DayKind` enum go? It's not directly related to either input or output, so conceptually it doesn't belong with either one. Let's create a new module for it. We'll call this one `day_kind`; it will go into `day_kind.rs`, and the only thing in it will be our new enum. We also need to add `mod day_kind;` to our `main.rs` file. These files should now look like the following listings.

5.1 Modules

Listing 5.8 Day kind in `main.rs`

```rust
use input::get_name;
use output::{goodbye, hello};

mod day_kind;
mod input;
mod output;

fn main() {
  let name = get_name();

  hello(&name);
  goodbye(&name);
}
```

Listing 5.9 Day kind in `day_kind.rs`

```rust
pub enum DayKind {
  Good,
  Bad,
}
```

⟵ **DayKind is now public so that it can be accessed from the other modules in our crate.**

Now, let's write our output function, which is responsible for printing a message to the user about how their day was. We will write it in `output.rs`.

Listing 5.10 Day kind in `output.rs`

```rust
use day_kind::DayKind;

pub fn print_day_kind_message(day_kind: DayKind) {
  match day_kind {
    DayKind::Good => println!("I'm glad to hear you're having a good day!"),
    DayKind::Bad => println!("I'm sorry to hear you're having a bad day"),
  }
}
```

Let's try to run our program now:

```
$ cargo run
error[E0432]: unresolved import `day_kind`
 --> src/output.rs:1:5
  |
1 | use day_kind::DayKind;
  |     ^^^^^^^^ help: a similar path exists: `crate::day_kind`
  |
```

Our code does not compile. The compiler provides us with help text that will make this code compile, but we are going to dive a little bit deeper into how Rust handles paths.

5.2 Paths

Everything with a name (variable, function, struct, enum, type, etc) in Rust can be referred to by a path. A *path* is a sequence of names called *path segments* separated by the :: characters, which combine to refer to an item or a variable (if the path contains only one segment). The following listing shows a few examples.

Listing 5.11 Examples of paths

```
fn main() {
  let value = true;

  // All of the lines below this are paths
  value;                    ← Path to the local Boolean variable value

  hello;                    ← Path to the function hello defined just under the main fn

  std::io::stdin;           ← Path to the stdin function in the standard library's io module

  std::collections::hash_map::ValuesMut::<i32, String>::len;   ←
}                           Path to the len function on a ValuesMut iterator for a hash map
                            containing i32 keys and String values from the hash_map
fn hello() { }              module within the standard library's collections module
```

As we can see, paths can be very small or very large, but they are all paths. If we try to build this program, the compiler will even warn us that all of our statements contain only paths (which is a no-op):

```
$ cargo build
warning: path statement with no effect
 --> src/main.rs:5:3
  |
5 |     value;
  |     ^^^^^^
  |
  = note: `#[warn(path_statements)]` on by default

warning: path statement with no effect
 --> src/main.rs:7:3
  |
7 |     hello;
  |     ^^^^^^

warning: path statement with no effect
 --> src/main.rs:9:3
  |
9 |     std::io::stdin;
  |     ^^^^^^^^^^^^^^

warning: path statement with no effect
  --> src/main.rs:11:3
   |
11 |     std::collections::hash_map::ValuesMut::<i32, String>::len;
   |     ^^^^^^^^^^^^^^^^^^^^^^^^^^^^^^^^^^^^^^^^^^^^^^^^^^^^^^^^^
```

The compiler warnings show up because paths by themselves are not too helpful. A path to a function on a line by itself is not useful; it's only useful when you actually *call* that function. A path to a struct is not useful (nor is it valid syntax); it's only useful when you construct an instance of that struct or call an associated function.

Paths contain an important gotcha that can trip up many new Rust developers—the subtle difference between relative and absolute paths.

5.2.1 Relative vs. absolute pathspaths

Relative paths, such as `hello` in listing 5.11, refer to variables or items within the current namespace, and *absolute paths*, such as `std::io::stdin`, refer to variables or items relative to the root of a crate.

It is helpful to compare paths in Rust with paths on the filesystem. Paths in Rust have a separation between crates (which always appear at the root of absolute paths) and modules (which may or may not appear in paths). This is similar to the way that paths are constructed on Windows operating systems. Relative paths use only directory names and filenames to indicate where something is located relative to some working directory, but absolute paths are rooted at a particular I/O drive, like `c:`. The distinction between drives and directories on Windows is similar to the distinction between crates and modules in Rust.

> **NOTE** On Unix-like operating systems, all paths very nicely begin with / as the root of the filesystem, with files and folders growing down from there. The Rust namespace system is not quite as simple.

When we need to use an absolute path to refer to items in the current crate, we need to use the `crate` keyword, which is a special path segment that means the root of the current crate. Another special path segment we can use, called `super`, is used in relative paths to refer to the namespace above the current namespace. Let's look at a small example to see relative and absolute paths in action. Imagine that we are writing the fictional `libsnack` crate, which has functions and types to acquire and consume delicious snacks. Currently, `libsnack` has a `lib.rs` file.

Listing 5.12 `libsnack` crate

```
pub mod treats {
  pub mod shop {}

  pub enum Treat {
    Candy,
    IceCream,
  }

  pub struct ConsumedTreat {
    treat: Treat,
  }
}
```

Notice that this example includes modules decorated with the `pub` keyword. We can add the `pub` keyword to modules just as we can with functions, structs, or enums. It means exactly the same thing for modules as it does for other items. A module without the `pub` keyword before its definition can only be accessed from the module where it was declared. If the `shop` module in listing 5.12 were not `pub`, we would not be able to access it from the crate root. We would only be able to access it from within the `treats` module.

Imagine that we want to add the following three functions to the modules in `libsnack` to handle the essential operations of snacking. The `buy` function will live in the `treats::shop` module:

```
fn buy() -> Treat
```

`eat` will be placed in the `treats` module:

```
fn eat(treat: Treat) -> ConsumedTreat
```

Finally, at the root of the crate, we provide the `regret` function:

```
fn regret(treat: ConsumedTreat)
```

All of these functions use types from the `treats` module of `libsnack` in their signatures. The paths to these types can all be expressed using either relative or absolute paths. We will write the functions in both ways to see how the code changes when we use each type of path. We'll begin with absolute paths.

Listing 5.13 Life cycle methods in `libsnack` using absolute paths

```
pub mod treats {
  pub mod shop {
    fn buy() -> crate::treats::Treat {
      crate::treats::Treat::IceCream
    }
  }

  pub enum Treat {
    Candy,
    IceCream,
  }

  pub struct ConsumedTreat {
    treat: Treat,
  }

  fn eat(treat: crate::treats::Treat) -> crate::treats::ConsumedTreat {
    crate::treats::ConsumedTreat { treat }
  }
}

fn regret(treat: crate::treats::ConsumedTreat) {
  println!("That was a mistake");
}
```

We can see that this code becomes verbose very quickly. The signature for `treats::eat` is particularly hard to read because it requires two large paths on the same line. Let's try using only relative paths.

Listing 5.14 Life cycle methods in `libsnack` using relative paths

```
pub mod treats {
  pub mod shop {
    fn buy() -> super::Treat {
      super::Treat::IceCream
    }
  }

  pub enum Treat {
    Candy,
    IceCream,
  }

  pub struct ConsumedTreat {
    treat: Treat,
  }

  fn eat(treat: Treat) -> ConsumedTreat {
    ConsumedTreat { treat }
  }
}

fn regret(treat: treats::ConsumedTreat) {
  println!("That was a mistake");
}
```

This code is a bit easier to read now. The `eat` function no longer needs any module qualification whatsoever since it is defined in the same module as the `Treat` and `ConsumedTreat` types that it uses. The downside to relative paths is that, if you move a function that has a relative type in its signature, you need to rewrite the types relative to the new location. If we move the `regret` function into the `shop` module, for example, we would need to change the signature to

```
fn regret(treat: super::ConsumedTreat)
```

Not a big deal when we have only a few functions and types, but these changes can add up and become frustrating. For that reason, it is often beneficial to combine the use of absolute and relative paths in Rust code using the `use` statement we learned about previously. Let's see how we can rewrite this crate with `use`.

Listing 5.15 Using both relative and absolute paths

```
pub mod treats {
  pub mod shop {
    use crate::treats::Treat;
```

```
    fn buy() -> Treat {
      Treat::IceCream
    }
  }

  pub enum Treat {
    Candy,
    IceCream,
  }

  pub struct ConsumedTreat {
    treat: Treat,
  }

  fn eat(treat: Treat) -> ConsumedTreat {
    ConsumedTreat { treat }
  }
}

use crate::treats::ConsumedTreat;

fn regret(treat: ConsumedTreat) {
  println!("That was a mistake");
}
```

Figure 5.2 shows all the relative and absolute paths that we use in listing 5.15.

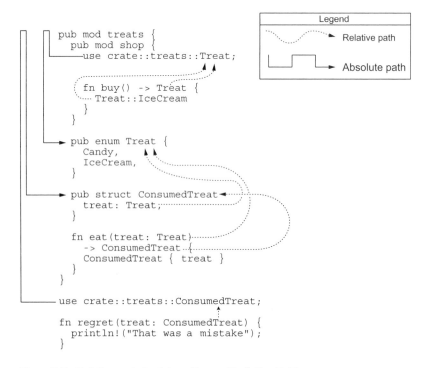

Figure 5.2   Relative and absolute paths used in listing 5.15

Notice that the arrows for the absolute paths go all the way to the top of the crate. This is intentional; it serves to remind us that absolute paths are always based at the root of the crate, and they take us from wherever we are in the crate back up to the root.

If we write `use` statements that rely on absolute paths, the rest of our code can rely on relative paths that do not need to worry about module hierarchies at all. This centralizes concerns about module hierarchies in our `use` statements, making the rest of our code easier to move around and easier to read.

Now let's jump back to our greeter program and get it to compile. Recall that we wrote the code in the following four listings, which did not compile.

Listing 5.16 `main.rs`

```
use input::get_name;
use output::{goodbye, hello};

mod day_kind;
mod input;
mod output;

fn main() {
  let name = get_name();

  hello(&name);
  goodbye(&name);
}
```

Listing 5.17 `day_kind.rs`

```
pub enum DayKind {
  Good,
  Bad,
}
```

Listing 5.18 `input.rs`

```
use std::io::stdin;

pub fn get_name() -> String {
  let mut name = String::new();

  println!("Please enter your name");
  stdin().read_line(&mut name).unwrap();

  name
}
```

Listing 5.19 `output.rs`

```
use day_kind::DayKind;                    ◁── Responsible for the compiler
                                              error unresolved import
pub fn print_day_kind_message(day_kind: DayKind) {    'day_kind'
  match day_kind {
    DayKind::Good => println!("I'm glad to hear you're having a good day!"),
```

```rust
    DayKind::Bad => println!("I'm sorry to hear you're having a bad day"),
  }
}

pub fn goodbye(name: &str) {
  println!("Goodbye, {}", name);
}

pub fn hello(name: &str) {
  println!("Hello, {}", name);
}
```

Knowing what we know now about paths, we should be able to fix it. The `day_kind` name does not exist within the `output` module, so we cannot use a relative path to get to it. We can use a special path segment called `super` that allows us to move up the module hierarchy, similar to the .. syntax in filesystem paths. However, outside of very simple cases, the use of `super` is generally discouraged. If we want to fix this error, we should use an absolute path. Since the `day_kind` module is just under the crate root, the absolute path to it is `crate::day_kind`. That means we can fix our code by changing that `use` statement to

```rust
use crate::day_kind::DayKind
```

The code should now compile. Now that we have that sorted, we can finish updating our greeter program by allowing it to ask the user how their day was. Let's write a new function in `input.rs` which does just that.

Listing 5.20 Asking the user about their day

```rust
use crate::day_kind::DayKind;

pub fn how_was_day() -> DayKind {
  let mut day = String::new();

  println!("How was your day?");
  stdin().read_line(&mut day).unwrap();

  let day_trimmed = day.trim();

  if day_trimmed == "good" {
    DayKind::Good
  } else {
    DayKind::Bad
  }
}
```

The read_line function generates a string that contains the newline character at the end of it. Calling .trim removes leading and trailing whitespace, which is necessary to compare this string to "good". If we did not call .trim, we would need to write if day == "good\n".

Now that we have a way to get a kind-of-day response from the user and a way to print out a message, let's combine them in our `main` function.

Listing 5.21 Calling kind-of-day functions from `main`

```rust
use input::{get_name, how_was_day};
use output::{goodbye, hello, print_day_kind_message};
```

```
mod day_kind;
mod input;
mod output;

fn main() {
  let name = get_name();

  hello(&name);

  let day_kind = how_was_day();
  print_day_kind_message(day_kind);

  goodbye(&name);
}
```

> We do not need to import the DayKind type to store a DayKind in a variable. Rust only requires importing structs and enums when they are used by name. If we wanted an explicit type annotation like let day_kind: DayKind, we would need to import it.

And now we can try running our program for both good and bad days:

```
$ cargo run
Please enter your name
Rose
Hello, Rose

How was your day?
good
I'm glad to hear you're having a good day!
Goodbye, Rose

$ cargo run
Please enter your name
Jack
Hello, Jack

How was your day?
bad
I'm sorry to hear you're having a bad day
Goodbye, Jack
```

So, we can now ask the user for their name and how their day was and respond accordingly. Two small matters remain that we should try to fix:

- The "Hello, {name}" text has a newline after it because we don't call .trim() on the name string. We can create a single function for pulling a line of text from stdin and trimming whitespace.
- It feels redundant to reference crate::day_kind::DayKind everywhere since the type name is the same as the module name. We can create an alias that makes it easier to use.

Let's start with the first problem. Given what we have seen from the other functions that read from stdin in the input module, we might come up with something that looks like this:

```
fn read_line() -> String {
  let mut line = String::new();
```

```
  stdin().read_line(&mut line).unwrap();

  line.trim()
}
```

But this code does not compile, and the Rust compiler is quick to tell us why:

```
$ cargo build
error[E0308]: mismatched types
 --> src/input.rs:9:3
  |
4 | fn read_line() -> String {
  |                   ------ expected `String` because of return type
...
9 |     line.trim()
  |     ^^^^^^^^^^^
  |     |
  |     expected struct `String`, found `&str`
  |     help: try using a conversion method: `line.trim().to_string()`
```

`String::trim` does not return another `String` with its own memory space; instead, it returns an `&str` string slice that references the same underlying memory as the original `String`. In most cases, this is a good thing because it means you do not need to reallocate strings when you only want to pull out whitespace. For our purposes, we need to reallocate. We can do this by following the compiler's instruction and adding `.to_string()` at the end of our line to reallocate the `&str` into a `String`.

Now, we need to rewrite our `get_name` and `how_was_day` functions to use the new helper function we created.

Listing 5.22 Greeter `input` module with `read_line` helper added

```
use crate::day_kind::DayKind;
use std::io::stdin;

fn read_line() -> String {              ◁── This function is not marked pub. It is not
  let mut line = String::new();              useful outside the context of the input
                                             module, so we do not need to export it
  stdin().read_line(&mut line).unwrap();     to the other modules of our crate.

  line.trim().to_string()
}

pub fn get_name() -> String {
  println!("Please enter your name");
  read_line()
}

pub fn how_was_day() -> DayKind {
  println!("How was your day?");
  let day = read_line();

  if day == "good" {
    DayKind::Good
  } else {
```

```
        DayKind::Bad
    }
}
```

Our code now runs without any gaps in the output after names:

```
$ cargo run
Please enter your name
Lonnie
Hello, Lonnie
How was your day?
good
I'm glad to hear you're having a good day!
Goodbye, Lonnie
```

Now that we have removed the gaps and centralized our `stdin` access, let's create an alias for `DayKind` to simplify importing it.

5.2.2 Path aliases

To create an alias for `DayKind`, we will combine two keywords that we have used many times before—pub use. When you combine these two things, they are called a *re-export* and act as an alias for the thing that is imported. Let's see how this works in practice; add the following line to the top of our `main.rs` file:

```
pub use crate::day_kind::DayKind;
```

This code both imports `DayKind` from the `day_kind` module and creates a new public-facing `DayKind` name, which is located at the crate root. We can then use it from our input and output modules:

```
use crate::DayKind;                 ← New way of writing the import statement

use crate::day_kind::DayKind;       ← Old way of writing the import statement
```

Both `use` statements refer to the exact same item, but one is shorter and relies on the `pub use` statement that we added to `main.rs` earlier.

The full contents of our greeter crate are shown in the following four listings.

Listing 5.23 Completed greeter application: `main.rs`

```rust
use input::{get_name, how_was_day};
use output::{goodbye, hello, print_day_kind_message};

pub use day_kind::DayKind;

mod day_kind;
mod input;
mod output;

fn main() {
    let name = get_name();
```

```
  hello(&name);

  let day_kind = how_was_day();
  print_day_kind_message(day_kind);

  goodbye(&name);
}
```

Listing 5.24 Completed greeter application: `input.rs`

```
use crate::DayKind;
use std::io::stdin;

fn read_line() -> String {
  let mut line = String::new();

  stdin().read_line(&mut line).unwrap();

  line.trim().to_string()
}

pub fn get_name() -> String {
  println!("Please enter your name");
  read_line()
}

pub fn how_was_day() -> DayKind {
  println!("How was your day?");
  let day = read_line();

  if day == "good" {
    DayKind::Good
  } else {
    DayKind::Bad
  }
}
```

Listing 5.25 Completed greeter application: `output.rs`

```
use crate::DayKind;

pub fn print_day_kind_message(day_kind: DayKind) {
  match day_kind {
    DayKind::Good => println!("I'm glad to hear you're having a good day!"),
    DayKind::Bad => println!("I'm sorry to hear you're having a bad day"),
  }
}

pub fn goodbye(name: &str) {
  println!("Goodbye, {}", name);
}

pub fn hello(name: &str) {
  println!("Hello, {}", name);
}
```

Listing 5.26 Completed greeter application: `day_kind.rs`

```rust
pub enum DayKind {
  Good,
  Bad,
}
```

`pub use` statements are often added to Rust code to hide the module hierarchy from the public API. This allows deeply nested and specific modules to be created within a crate without requiring end users to care about them. Imagine you are using a crate called `forest` that has the following `lib.rs`:

```rust
pub mod the {
  pub mod secret {
    pub mod entrance {
      pub mod to {
        pub mod the {
          pub mod forest {
            pub fn enter() { }
          }
        }
      }
    }
  }
}

pub use the::secret::entrance::to::the::forest::enter;
```

You could construct the very large path to the `enter` function yourself, or you could call `forest::enter`. Which one would you rather do? As a library maintainer, do you want to commit to maintaining that very long path as a part of your public API? If you change any part of that path, people using the long version of the path will have compiler errors.

A few more items are left to discuss with respect to paths and modules. Let's consider a significantly simpler version of our `forest` crate. This crate contains many modules representing various areas in a forest, each containing an `enter` function used to walk into this area of the forest. All of these `enter` functions use the shared `forest::enter_area` function for their implementation.

Listing 5.27 `forest` crate

```rust
pub mod forest {
  pub fn enter_area(area: &str) {
    match area {
      "tree cover" => println!("It's getting darker..."),
      "witches coven" => println!("It's getting spookier..."),
      "walking path" => println!("It's getting easier to walk..."),
      x => panic!("Unexpected area: {}", x),
    }
  }
}
```

```
pub mod tree_cover {
  pub fn enter() {
    crate::forest::enter_area("tree cover");
  }
}

pub mod walking_path {
  pub fn enter() {
    crate::forest::enter_area("walking path");
  }
}

pub mod witches_coven {
  pub fn enter() {
    crate::forest::enter_area("witches coven");
  }
}
```

Users of the `forest` crate should call `tree_cover::enter`, `walking_path::enter`, and `witches_coven::enter`. They should not call the generic `forest::enter_area` function, as it is only intended to work with the strings that come from other functions in this crate. The current `forest` crate does not protect users from misusing this API. The `forest` and its `enter_area` function are both exposed publicly and can be used directly by crate users. We should not expose these items publicly; we should hide them. Let's remove the `pub` keyword from the `forest` module and the `enter_area` function.

Listing 5.28   `forest` module with `pub` removed

```
mod forest {
  fn enter_area(area: &str) {
    match area {
      "tree cover" => println!("It's getting darker..."),
      "witches coven" => println!("It's getting spookier..."),
      "walking path" => println!("It's getting easier to walk..."),
      x => panic!("Unexpected area: {}", x),
    }
  }
}

...
```

If we try to compile this code now, we run into a bit of a snag:

```
$ cargo build
error[E0603]: function `enter_area` is private
  --> src/lib.rs:14:20
   |
14 |      crate::forest::enter_area("tree cover");
   |                     ^^^^^^^^^^ private function
   |
note: the function `enter_area` is defined here
```

```
--> src/lib.rs:2:3
  |
2 |     fn enter_area(area: &str) {
  |     ^^^^^^^^^^^^^^^^^^^^^^^^^
```

... (same error on lines 20 and 26)

The compiler is complaining because we made the `enter_area` function private, which is not a crate-level distinction but a module-level distinction. We could only call `enter_area` from another function inside of the `forest` module now. We don't want to add `pub` to `enter_area` since we don't want it to be available outside of the crate, but we also don't want it to be hidden from other modules *within* the crate. We can fulfill both requirements here by using a different kind of visibility modifier—`pub(crate)`.

As the syntax implies, `pub(crate)` means that the item is visible to all other modules within the crate but is not visible from any other crate. This is useful when writing utility functions that are used throughout a crate, which you do not want to expose publicly. It exactly describes the `enter_area` function in our `forest` module. Let's add that annotation now.

Listing 5.29 A module with the function visible within the crate

```
mod forest {
  pub(crate) fn enter_area(area: &str) {
    match area {
      "tree cover" => println!("It's getting darker..."),
      "witches coven" => println!("It's getting spookier..."),
      "walking path" => println!("It's getting easier to walk..."),
      x => panic!("Unexpected area: {}", x),
    }
  }
}

...
```

The crate now compiles with no problem:

```
$ cargo build
   Compiling forest
    Finished dev [unoptimized + debuginfo] target(s) in 0.13s
```

But hold on a moment: Why does this compile? The `forest` module is not marked as `pub(crate)`. Why can we use it from other modules? To answer this question, we need to look at the upward visibility rules for modules.

5.3 Upward visibility

Code within a module inherits the visibility rules from the module above itself. This concept can be a little tricky to understand, so let's look at a short example.

Listing 5.30 Upward visibility without pub

```
fn function() {}

mod nested {
  fn function() {
    crate::function();
  }

  mod very_nested {
    fn function() {
      crate::function();
      crate::nested::function();
    }

    mod very_very_nested {
      fn function() {
        crate::function();
        crate::nested::function();
        crate::nested::very_nested::function();
      }
    }
  }
}
```

Notice that no functions or modules are marked `pub`. Everything is private, but it works because the function only attempts to call functions that are higher in the module tree than themselves. We can make the code fail to compile by changing the code to call down the module tree.

Listing 5.31 Downward visibility without pub (doesn't work)

```
fn function() {
  nested::function();
}

mod nested {
  fn function() {
    very_nested::function();
  }

  mod very_nested {
    fn function() {
      very_very_nested::function();
    }

    mod very_very_nested {
      fn function() {}
    }
  }
}
```

Now, every line that attempts to call down results in a compile error:

```
$ cargo build
error[E0603]: function `function` is private
```

```
  --> src/lib.rs:2:11
   |
 2 |     nested::function();
   |             ^^^^^^^^ private function
   |
error[E0603]: function `function` is private
  --> src/lib.rs:7:18
   |
 7 |         very_nested::function();
   |                      ^^^^^^^^ private function
   |
error[E0603]: function `function` is private
  --> src/lib.rs:12:25
   |
12 |             very_very_nested::function();
   |                               ^^^^^^^^ private function
   |
```

Figure 5.3 shows the functions at each point in the module tree that are legal to call.

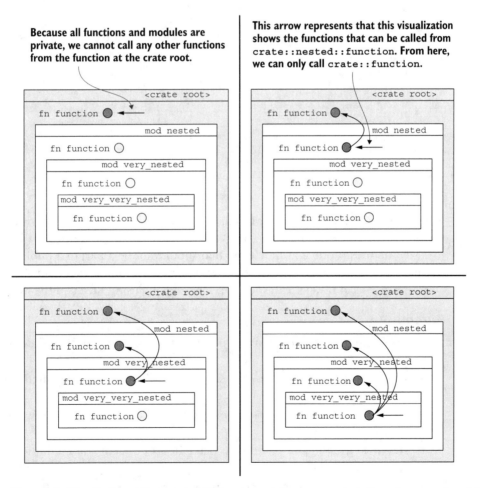

Figure 5.3 Visualization of the parent visibility rule: modules can use private items from parent modules.

So, because of Rust's implicit visibility rules for members of a parent module, the code in listing 5.29 works. Here is the final code for our `forest` crate.

Listing 5.32 Final code for the `forest` crate

```
mod forest {
  pub(crate) fn enter_area(area: &str) {
    match area {
      "tree cover" => println!("It's getting darker..."),
      "witches coven" => println!("It's getting spookier..."),
      "walking path" => println!("It's getting easier to walk..."),
      x => panic!("Unexpected area: {}", x),
    }
  }
}

pub mod tree_cover {
  pub fn enter() {
    crate::forest::enter_area("tree cover");
  }
}

pub mod walking_path {
  pub fn enter() {
    crate::forest::enter_area("walking path");
  }
}

pub mod witches_coven {
  pub fn enter() {
    crate::forest::enter_area("witches coven");
  }
}
```

Now we have a much more thorough understanding of the Rust module system, which will come in very handy as we create larger programs and libraries. Being able to easily subdivide code and hide code that should not be a part of a public interface is crucial for creating software that is easy to understand and maintain. In the next chapter, we look at how we can speed up Python code using Rust and the `pyo3` crate.

Summary

- Using the `mod` keyword allows us to separate code into logical modules with specific purposes.
- Writing `mod your_mod_name { contents; }` allows you to keep modules within one file.
- Writing `mod your_mod_name;` allows you to write the contents of the module in `your_mod_name.rs`.
- You must use the `pub` keyword to make items public if you intend to use them between modules.
- Modules can be nested as deeply as you want.

- Relative and absolute paths are used to access items within modules.
- Relative paths are evaluated relative to the current module.
- Absolute paths begin with the name of a crate.
- The `crate` keyword refers to the root of the current crate.
- `pub use` allows you to alias items.
- Modules inherit visibility from their parents.
- `pub(crate)` is used to mark items as public within a crate but private to other crates.

Integrating with dynamic languages

This chapter covers

- Writing Rust code that can be easily called from Python
- Calling Python code from Rust
- Benchmarking Rust code with Criterion

So far, we have devoted a lot of time to Rust fundamentals and C FFI. This chapter will more directly cover how we can integrate Rust code into dynamic programming languages and reap huge performance benefits from it.

6.1 Data processing in Python

Let's imagine we are working on a Python program that aggregates some newline-separated JSON data. Here is our input data file; let's call it `data.jsonl`:

```
{ "name": "Stokes Baker", "value": 954832 }
{ "name": "Joseph Solomon", "value": 279836 }
{ "name": "Gonzalez Koch", "value": 140431 }
{ "name": "Parrish Waters", "value": 490411 }
{ "name": "Sharlene Nunez", "value": 889667 }
```

```
{ "name": "Meadows David", "value": 892040 }
{ "name": "Whitley Mendoza", "value": 965462 }
{ "name": "Santiago Hood", "value": 280041 }
{ "name": "Carver Caldwell", "value": 632926 }
{ "name": "Tara Patterson", "value": 678175 }
```

Our program calculates the total sum of each of the `"value"` entries and the sum of the length of all of the `"name"` strings. This process is relatively straightforward in normal Python code. Let's save this in a file called main.py.

Listing 6.1 Python program to aggregate JSON lines

```
import sys
import json

s = 0

for line in sys.stdin:
  value = json.loads(line)
  s += value['value']
  s += len(value['name'])

print(s)
```

Let's run it to see what we get:

```
$ python main.py < data.jsonl
6203958
```

The code works, but we have heard some complaints that this aggregation code does not sufficiently meet the needs of users. People have very high expectations for the performance of this feature. Consequently, you decide to try moving the JSON parsing piece of functionality into Rust while keeping the I/O in Python, since it is part of a larger Python application. Let's look at the plan for how we can accomplish this move.

6.2 Planning the move

As we rewrite this JSON aggregation functionality, we're going to do a few things:

- Implement a pure-Rust version of the aggregation functionality.
- Use PyO3 to wrap the Rust code in a format that can be called from Python.
- Create a benchmarking harness to compare the original pure Python versus pure Rust versus Rust in Python.

Let's start by writing the functionality in Rust. First, we should identify which piece of the code we want to rewrite. We want to keep the I/O piece of the code in Python, since we are assuming that this JSON aggregation code is part of a larger Python program, such as an HTTP server. The Python code is also responsible for summing the total of each call to our Rust code. The Python code looks something like the following listing.

> **Listing 6.2 The Python code**

```python
import sys
import rust_json

s = 0

for line in sys.stdin:
    s += rust_json.sum(line)

print(s)
```

Our Rust function needs to do the things we removed from the Python code:

1. Take in a string as input.
2. Parse this string as a JSON object containing a `"name"` string property and a `"value"` numeric property.
3. Return the sum of the `"value"` property and the length of the `"name"` property.

We can sketch this code in Rust pseudocode.

> **Listing 6.3 Rust pseudocode for JSON summing**

```rust
pub fn sum(line: &str) -> i32 {
    let data = parse_as_json(line);    ◁── We don't know how to write this JSON
                                            parsing code in Rust yet, but we
    data.value + data.name.len()            explore it in the next section.
}
```

We're almost there with our Rust code, but we do need to take a small detour to look into how to parse JSON in Rust.

6.3 JSON Parsing

Many data formats in Rust can be easily parsed into Rust data structures using Serde. Serde is "a framework for *ser*ializing and *de*serializing Rust data structures efficiently and generically (https://serde.rs)." The name *Serde* comes from the first parts of the words *serialize* and *deserialize*. Serde acts as a generic framework that doesn't care about any one data format in particular, and other crates like `serde_json` act as a bridge between the generic Serde data model and the JSON data format. The Serde ecosystem has a huge number of crates for all manner of different formats. The official website lists over 20 different data formats that Rust data types can serialize into and/or deserialize from using Serde. Figure 6.1 shows how the various pieces of the ecosystem fit together.

6.3 JSON Parsing

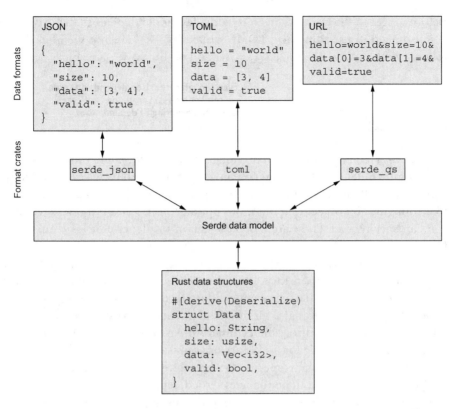

Figure 6.1 The Serde ecosystem

At the core of Serde are two traits. The `Serialize` trait is used for taking a Rust datatype and rendering it into some data format. Conversely, the `Deserialize` trait is used for parsing a data format into a Rust data type. We can write the code to implement these traits manually, but we can also use the Rust compiler to do the work for us. Let's take a look at how we can do that. Recall that we need to parse JSON objects that look like this:

```
{ "name": "Rachelle Ferguson", "value": 948129 }
```

A `name` field contains a string, and a `value` field contains a number. If we wanted to create a Rust struct to store this data, it might look like

```
struct Data {
  name: String,
  value: i32,
}
```

Let's build up the parsing code for this struct. Create a new Rust project called `rust_json`:

```
$ cargo new rust_json
```

Before we get to the code, we need to add a few dependencies to the `Cargo.toml` file. We also need to use some new TOML syntax that we have not seen before. Add the following lines to the `[dependencies]` section of the `Cargo.toml` file:

```
[dependencies]
serde_json = "1.0"
serde = { version = "1.0", features = ["derive"] }
```

> Even though serde_json depends on serde, we can list it first. Cargo does not care about the ordering of dependencies.

The `serde_json` line looks familiar enough, but the dependency line for `serde` is a bit odd. Similar to JSON, TOML can contain objects with arbitrary keys and values. Cargo accepts dependencies as either a name mapped to a version string or a name mapped to a configuration object that has more options on it. For a full reference of the keys you can specify, visit The Cargo Book's section on dependencies (https://mng.bz/N1qX).

For our purposes, we include a version number for `serde` and an array of features. *Features* are the mechanism Rust uses for conditional compilation. Crates can specify any number of features that may enable different code paths, include additional dependencies, or enable features in their own dependencies. The specific feature we need to enable is the `derive` feature, which contains the code that allows the Rust compiler to generate the parsing code for us. We are not only saved from a lot of typing, but we also generate parsing code that is specific to whatever data type we provide it.

Now that we have our dependencies settled, let's jump over to the code. Open the `main.rs` file, and add the code in the following listing.

Listing 6.4 First pass at JSON parsing code

```rust
struct Data {
  name: String,
  value: i32,
}

fn main() {
  let input = "{ \"name\": \"Sharpe Oliver\", \"value\": 134087 }";

  let parsed = serde_json::from_str(input).unwrap();

  println!("{:?}", parsed);
}
```

The program should try to parse the JSON string that we provide and print out the resulting Rust data type. Let's try running it:

```
$ cargo run
error[E0282]: type annotations needed
 --> src/main.rs:9:7
  |
9 |     let parsed = serde_json::from_str(input).unwrap();
  |         ^^^^^^ consider giving `parsed` a type
```

We run into an error now because the compiler is not smart enough to infer that we expect `serde_json::from_str` to return a `Data` instance. This function has a generic return type, similar to the `parse` function we learned about in chapter 3. Similar to `parse`, we need to give the compiler a hint as to what type it should return. Add an explicit type annotation to the `parsed` variable:

```rust
let parsed: Data = serde_json::from_str(input).unwrap();
```

Let's try running the program again:

```
$ cargo run
error[E0277]: the trait bound `Data: serde::de::Deserialize<'_>` is not
              satisfied
    --> src/main.rs:9:22
     |
9    |     let parsed: Data = serde_json::from_str(input).unwrap();
     |                        ^^^^^^^^^^^^^^^^^^^^ the trait
     |                        `serde::de::Deserialize<'_>` is not implemented
     |                        for `Data`
     |
    ::: serde_json-1.0.68/src/de.rs:2587:8
     |
2587 |         T: de::Deserialize<'a>,
     |            ------------------ required by this bound in
     |                               `serde_json::from_str`

error[E0277]: `Data` doesn't implement `Debug`
    --> src/main.rs:11:20
     |
11   |     println!("{:?}", parsed);
     |                      ^^^^^^ `Data` cannot be formatted using `{:?}`
     |
```

Now, there are two different error messages. We may recognize the error caused when `Data` does not implement the `Debug` trait. If you want to print out Rust values using the `{:?}` formatter, you must be sure to implement `Debug`. The other error is from `serde_json`: `Data` does not implement the `Deserialize` trait. Similar to `Debug`, if we want to deserialize into our struct, we need to implement the `Deserialize` trait. Thanks to the `derive` feature we included in our `serde` dependency, we can solve both errors with a single line.

Listing 6.5 Working JSON parsing code

```rust
#[derive(Debug, serde::Deserialize)]     ⬅ Note the new
struct Data {                                derive line here.
  name: String,
  value: i32,
}

fn main() {
  let input = "{ \"name\": \"Sharpe Oliver\", \"value\": 134087 }";
```

```rust
    let parsed: Data = serde_json::from_str(input).unwrap();

    println!("{:?}", parsed);
}
```

Let's try running the code now:

```
$ cargo run
Data { name: "Sharpe Oliver", value: 134087 }
```

It works! For most simple data types, adding `#[derive(serde::Deserialize)]` is all that's required to parse them from any data format that `serde` supports. Notice that the struct definition doesn't have any JSON-specific code on it. If we added the correct dependencies, we could just as easily parse our `Data` struct from YAML, TOML, MessagePack, or even environment variables. It is common for library authors to have simple data types like this implement `Deserialize` and/or `Serialize`, and then the library consumers can serialize and/or deserialize those types into whatever formats they want.

Serde has many more complex configuration options for renaming fields, providing defaults, or even nesting behavior. They are all well documented at https://serde.rs, but we do not discuss them.

Serde also provides type checking for us. Let's try changing the `name` field to an `i32`.

Listing 6.6 JSON parsing code with a run-time type error

```rust
#[derive(Debug, serde::Deserialize)]
struct Data {
    name: i32,       ◁── The expected type of name is now i32.
    value: i32,
}

fn main() {
    let input = "{ \"name\": \"Sharpe Oliver\", \"value\": 134087 }";   ◁── We provide a string value for name.

    let parsed: Data = serde_json::from_str(input).unwrap();

    println!("{:?}", parsed);
}
```

Now let's run the code to see what happens:

```
$ cargo run
thread 'main' panicked at called `Result::unwrap()` on an `Err` value:
Error("invalid type: string \"Sharpe Oliver\", expected i32", line: 1,
  column: 19)
```

Since we use `unwrap` on the `Result` returned from `serde_json::from_str`, the program panics when the function returns an error. But we can see that this error includes line and column information, as well as the exact type error that occurred.

These details represent work that we're not doing in generating error messages and validation ourselves; they come essentially for free when we use `serde`.

Now that we understand how to parse simple JSON structures in Rust, let's recreate the rest of the Python functionality. Recall that we need to sum the `value` property and the length of the `name` property. Let's create a function that parses the JSON and returns the math expression.

> **Listing 6.7 Rust program mimicking the functionality of Python**

```rust
#[derive(Debug, serde::Deserialize)]
struct Data {
  name: String,
  value: i32,
}

fn main() {
  let result =
    sum("{ \"name\": \"Rachelle Ferguson\", \"value\": 948129 }");

  println!("{}", result);
}

fn sum(input: &str) -> i32 {
  let parsed: Data = serde_json::from_str(input).unwrap();

  parsed.name.len() as i32 + parsed.value      // String::len() returns a
}                                              // usize, which must be
                                               // cast to an i32 manually.
```

We can run this code now and check its return value:

```
$ cargo run
948146
```

Let's run this JSON string through the Python version to validate the results:

```
$ echo '{ "name": "Rachelle Ferguson", "value": 948129 }' | python main.py
948146
```

The results match! Now that we have Rust code that performs the same functionality as a small piece of the Python code, we need to write some glue code that allows our Rust function to be called from Python.

6.4 Writing a Python extension module in Rust

We will be creating a Python extension module. Similar to Rust, Python uses *modules* as the organizational unit for functions, classes, and other top-level items. An *extension module* is a module that is compiled against the Python C/C++ libraries as opposed to being written in Python. As a result, they are significantly faster than normal Python modules but have public APIs that work the same as normal Python modules. We can use Rust to define Python classes, functions, global variables, and other items. For our purposes here, though, we only look at functions. Let's begin.

First, we need to update our `Cargo.toml` file to include a new dependency. We will use the pyo3 crate. PyO3 provides high-level Rust bindings to the Python interpreter. These bindings can be used both to create extension modules and to run arbitrary Python code from within Rust. We explore both in this chapter, but first, we will look at writing an extension module. Open `Cargo.toml` and update it to look like this:

```toml
[package]
name = "rust_json"
version = "0.1.0"
edition = "2018"

[lib]                                ◁── The new [lib] section that we added when creating Rust libraries to be called from C
crate-type = ["cdylib"]

[dependencies]
serde_json = "1.0"
serde = { version = "1.0", features = ["derive"] }
pyo3 = { version = "0.14", features = ["extension-module"] }   ◁── The new pyo3 dependency and the extension-module feature that we've enabled
```

Because PyO3 has a lot of different functionality, it does not include the extension module API by default. We must enable it by including it in the list of features that we're using.

Next, we need to turn our executable crate into a library crate. An *executable* crate contains a `main.rs` and can be compiled into a self-contained executable. A *library* crate, by comparison, contains a `lib.rs` and cannot be executed by itself; it must be included in some other executable. Recall that we made this distinction previously by passing `--lib` to the `cargo new` command. In this case, the only thing that `cargo new` does differently is to create a `lib.rs` instead of a `main.rs`. Therefore, the migration for us is quite simple. We must rename the `main.rs` file to `lib.rs` and delete the `main` function:

Listing 6.8 rust_json as a library (lib.rs)

```rust
#[derive(Debug, serde::Deserialize)]
struct Data {
  name: String,
  value: i32,
}

fn sum(input: &str) -> i32 {
  let parsed: Data = serde_json::from_str(input).unwrap();

  parsed.name.len() as i32 + parsed.value
}
```

Now that's sorted, let's write our Python glue code! Our first goal should be to create a module that can successfully be imported by Python. Then we can add the `sum` function to that module. Let's create our skeleton module by updating our `lib.rs` now.

Listing 6.9 Empty extension module

```
use pyo3::prelude::*;

#[derive(Debug, serde::Deserialize)]
struct Data {
  name: String,
  value: i32,
}

fn sum(input: &str) -> i32 {
  let parsed: Data = serde_json::from_str(input).unwrap();

  parsed.name.len() as i32 + parsed.value
}

#[pymodule]
fn rust_json(_py: Python, m: &PyModule) -> PyResult<()> {
  Ok(())
}
```

There are a few new interesting things going on here. Let's start with the `use` statement on the first line. Notice that it ends with `*`, which is called a *wildcard* and indicates that we will be importing all names from the `prelude` module. A *prelude* is a special module that (by convention) includes many types that are required for users of a particular crate. It is common for crates to create `prelude` modules that re-export commonly used types so that users do not need to name them all individually. It is important when designing one of these preludes to ensure that your re-exports will not conflict with other global names. For instance, notice that the items we import from PyO3 all begin with the `py` prefix.

Next, let's look at the declaration of the `rust_json` function. First, it has a `#[pymodule]` attribute on it. Similar to `#[no_mangle]`, this attribute performs a special function at compile time. Unlike `#[no_mangle]`, this attribute does not turn off Rust's name mangling but instead runs code at compile time to generate a Python extension module named `rust_json`. It is important that our function is named `rust_json` (the same as the name of our crate), or we will run into problems with name resolution when we try to import our module in Python.

`rust_json` also includes two unused parameters, a `Python` and an `&PyModule`. Both are required even though they are both unused. If we try to remove either, the `#[pymodule]` attribute will reject our function. `Python` is a marker type that indicates that the Python Global Interpreter Lock (GIL) is held, and `PyModule` represents our newly created Python module. We will add our `sum` function to the `PyModule` later. The function returns a `PyResult`, which is a wrapper type around a Rust `Result` where the error variant is a Python-compatible `PyError`.

Now that we understand the structure of our empty module, let's try to import it from Python:

```
$ python
>>> import rust_json
Traceback (most recent call last):
```

```
  File "<stdin>", line 1, in <module>
ModuleNotFoundError: No module named 'rust_json'
```

It's never that easy, is it? Before we can import `rust_json` in Python, we need to compile our extension module in a fashion that Python understands. The PyO3 developers created a tool, `maturin`, to make this process easier. It can set up development environments for Rust-based Python extensions or build distribution-ready packages. We can install it with `pip`, the Python package manager:

```
$ pip install maturin
```

`maturin` has a `develop` subcommand that will compile our Rust code and install the resulting Python module for immediate use. It has one caveat: we must run it from within a Python virtual environment. We will not linger on virtual environments but know that they are used for dependency isolation in Python projects to prevent users from accidentally overwriting a globally installed (possibly stable) version of their package while it's still being developed. Let's now create and activate a virtual environment for our development purposes:

```
$ virtualenv rust-json
$ source rust-json/bin/activate
(rust-json) $
```

The exact name we give this virtual environment is not important, but notice that the `(rust-json)` name now appears before the shell prompt. In future listings, this prefix indicates that the command must be run from within this virtual environment. If you open a new shell or leave this environment, you can reenter it by running `source rust-json/bin/activate` again. To leave, you can run `deactivate`.

Now that we have a virtual environment set up, we should be able to build, install, and import our module! Let's give it a try:

```
(rust-json) $ maturin develop
  Found pyo3 bindings
  Found CPython 3.8 at python
    ... lots of cargo output
  Finished dev [unoptimized + debuginfo] target(s) in 7.49s

(rust-json) $ python
>>> import rust_json
>>> print(rust_json)
<module 'rust_json' from 'rust_json/__init__.py'>
```

We did it! We can import a Python module written in Rust, and it doesn't spit out an error! Now that we have an empty module, let's add our `sum` function to it. We can accomplish this with some minor edits to our `lib.rs`.

Listing 6.10 `rust_json` extension module that works

```
use pyo3::prelude::*;

#[derive(Debug, serde::Deserialize)]
struct Data {
```

6.4 Writing a Python extension module in Rust

```
  name: String,
  value: i32,
}
#[pyfunction]          ◁──── This pyfunction attribute is added.
fn sum(input: &str) -> i32 {
  let parsed: Data = serde_json::from_str(input).unwrap();

  parsed.name.len() as i32 + parsed.value
}

#[pymodule]
fn rust_json(_py: Python, m: &PyModule) -> PyResult<()> {
  m.add_function(wrap_pyfunction!(sum, m)?)?;          ◁──── This add_function call is added.

  Ok(())
}
```

We added two new things: the `pyfunction` attribute macro on the `sum` function, and the `add_function` method is now being called on our `PyModule`. Just like `#[pymodule]` is used to declare a Python module, `#[pyfunction]` is required to wrap a Rust function in a format that Python understands.

The `add_function` line has a few interesting things on it; the slightly odd `wrap_pyfunction` macro is required to wrap our `sum` function in an additional layer of Python-compatible goodness. Now that we have added the `sum` function to our module, let's try to call it from Python:

```
(rust-json) $ maturin develop
(rust-json) $ python
>>> import rust_json
>>> rust_json.sum('{ "name": "Rachelle Ferguson", "value": 948129 }')
948146
```

We've done it! We reimplemented a small piece of the code in Rust and called it from Python. Let's try to integrate it into our original Python program.

> **Listing 6.11 Python program using our `rust_json` module**

```
import sys
import json
import rust_json

s = 0

for line in sys.stdin:
  s += rust_json.sum(line)

print(s)
```

And let's try to run it, recalling that the original all-Python code output `6203958`:

```
(rust-json) $ python main.py < data.jsonl
6203958
```

We get the same result! So, we have successfully duplicated the original functionality from our Python code in Rust. We believe that it's faster, but we currently don't have a great way to validate that. To really know the effects of what we've done, we need to do some benchmarking.

6.5 *Benchmarking in Rust*

Benchmarking is a topic fraught with opportunities for misunderstanding and confusion. If not constructed properly, benchmarks can provide misleading results that give one experimental path an unfair advantage over another. Benchmarks are often conducted under best-case scenarios to test the theoretical performance limits of a system, with real-world results never approaching those seen during testing.

To try to minimize this risk, we will use a benchmarking harness called Criterion, which was designed from the ground up to be easy to use and provide users with reliable and correct results. Criterion is a Rust crate that allows us to benchmark our code. We can use Criterion to benchmark both the Rust code and the Python code using the `pyo3` library to run Python from within our Rust code. This process is a little bit more complicated. Figure 6.2 shows how it all fits together.

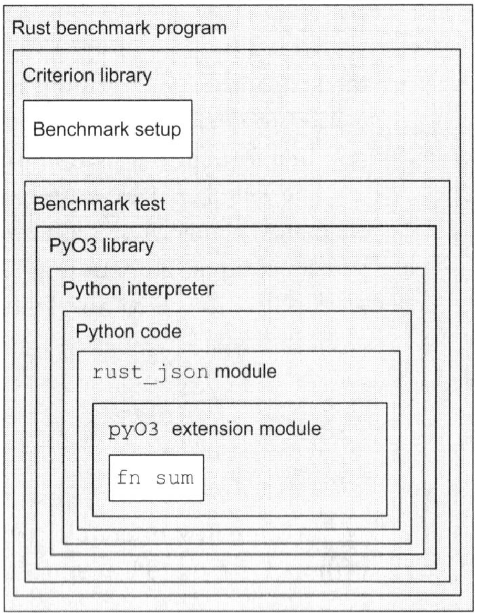

We begin by creating a new crate that will hold the benchmarking code. It needs to be a separate crate due to linking restrictions that come along with our main crate being a `pyo3` extension module. If it were a normal Rust crate, we would be able to keep the benchmark code in the main crate. Let's create this crate as a sibling directory of the `rust_json` crate:

Figure 6.2 **Anatomy of our benchmark program**

```
$ cargo new --lib rust_json
$ ls
main.py
json-sum-benchmark
rust_json
```

This new crate has dependencies on Criterion and PyO3. PyO3 needs to have a different feature enabled rather than `extension-module` this time. We must add the `auto-initialize` feature, which makes it easier to run Python code from within Rust.

Normally, we add dependencies to the `dependencies` section, but we are going to put them somewhere else in this case. `dev-dependencies` is the section of a

Cargo.toml file for dependencies that are only required when running examples, tests, and benchmarks. When adding crates that are only useful at test time, such as Criterion, they should be included in this section so that they are not compiled or linked with any final library or executable produced by our crate.

We also need to tell Cargo about the new benchmark file that we're going to create. Let's name our new file py-vs-rust.rs. Cargo needs to know the name of the benchmark file, and we need to disable the default benchmarking harness. Rust has a benchmark harness built in, but it is unstable and cannot be used with a standard compiler. Criterion is a more full-featured crate, so we are not losing anything by skipping it.

Let's add these crates to the dev-dependencies section and our new benchmark now.

Listing 6.12 Cargo.toml with criterion and pyo3

```toml
[package]
name = "json-sum-benchmark"
version = "0.1.0"
edition = "2018"

[[bench]]
name = "py-vs-rust"
harness = false

[dependencies]

[dev-dependencies]
criterion = "0.3.5"
pyo3 = { version = "0.14", features = ["auto-initialize"] }
```

- The two sets of square brackets are required; they are TOML syntax indicating the potential for multiple bench items.
- Only the basename of the file, without the .rs extension
- Tells Cargo to ignore the built-in benchmarking harness, which we replace with Criterion

Now that we have our dependencies sorted, we can create the benchmark harness file. We're going to start out by benchmarking something far simpler than Python code: the performance of addition operations using u8 values and u128 values. Open benches/py-vs-rust.rs and add the code in the following listing.

Listing 6.13 Basic benchmark example in benches/py-vs-rust.rs

```rust
use criterion::{black_box, criterion_group, criterion_main, Criterion};

criterion_main!(python_vs_rust);
criterion_group!(python_vs_rust, bench_fn);

fn bench_fn(c: &mut Criterion) {
    c.bench_function("u8", |b| {
        b.iter(|| {
            black_box(3u8 + 4);
        });
    });
}
```

```
    c.bench_function("u128", |b| {
      b.iter(|| {
        black_box(3u128 + 4);
      });
    });
}
```

This Criterion benchmark program is about the simplest we can write. There are a lot of pieces here, but they all build on things that we've seen before. Let's take a look at them individually.

The first use line brings in some items from the Criterion crate but use as a statement is not new to us, so we won't linger here. Next up is the criterion_main macro. Because we disabled the built-in benchmarking harness, we need to provide our own. We have to provide a main function to be called when our program starts up. Criterion provides the criterion_main macro to construct this main function, and it takes as input a number of Criterion *groups* to run. These groups are created via the criterion_group macro, and each one contains a number of functions to run. These groups are collections of benchmarking functions that run with the same configuration. In this case, it is the default configuration, as we don't specify any overrides.

After the macro calls, we have our bench_fn:

```
fn bench_fn(c: &mut Criterion) {
    ...
}
```

The name of this function is not important, but it is important that it matches the name provided to the criterion_group macro call. This function must take as input an &mut Criterion, which is the benchmarking manager struct. We call .bench_function, which takes a benchmark name (in this case, u8) and a closure:

```
c.bench_function("u8", |b| {
  b.iter(|| {
    black_box(3u8 + 4);
  });
});
```

This closure takes an &mut Bencher as an argument, and we can call .iter on this bencher. The actual running, looping, and measurement takes place here. Everything inside the closure of .iter will be run many times and measured for performance. Within this closure, we compute the result of the math expression 3 + 4, and we pass it to the black_box function, which is provided by Criterion to ensure that the compiler does not optimize away a computation that it detects as unused. We have another call to .bench_function and .iter for the u128 example, and it works in the same way:

```
c.bench_function("u128", |b| {
  b.iter(|| {
    black_box(3u128 + 4);
  });
});
```

NOTE It is important to pass the final results of benchmark tests to `black_box` to ensure that the compiler does not optimize away your entire test!

Figure 6.3 shows a visual idea of what's happening in the benchmark file.

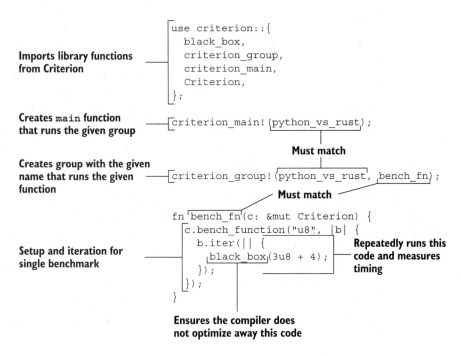

Figure 6.3 Anatomy of a benchmark file

Now that we understand a bit about what's happening in the benchmark file, let's run our benchmark test and see what results it spits out. We can run it with `cargo bench`. You should get output that looks roughly like this:

```
$ cd json-sum-benchmark
$ cargo bench
   Compiling json-sum-benchmark v0.1.0
    Finished bench [optimized] target(s) in 2.09s
     Running unittests

running 1 test
test tests::it_works ... ignored

test result: ok. 0 passed; 0 failed; 1 ignored; 0 measured; 0 filtered out;

     Running unittests
Benchmarking u8: Warming up for 3.0000 s
Benchmarking u8: Collecting 100 samples in estimated 5.0000 s (20B iters)
u8                      time:   [257.13 ps 261.71 ps 266.79 ps]
```

```
Benchmarking u128: Warming up for 3.0000 s
Benchmarking u128: Collecting 100 samples in estimated 5.0000 s (10B iters)
u128                    time:   [502.27 ps 510.24 ps 521.03 ps]
```

After compilation finishes, we first get a run through all the unit tests and an ignored line for each. The it_works unit test is written by Cargo when we run cargo new --lib by default. Benchmark tests are considered a subset of tests, and the built-in unit testing harness allow users to write benchmark tests alongside unit tests, which is why they show up in this output.

Next, the output from Criterion runs the benchmark as many times as possible in 3 seconds to warm the CPU and memory caches and get a clean measurement. It then attempts to run the benchmark as many times as possible within 5 seconds and measures the execution time of these iterations. It estimates that it will be able to perform 20 billion iterations for the u8 version and 10 billion iterations for the u128 version.

Finally, for each test, we get a line showing the estimated run time of a single iteration of the benchmark within a confidence interval. This confidence interval is configurable, but it defaults to 95%. The first and last numbers are the lower and upper bounds of the interval, and the middle number is Criterion's best guess for the time taken on each interval. It's a great way to reduce the data from 20 billion iterations of a test down to three numbers. Figure 6.4 shows the data output for each benchmark test.

In addition to its simplicity, this program is a great example of using Criterion because it highlights how precise the library is. We captured a factor of two differences at the 0.1 nanosecond level—a difference of 250 trillionths of a second. Criterion is very precise and has low overhead. You can time and measure almost anything you throw at it.

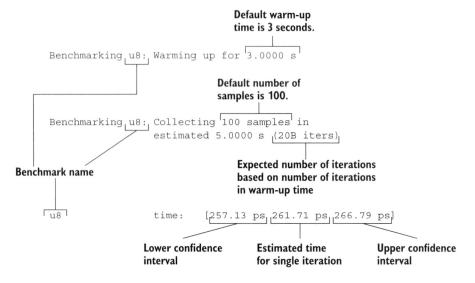

Figure 6.4 Anatomy of Criterion's command-line output

Now let's try to apply Criterion to our use case. Remember that we're trying to benchmark Python's built-in `json` module against the custom `rust_json.sum` method that we wrote in Rust and exposed via a PyO3 extension module.

To benchmark our Python code from within Rust, we need to write some code that uses a different part of the `pyo3` API. We already used it to create Rust code that can be called from Python, but we can also use PyO3 to run Python code from within Rust.

Let's write a function now called `bench_py` that allows us to do this. The function needs a few parameters: a Criterion `Bencher` so that it can run the benchmark test, the input string to use for parsing, and the Python code that will be run in the test. Here's what that function will look like:

```
use criterion::Bencher;
use pyo3::prelude::*;
use pyo3::types::PyDict;

fn bench_py(b: &mut Bencher, code: &str, input: &str) {
  Python::with_gil(|py| {
    let locals = PyDict::new(py);

    locals.set_item("json", py.import("json").unwrap()).unwrap();
    locals
      .set_item("rust_json", py.import("rust_json").unwrap())
      .unwrap();
    locals.set_item("INPUT", input).unwrap();

    b.iter(|| black_box(py.run(code, None, Some(&locals)).unwrap()));
  });
}
```

A lot is going on in this function. Let's break it down. The function begins with a call to `Python::with_gil`. The Python interpreter requires that most operations run from a single thread per process by utilizing the GIL data structure. The core data structures of Python require that users are holding the GIL and are not thread safe. These requirements do not matter too much from normal Python code (beyond the performance problems they raise), but it is very important when using the Python C API. PyO3 enforces the rule that the GIL is always held when required, and we acquire it using this `with_gil` function. It takes as its only parameter a function that itself is passed a handle to the Python GIL. This handle is required for interfacing with many PyO3 types.

After the GIL is acquired, we create a new `PyDict` to hold the local variables that will be injected into our code sample. `PyDict` is the PyO3 equivalent of creating a Python dict. Notice that this action requires us to use the handle to the GIL that we previously acquired.

The next few lines place items within our newly created `locals` dict. The first two are importing libraries—the `json` library, which is used by the pure-Python benchmark code, and then the `rust_json` library for the `pyo3` extension module benchmark. The `import` method on the GIL handle is used to import a Python library and returns a module instance. The `set_item` function we use on the `PyDict` is generic and can be passed any key and value types that can be converted into Python objects. The last `set_item` line is used to pass the input string from the Rust code to the Python code in the form of a variable called INPUT.

The final section of the function is running the actual benchmark. Recall from our previous example that b.iter takes in a function that is run over and again many times by Criterion and measured for its performance. Notice that we do not include the initialization code as a part of this iteration to save benchmark run time and to eliminate possible sources of noise. Within this function, we again use black_box to ensure that the compiler does not optimize away any computations. The py.run function we call here takes in a string containing Python code to run and two Option<&PyDict> values to hold global variables and local variables. We store our inputs as local variables. Figure 6.5 shows how all the pieces work together.

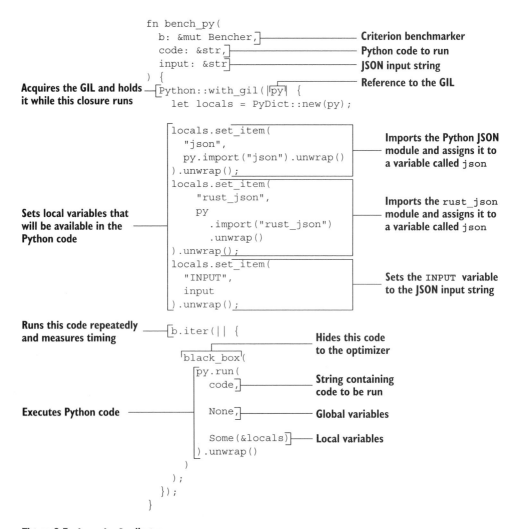

Figure 6.5 bench_fn diagram

6.5 Benchmarking in Rust

Let's use that function to compare the performance of the two versions of the code.

Listing 6.14 Benchmarking pure Python vs. a Rust extension module

```rust
use criterion::{
  black_box, criterion_group, criterion_main, Bencher, Criterion,
};
use pyo3::prelude::*;
use pyo3::types::PyDict;

criterion_main!(python_vs_rust);
criterion_group!(python_vs_rust, bench_fn);

fn bench_py(b: &mut Bencher, code: &str, input: &str) {
  Python::with_gil(|py| {
    let locals = PyDict::new(py);

    locals.set_item("json", py.import("json").unwrap()).unwrap();
    locals
      .set_item("rust_json", py.import("rust_json").unwrap())
      .unwrap();
    locals.set_item("INPUT", input).unwrap();

    b.iter(|| black_box(py.run(code, None, Some(&locals)).unwrap()));
  });
}

fn bench_fn(c: &mut Criterion) {
  let input = r#"{"name": "lily", "value": 42}"#;

  c.bench_function("pure python", |b| {
    bench_py(
      b,
      "
value = json.loads(INPUT)
s = value['value'] + len(value['name'])
",
      input,
    );
  });

  c.bench_function("rust extension library", |b| {
    bench_py(b, "s = rust_json.sum(INPUT)", input);
  });
}
```

Now, let's try running our benchmark, ensuring that we're within the virtual environment that we created earlier:

```
(rust-json) $ cd json-sum-benchmark
(rust-json) $ cargo bench
Benchmarking pure python: Collecting 100 samples in estimated
                         5.1074 s (202k iterations)
pure python             time:   [25.415 us 25.623 us 25.842 us]
```

```
Benchmarking rust extension library: Collecting 100 samples in estimated
                                5.0931 s (232k iterations)
rust extension library  time:   [21.746 us 21.987 us 22.314 us]
```

Wait a minute. The Rust version is barely faster than the pure Python version. We put in an awful lot of work to get a 10% speed boost beyond base Python. We are forgetting one important thing that Rust has that Python does not: an optimizing compiler. Let's take a small detour to look at that.

6.6 Optimized builds

You may recall the following line from the end of all our `cargo build` commands:

```
Finished dev [unoptimized + debuginfo] target(s) in 2s
```

This code line indicates that Cargo is not compiling our code with any optimizations enabled. Running compile-time optimizations increases compile time, so they are not enabled by default. If you're running your code on a development machine for testing purposes, you can generally get away with this, as we have been able to up to this point. When you want to distribute your code or run it in production somewhere, you should be using optimized builds. It's quite straightforward to get Cargo to produce optimized builds; we simply need to add the `--release` flag to any `cargo build` or `cargo run` commands that we're using.

In this particular case, we're building a `pyo3` extension module and using the `maturin develop` command to do it. This command is a small wrapper around `cargo build` and accepts many of the same parameters and flags that Cargo does. It accepts the `--release` flag, so let's recompile our extension module with this flag to produce an optimized binary:

```
$ (rust-json) cd rust_json
$ (rust-json) maturin develop --release
   Found pyo3 bindings
   Found CPython 3.8 at python
   Compiling pyo3-build-config v0.14.5
   Compiling pyo3-macros-backend v0.14.5
   Compiling pyo3 v0.14.5
   Compiling pyo3-macros v0.14.5
   Compiling rust-json v0.1.0
    Finished release [optimized] target(s) in 7.91s
```

Notice that the last line now indicates that Cargo has produced an [optimized] build in release mode.

Now let's rerun our benchmarks to see how that affects the performance:

```
$ (rust-json) cd json-sum-benchmark
$ (rust-json) cargo bench
   Compiling pyo3-build-config v0.14.5
   Compiling pyo3-macros-backend v0.14.5
   Compiling pyo3 v0.14.5
   Compiling pyo3-macros v0.14.5
```

```
Compiling json-sum-benchmark v0.1.0
  Finished bench [optimized] target(s) in 9.21s
  Running unittests
```
> Cargo compiles benchmark tests in release mode by default.

```
Benchmarking pure python: Collecting 100 samples in estimated
                         5.1069 s (202k iterations)
pure python             time:    [25.019 us 25.188 us 25.377 us]

Benchmarking rust extension library: Collecting 100 samples in estimated
                         5.0306 s (454k iterations)
rust extension library  time:    [10.843 us 10.918 us 10.996 us]
```

We see some interesting results. Just by switching to a release build, we've doubled the performance of our Rust code. The Rust version is now over twice as fast as the pure Python code. This example is isolated, and in many cases, replacing Python with Rust can lead to even more significant performance gains. You will need to measure your own code to determine how much benefit you gain from adopting Rust.

In sum, we walked through the process of incrementally adding Rust to an existing Python application. These steps are

1. Identifying isolated code that can be extracted
2. Writing Rust code that performs the expected behavior
3. Wrapping the Rust code in language-specific bindings
4. Compiling the extension module with `--release`
5. Importing your new module in the non-Rust language
6. Benchmarking the old and new code paths to validate that performance has improved

We looked at a specific example of integrating with Python, but similar steps can be taken with many other dynamic languages. Just as `pyO3` is used for Python integration with Rust, similar crates are available for other languages. Rutie integrates with Ruby, Neon is for Node.js, j4rs and JNI work with Java, and flutter_rust_bridge can be used to integrate with Flutter applications.

Summary

- `serde` is the de facto standard ecosystem for serializing and deserializing in Rust.
- `#[derive(serde::Deserialize)]` allows structs to easily be parsed from many different data formats.
- The `derive` feature of `serde` must be enabled to use the derive macros.
- `serde_json::from_str` is used to parse a Rust data structure from a JSON string.
- `pyO3` is a Rust crate that can be used to interface with the Python interpreter.
- Enabling the `extension-module` feature of PyO3 allows you to easily expose Rust functions to Python.

- `maturin` is a command-line tool that makes developing Python modules in Rust easier.
- `maturin develop` compiles and installs a Rust-based Python module in a virtual environment.
- The `auto-initialize` feature of PyO3 should be enabled when running Python code from within Rust.
- `dev-dependencies` in `Cargo.toml` holds dependencies used for unit, integration, and benchmark tests.
- Criterion is a Rust crate for benchmarking code.
- The `bench` sections of `Cargo.toml` hold information about benchmark test files.
- Each `bench` section requires a `name` field and `harness = false`.
- Within a benchmarking group function, use `.bench_function` and `.iter` to run the code you want to measure.
- Use `criterion::black_box` to ensure the compiler does not optimize out code.
- `Python::with_gil` acquires the GIL with PyO3.
- `PyDict` are the PyO3 equivalent of Python dict objects.
- `.run` can be used to run Python code strings from Rust.
- Passing `--release` to many Cargo commands will cause the compiler to apply optimizations, which may lead to multiple-times performance improvements.

Testing your Rust integrations

This chapter covers

- Writing automated tests in Rust
- Testing Rust code from a dynamic language
- Reusing existing tests using monkey patching
- Testing new code against old code with randomized inputs

When shipping large refactors, it is important to validate that the code will behave as expected. Some form of automated testing is generally considered best practice across the industry. In this chapter, we will create automated tests for the JSON summing code that we wrote in the last chapter. Let's get started by adding some unit tests to our Rust code.

7.1 Writing tests with Rust

Rust has a minimal testing system built into the language itself. You may recall a brief mention of it from chapter 3. As we discussed in chapter 2, beginning a new Rust application will automatically create a "Hello world!" program for you. When we create a blank library, we similarly are presented with automated test scaffolding. Let's create a blank library crate called `testing` to play around with some tests before we apply what we learn to the JSON library:

```
$ cargo new --lib testing
```

Now, open `testing/src/lib.rs`, and look at the prebuilt test code that we get from Cargo.

Listing 7.1 Contents of a newly initialized Rust library

```
#[cfg(test)]
mod tests {
  #[test]
  fn it_works() {
    let result = 2 + 2;
    assert_eq!(result, 4);
  }
}
```

Let's break down all of the parts of this file to understand how they are all useful and come together to create a test suite. We'll start with the first two lines of the file, which contain some syntax we have not seen before:

```
#[cfg(test)]
mod tests {
```

The second line is similar to inline modules that we have seen before, but the first line is something new. Here we create a new module called `tests` that will hold all of the test functions for our library. The first line is an attribute macro called `cfg`, which allows us to tell the compiler to compile or skip certain parts of the code when operating under certain circumstances. For example, we might create OS-specific versions of a function and use `cfg` to control which version should be compiled depending on the target operating system. Developers can create custom conditional compilation flags that allow users to specify whole features to include or exclude from compilation.

These flags can be attached to any item—function, struct, trait, block, or, in this case, module. Because `cfg(test)` is at the module level, everything within the `tests` module will only be compiled when the compiler is compiling tests. As a result, builds of an executable or library will not include our tests. This keeps binary size down and limits the number of lines of code that need to be validated by the compiler.

> **NOTE** It is not strictly required to put tests within a module with `#[cfg(test)]` on it, but it is considered best practice.

Placing all tests within a module allows us to easily exclude testing code from production builds without needing to attach `#[cfg(test)]` to all test functions. This reduces the risk that a test value or function will be used accidentally and keeps binary sizes down.

7.1 Writing tests with Rust

Next, let's take a look at the function within the module `it_works`:

```
#[test]
fn it_works() {
```

Like many other languages, the individual unit of testing in Rust (the minimum thing that can fail or pass) is a function. Unlike some other languages, test function names are not significant in Rust. They are only useful for communicating with the developer. Instead, the `#[test]` attribute macro signals to the compiler whose functions contain tests. In this case, the `it_works` test validates that 2 + 2 equals 4. Let's look inside the function to see how we do this:

```
let result = 2 + 2;
assert_eq!(result, 4);
```

The `assert_eq` macro will compare the two values passed into it for equality. If they are not equal, it will panic the thread running the test. The test framework will catch the panic, and the test will be marked as "failed" with a message containing the `Debug` representation of both values to aid in debugging the test. `assert_eq` is not a test-specific macro; it can be used in any and all Rust code, but due to the nature of most automated tests, it appears in them quite regularly.

We could write tests that don't use `assert_eq!`. The `assert!` macro similarly validates that whatever Boolean passed into it is `true` and will panic if it is not. We might also write tests that only validate that functions do not return errors, and these might accomplish that by using `.unwrap()` or `.expect()` and contain no `assert!`/`assert_eq!` macros. Figure 7.1 shows the most important parts of our test module.

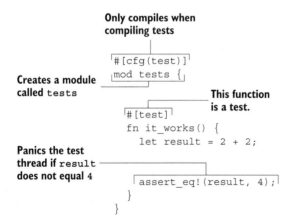

Figure 7.1 Diagram of a test module

Now that we understand how the parts of our test fit together, let's see what it looks like to run a test:

```
$ cargo test
   Compiling testing v0.1.0
```

```
    Finished test [unoptimized + debuginfo] target(s) in 0.31s
     Running unittests

running 1 test
test tests::it_works ... ok

test result: ok. 1 passed; 0 failed;

   Doc-tests testing

running 0 tests
```

The most important part of this output is the line that has the name of the test we wrote alongside `ok`, which indicates that the test ran successfully. Let's also take a look at what we see when a failing test is added to the mix. Add the `it_does_not_work` test to our `lib.rs` file.

Listing 7.2 A test that fails

```
#[cfg(test)]
mod tests {
  #[test]
  fn it_works() {
    let result = 2 + 2;
    assert_eq!(result, 4);
  }

  #[test]
  fn it_does_not_work() {
    let result = 2 + 2;
    assert_eq!(result, 5);          ◁──┤ We assert 2 + 2 = 5,
  }                                     something that always fails.
}
```

Let's run this:

```
$ cargo test
   Compiling testing v0.1.0
    Finished test [unoptimized + debuginfo] target(s) in 0.33s
     Running unittests

running 2 tests
test tests::it_works ... ok
test tests::it_does_not_work ... FAILED

failures:

---- tests::it_does_not_work stdout ----
thread 'tests::it_does_not_work' panicked at 'assertion failed:
  left: `4`,
 right: `5`', testing/src/lib.rs:12:5
note: run with `RUST_BACKTRACE=1` environment variable to display backtrace

failures:
    tests::it_does_not_work
```

```
test result: FAILED. 1 passed; 1 failed;

error: test failed, to rerun pass '--lib'
```

This output contains a lot of information. We still get the passing `it_works` test, but the `it_does_not_work` test is highlighted as failing. After the list of tests, we can see the captured `stdout` from the failing test, which shows us the two values passed to `assert_eq`. We can use these values to determine where we went wrong. We also get the filename and line number of the failing `assert_eq` macro. Recall from chapter 2 that the note about `RUST_BACKTRACE` is generic and printed any time a thread panics.

By default, `stdout` and `stderr` are captured by the Rust test framework and not emitted to the console. They are stored in memory and only emitted when a test fails. Consequently, you can print out as many log messages as you'd like during test execution, and your output will stay clean. Let's take a look at how this works by adding some output to our tests.

Listing 7.3 Writing to `stdout` and `stderr` from tests

```rust
#[cfg(test)]
mod tests {
  #[test]
  fn it_works() {
    eprintln!("it_works stderr");
    println!("it_works stdout");
    let result = 2 + 2;
    assert_eq!(result, 4);
  }

  #[test]
  fn it_does_not_work() {
    eprintln!("it_does_not_work stderr");
    println!("it_does_not_work stdout");
    let result = 2 + 2;
    assert_eq!(result, 5);
  }
}
```

And let's see what the console output of this looks like:

```
$ cargo test
   Compiling testing v0.1.0
    Finished test [unoptimized + debuginfo] target(s) in 0.31s
     Running unittests

running 2 tests
test tests::it_works ... ok
test tests::it_does_not_work ... FAILED

failures:

---- tests::it_does_not_work stdout ----
it_does_not_work stderr
```

```
it_does_not_work stdout
thread 'tests::it_does_not_work' panicked at 'assertion failed:
  left: `4`,
 right: `5`', testing/src/lib.rs:16:5
note: run with `RUST_BACKTRACE=1` environment variable to display backtrace

failures:
    tests::it_does_not_work
```

Notice that we get stdout and stderr streams unified under the stdout banner from the test output, but we don't get either message from the it_works test. Sometimes it can be beneficial to get full output streams from all tests by disabling capturing. We can do this by passing the --nocapture flag to the test binary. It is important to note that we are passing this flag to the test binary and not to Cargo. We can do this using an extra -- to separate the arguments for Cargo with arguments for the test binary. Let's do that now:

```
$ cargo test -- --nocapture
    Finished test [unoptimized + debuginfo] target(s) in 0.03s
     Running unittests

running 2 tests
it_does_not_work stderr
it_does_not_work stdout
thread 'tests::it_does_not_work' panicked at 'assertion failed:
  left: `4`,
 right: `5`', testing/src/lib.rs:16it_works stderr
:5it_works stdout

note: run with `RUST_BACKTRACE=1` environment variable to display backtrace
test tests::it_works ... ok
test tests::it_does_not_work ... FAILED

failures:


failures:
    tests::it_does_not_work

test result: FAILED. 1 passed; 1 failed;

error: test failed, to rerun pass '--lib'
```

Notice it_works stderr at the end of this line.

Notice it_works stdout at the end of this line.

It may be a bit difficult to see, but notice that we're now getting the output of the it_works test along with the it_does_not_work test. The output streams are muddied together, though, because Rust runs tests in parallel by default. We can clean this up a bit by running the tests only from a single thread, which is controlled via the --test-threads argument:

```
$ cargo test -- --nocapture --test-threads=1
    Finished test [unoptimized + debuginfo] target(s) in 0.03s
     Running unittests
```

7.1 Writing tests with Rust

```
running 2 tests
test tests::it_does_not_work ... it_does_not_work stderr
it_does_not_work stdout
thread 'main' panicked at 'assertion failed: `(left == right)`
  left: `4`,
 right: `5`', chapter-07/listing_03_stdout/src/lib.rs:16:5
note: run with `RUST_BACKTRACE=1` environment variable to display backtrace
FAILED
test tests::it_works ... it_works stderr
it_works stdout
ok

failures:

failures:
    tests::it_does_not_work

test result: FAILED. 1 passed; 1 failed;
```

Now, we see the outputs independently, but serial test execution isn't great for run time. Usually, when running tests, we won't want to print out all the output, and we won't want to run all the tests serially like this. For now, let's delete the output code and the failing test. Your code should now look like the library crate starter code:

```rust
#[cfg(test)]
mod tests {
  #[test]
  fn it_works() {
    let result = 2 + 2;
    assert_eq!(result, 4);
  }
}
```

When writing Rust crates that will be used by others, it is also considered best practice to document your functions. Unfortunately, documentation and examples can frequently become out of date. Rust has a system in place to help; it supports running code examples in documentation via the testing system. Let's look at a short example to see how it works.

7.1.1 Documentation tests

Imagine you are writing a small function called `add` that takes in two numbers and adds them together. You want to make the code as easy to use as possible for the developer consuming your library, so you write some comments. Let's add this function to our `lib.rs` file outside of the `tests` module.

Listing 7.4 Add function

```rust
// Add together two i32 numbers and return the result of that addition
pub fn add(x: i32, y: i32) -> i32 {
  x + y
}
```

Now this comment looks reasonable enough when looking at the source code, but Rust has a powerful documentation system built in that we can access by changing our comment slightly. Instead of using the standard comment with two slash symbols, using three slashes creates a *documentation comment,* or *doc comment* for short. These comments are associated with items that will be picked up by Rust's documentation system. Let's make one now.

> **Listing 7.5 Giving the add function a documentation comment**

```
/// Add together two i32 numbers and return the result of that addition
pub fn add(x: i32, y: i32) -> i32 {
  x + y
}
```

The difference is subtle from a code perspective, but let's see what we can do with it. Let's generate the documentation for our library and look at the output:

```
$ cargo doc --open
```

This command generates documentation for all public items in your crate and opens a web browser to that documentation. Click the add function to see its type signature and the doc comment that we just wrote, as shown in figure 7.2.

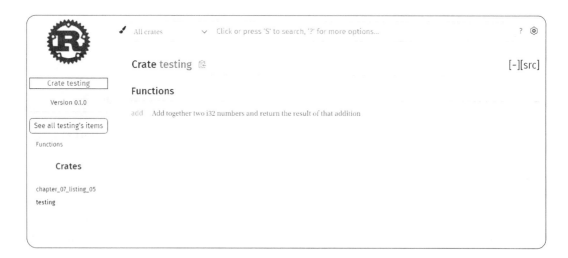

Figure 7.2 Screenshot of documentation for the add function

In addition to the documentation itself, we can add examples to doc comments that are validated when running tests. Let's add a few now. For the sake of completeness, we will add one that passes, one that fails, and one that does not compile.

Listing 7.6 Documentation tests

```
/// Add together two i32 numbers and return the result of that addition
/// ```
/// assert_eq!(testing::add(2, 2), 4);
/// ```
///
/// ```
/// use testing::add;
/// assert_eq!(add(2, 2), 5);
/// ```
///
/// ```
/// use testing::add;
/// assert_eq!(add("hello", 2), 5);
/// ```
pub fn add(x: i32, y: i32) -> i32 {
  x + y
}
```

Notice that these are Markdown code blocks. Doc comments support Markdown syntax for making lists, links, bolding, italics, and more. It is also important to note that each doc comment is compiled as a separate crate. As a result, it only has access to the public API of your crate, and you must either import items from your crate or use a fully qualified path; these items are meant to be examples of the public API for the users of your crate.

Notice that the second doc test will fail. It contains an assertion that 2 + 2 = 5, which is nonsense. The third test won't even compile as it tries to pass the string slice `"hello"` where an `i32` is required. Let's see how Rust's testing system shows us this failure to document:

```
$ cargo test
   Compiling testing v0.1.0
    Finished test [unoptimized + debuginfo] target(s) in 0.30s
     Running unittests

running 1 test
test tests::it_works ... ok

test result: ok. 1 passed; 0 failed;

   Doc-tests chapter-07-listing-06

running 3 tests
test src/lib.rs - add (line 11) ... FAILED
test src/lib.rs - add (line 2) ... ok
test src/lib.rs - add (line 6) ... FAILED

failures:

---- src/lib.rs - add (line 11) stdout ----
error[E0308]: mismatched types
```

```
  --> src/lib.rs:13:16
   |
 5 | assert_eq!(add("hello", 2), 4);
   |                ^^^^^^^ expected `i32`, found `&str`

error: aborting due to previous error

For more information about this error, try `rustc --explain E0308`.
Couldn't compile the test.
---- src/lib.rs - add (line 6) stdout ----
Test executable failed (exit code 101).

stderr:
thread 'main' panicked at 'assertion failed: `(left == right)`
  left: `4`,
 right: `5`', src/lib.rs:5:1
note: run with `RUST_BACKTRACE=1` environment variable to display a backtrace


failures:
    src/lib.rs - add (line 11)
    src/lib.rs - add (line 6)

test result: FAILED. 1 passed; 2 failed;
```

This code has no separate doc test command; all types of tests run when we run `cargo test`. We get the `ok` from the `it_works` test, and it then immediately go into running the doc tests.

The doc test that fails to compile does not block the compilation of the entire test. It is reported only as a part of the individual doc test that failed.

Notice how these failures appear. Both indicate failure on line 5, but that does not match the line of the file where the errors appear. This is because doc tests are wrapped in an implicit `main` function, and the line numbers coming from these panic messages are not reliable. Instead, we should look at the line number of the test. `src/lib.rs - add (line 6)` and `src/lib.rs - add (line 11)` point us to the code blocks where the failing doc tests begin. Now we can update our example so that it contains the correct code.

Listing 7.7 Passing doc tests

```
/// Add together two i32 numbers and return the result of that addition
/// ```
/// assert_eq!(testing::add(2, 2), 4);
/// ```
///
/// ```
/// use testing::add;
/// assert_eq!(add(3, 2), 5);
/// ```
pub fn add(x: i32, y: i32) -> i32 {
```

```
    x + y
}
```

Running the tests now shows that they pass as expected:

```
$ cargo test
   Compiling testing v0.1.0
    Finished test [unoptimized + debuginfo] target(s) in 0.41s
     Running unittests

running 1 test
test tests::it_works ... ok

test result: ok. 1 passed; 0 failed;

   Doc-tests testing

running 2 tests
test src/lib.rs - add (line 2) ... ok
test src/lib.rs - add (line 6) ... ok

test result: ok. 2 passed; 0 failed;
```

Let's also regenerate our documentation to see how the examples will look for our crate's users, as shown in figure 7.3:

```
$ cargo doc --open
```

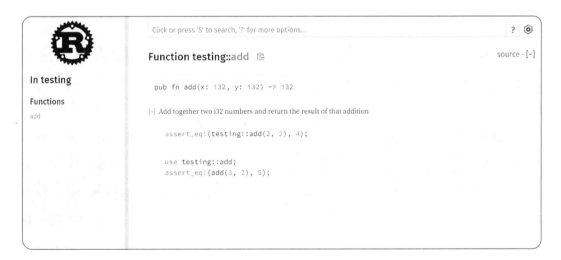

Figure 7.3 Screenshot of documentation for the `add` function with a doctest

Now that we understand how to write tests more generally, let's add some tests for the `rust_json` crate that we created in chapter 6.

7.1.2 Adding tests to existing code

Open the `lib.rs` file from the `rust_json` crate. It should look like the following listing.

Listing 7.8 `rust_json/src/lib.rs` from chapter 6

```rust
use pyo3::prelude::*;

#[derive(Debug, serde::Deserialize)]
struct Data {
  name: String,
  value: i32,
}

#[pyfunction]
fn sum(input: &str) -> i32 {
  let parsed: Data = serde_json::from_str(input).unwrap();

  parsed.name.len() as i32 + parsed.value
}

#[pymodule]
fn rust_json(_py: Python, m: &PyModule) -> PyResult<()> {
  m.add_function(wrap_pyfunction!(sum, m)?)?;

  Ok(())
}
```

Now, let's create a `test` module and write a basic test.

Listing 7.9 Basic test for `rust_json::sum`

```rust
...
#[cfg(test)]
mod tests {
  use crate::sum;

  #[test]
  fn test_stokes_baker() {
    assert_eq!(
      sum("{ \"name\": \"Stokes Baker\", \"value\": 954832 }"),
      954844
    );
  }
}
```

Let's run the test to ensure that it works:

```
$ cargo test
   Compiling rust_json
    Finished test [unoptimized + debuginfo] target(s) in 7.56s
     Running unittests
```

```
running 1 test
test tests::test_stokes_baker ... ok

test result: ok. 1 passed; 0 failed;
```

This test validates that our code behaves as expected with this small input, but we can improve a few things. First, all of those escapes in the string to allow us to put a literal double quote are a bit annoying. Thankfully, Rust has a way for us to get around this. We can use a *raw string*.

RAW STRINGS

Raw strings are string literals that do not parse escape sequences and can be opened/closed by something other than a single double-quote character. We can turn a normal string into a raw string by putting an `r` just before the opening quotation mark. This `r` disables escape sequences within the string. Let's try to do this on the JSON string literal in our new test:

```
sum(r"{ \"name\": \"Stokes Baker\", \"value\": 954832 }"),
```

If we try to run the test now, it will not compile! The error is also quite long and difficult to understand:

```
$ cargo test
   Compiling rust_json v0.1.0
error: unknown start of token: \
  --> src/lib.rs:30:21
   |
30 |         sum(r"{ \"name\": \"Stokes Baker\", \"value\": 954832 }"),
   |                     ^

error: suffixes on a string literal are invalid
  --> src/lib.rs:30:11
   |
30 |         sum(r"{ \"name\": \"Stokes Baker\", \"value\": 954832 }"),
   |             ^^^^^^^^^^ invalid suffix `name`

error: expected one of `)`, `,`, `.`, `?`, or an operator,
       found `": \"Stokes Baker\", \"value\": 954832 }"`
  --> src/lib.rs:30:22
   |
30 |         sum(r"{ \"name\": \"Stokes Baker\", \"value\": 954832 }"),
   |                      -^^^^^^^^^^^^^^^^^^^^^^^^^^^^^^^^^^^^^^^^^^^^
   |                       |
   |                       expected one of `)`, `,`, `.`, `?`, or an operator
   |                       |
   |                       help: missing `,`

error[E0061]: this function takes 1 argument but 2 arguments were supplied
  --> src/lib.rs:30:7
   |
30 |         sum(r"{ \"name\": \"Stokes Baker\", \"value\": 954832 }"),
   |         ^^^ ---------- -----------------------------------------
   |             |
   |             | supplied 2 arguments
   |
```

```
    |         expected 1 argument
    |
```

This error occurs because turning our string literal into a raw string turns off the escape sequences that allow us to use literal double-quote characters. When the compiler sees the first double-quote character before the n in name, it now treats it as the end of the string. Figure 7.4 shows how the compiler now parses this code.

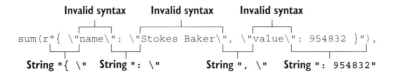

Figure 7.4 Parsing our raw string

This code is currently worse than the code we had before, which can be compiled and executed. We can fix these errors with a clever addition Rust has on its raw strings. We can use a delimiter other than a single double-quote character for the beginning and end of the string. We can also pad the double quotes with any number of octothorpes (aka "number sign," "pound sign," "hash sign," #). By taking these steps, we unlock the ability to write string literals that contain double-quote characters without escaping them. The code looks like this:

```
sum(r#"{ "name": "Stokes Baker", "value": 954832 }"#),
```

This method makes it easier to read our JSON strings. We used only a single octothorpe, but if we needed to write a literal "# inside of our string, we could add as many octothorpes as we wanted to the start and end of the string to denote its beginning and end—for example:

```
println!("{}", r###"hello"#world"##how are you today?"###);
```

This line prints out the string

```
hello"#world"##how are you today?
```

This code works because we need to provide a double quote and three octothorpes to end the string, and the interior items provide only one or two octothorpes. Placed in the full code, our new raw string looks like the following listing.

Listing 7.10 Raw string used in JSON test

```
use pyo3::prelude::*;

#[derive(Debug, serde::Deserialize)]
struct Data {
```

```
    name: String,
    value: i32,
}

#[pyfunction]
fn sum(input: &str) -> i32 {
    let parsed: Data = serde_json::from_str(input).unwrap();

    parsed.name.len() as i32 + parsed.value
}

#[pymodule]
fn rust_json(_py: Python, m: &PyModule) -> PyResult<()> {
    m.add_function(wrap_pyfunction!(sum, m)?)?;

    Ok(())
}

#[cfg(test)]
mod tests {
    use crate::sum;

    #[test]
    fn test_stokes_baker() {
        assert_eq!(
            sum(r#"{ "name": "Stokes Baker", "value": 954832 }"#),    ◁──┤ The line we changed
            954844
        );
    }
}
```

And let's validate that our test still passes:

```
$ cargo test
    Finished test [unoptimized + debuginfo] target(s) in 8.33s
     Running unittests

running 1 test
test tests::test_stokes_baker ... ok

test result: ok. 1 passed; 0 failed;
```

Before we move on to testing our Rust code from Python, let's add a few more test cases for posterity.

Listing 7.11 Additional test cases for our Rust code

```
...

#[cfg(test)]
mod tests {
    use crate::sum;

    #[test]
    fn test_stokes_baker() {
```

```
    assert_eq!(
      sum(r#"{ "name": "Stokes Baker", "value": 954832 }"#),
      954844
    );
  }

  #[test]
  fn test_william_cavendish() {
    assert_eq!(
      sum(r#"{ "name": "William Cavendish", "value": -4011 }"#),
      -3994
    );
  }

  #[test]
  fn test_ada_lovelace() {
    assert_eq!(
      sum(r#"{ "name": "Ada Lovelace", "value": 18151210 }"#),
      18151222
    );
  }
}
```

And they should all now pass:

```
$ cargo test
   Finished test [unoptimized + debuginfo] target(s) in 7.15s
     Running unittests

running 3 tests
test tests::test_ada_lovelace ... ok
test tests::test_stokes_baker ... ok
test tests::test_william_cavendish ... ok

test result: ok. 3 passed; 0 failed;
```

Great! Now that we have some basic tests written in Rust, let's look at how our new Rust code can use existing tests written against the original Python implementation.

7.2 Testing Rust code using Python

In this section, we discuss updating existing Python tests to cover our new Rust code in addition to the existing Python code. The existing tests we will be updating are written in Python using the `pytest` framework. `pytest` is a Python testing framework designed to make it easy to write small, readable tests.

> **NOTE** This section requires us to manipulate Python virtual environments and assumes that you are using a virtual environment setup based on the instructions from chapter 6. If you do not have this setup, you will not be successful in this section.

First, let's install `pytest` in our `rust-json` virtual environment:

```
(rust-json) $ pip install pytest
...
```

```
Successfully installed
  attrs-21.4.0
  iniconfig-1.1.1
  packaging-21.3
  pluggy-1.0.0
  py-1.11.0
  pyparsing-3.0.7
  pytest-7.0.1
  tomli-2.0.1
```

For a refresher, the following listing shows our original Python source code.

Listing 7.12 Python program we will be testing

```python
import sys
import json

s = 0

for line in sys.stdin:
    value = json.loads(line)
    s += value['value']
    s += len(value['name'])

print(s)
```

To be more testable, we're going to turn this code into a function with defined inputs and outputs, rather than something that just operates on `stdin`/`stdout`. The program will now look like the following listing.

Listing 7.13 Python program after being updated to use a function

```python
import sys
import json

def sum(lines_iter):
    s = 0

    for line in lines_iter:
        value = json.loads(line)
        s += value['value']
        s += len(value['name'])

    return s

if __name__ == '__main__':        ⟵  This Python construct is similar to the main function in other languages.
    print(sum(sys.stdin))
```

Let's imagine that we already have a `pytest` file set up with a single test in it to start. This test runs through 10 lines of data with known properties and a known sum value. This test file is called `main_test.py`.

Listing 7.14 The test file `main_test.py`

```python
import main

def test_10_lines():
  lines = [
    '{ "name": "Stokes Baker", "value": 954832 }',
    '{ "name": "Joseph Solomon", "value": 279836 }',
    '{ "name": "Gonzalez Koch", "value": 140431 }',
    '{ "name": "Parrish Waters", "value": 490411 }',
    '{ "name": "Sharlene Nunez", "value": 889667 }',
    '{ "name": "Meadows David", "value": 892040 }',
    '{ "name": "Whitley Mendoza", "value": 965462 }',
    '{ "name": "Santiago Hood", "value": 280041 }',
    '{ "name": "Carver Caldwell", "value": 632926 }',
    '{ "name": "Tara Patterson", "value": 678175 }',
  ]

  assert main.sum(lines) == 6203958
```

`pytest` will detect any function that begins with `test_` and run it automatically. In this case, it will treat `test_10_lines` as a test and run it when we invoke `pytest`. Let's do that now to validate that it works as expected before we start to make modifications:

```
(rust-json) $ pytest -v
============================================================================
platform linux -- Python 3.8.10, pytest-7.0.1, pluggy-1.0.0
cachedir: .pytest_cache
collected 1 item

main_test.py::test_10_lines PASSED                                     [100%]

============================================================================
```

It's good practice to make a test fail once, so let's modify our source code and rerun the test. We'll update the `sum` function to add 1 to the returned value, which should make the test fail.

Listing 7.15 A version of `main.py` that fails our test

```python
import sys
import json

def sum(lines_iter):
  s = 0

  for line in lines_iter:
    value = json.loads(line)
    s += value['value']
    s += len(value['name'])

  return s + 1               ◁── Note the extra + 1.

if __name__ == '__main__':
  print(sum(sys.stdin))
```

7.2 Testing Rust code using Python

Now, if we rerun the test, it fails and includes an error message:

```
(rust-json) $ pytest -v
=========================== test session starts ===========================
platform linux -- Python 3.8.10, pytest-7.0.1, pluggy-1.0.0
cachedir: .pytest_cache
collected 1 item

main_test.py::test_10_lines FAILED                                   [100%]

================================= FAILURES ================================
_____ test_10_lines _____
    def test_10_lines():
      lines = [
        '{ "name": "Stokes Baker", "value": 954832 }',
        '{ "name": "Joseph Solomon", "value": 279836 }',
        '{ "name": "Gonzalez Koch", "value": 140431 }',
        '{ "name": "Parrish Waters", "value": 490411 }',
        '{ "name": "Sharlene Nunez", "value": 889667 }',
        '{ "name": "Meadows David", "value": 892040 }',
        '{ "name": "Whitley Mendoza", "value": 965462 }',
        '{ "name": "Santiago Hood", "value": 280041 }',
        '{ "name": "Carver Caldwell", "value": 632926 }',
        '{ "name": "Tara Patterson", "value": 678175 }',
      ]
>     assert main.sum(lines) == 6203958
E     assert 6203959 == 6203958
E      +6203959
E      -6203958

main_test.py:17: AssertionError
========================= short test summary info =========================
FAILED main_test.py::test_10_lines - assert 6203959 == 6203958
============================ 1 failed in 0.01s ============================
```

Now remove the + 1 from the end of the return statement and rerun the test to validate that we've restored to working functionality. Next, let's update our Python program to use the Rust JSON summing library.

> **Listing 7.16 Python program rewritten to use our Rust library**

```python
import sys

import rust_json

def sum(lines_iter):
  s = 0

  for line in lines_iter:
    s += rust_json.sum(line)

  return s

if __name__ == '__main__':
  print(sum(sys.stdin))
```

The test should continue to pass after this change is made:

```
(rust-json) $ pytest -v
========================== test session starts ==========================
platform linux -- Python 3.8.10, pytest-7.0.1, pluggy-1.0.0
cachedir: .pytest_cache
collected 1 item

main_test.py::test_10_lines PASSED                                 [100%]

=========================== 1 passed in 0.01s ===========================
```

In a larger existing application, hopefully more existing tests would exercise more code paths in the Rust code. Updating tests to use a new code path is all well and good, but it would be nice to test the Rust version against the original Python version more directly so we can determine whether and, if so, how the two differ. We can create a test that runs the two versions on randomized inputs and compares the outputs.

Before we add the randomization, let's write a utility function that allows us to run the sum function backed by either the original Python code or the new Rust function. We're going to do this using *monkey patching*.

7.2.1 Monkey patching

Monkey patching is a process for dynamically redefining items in programs, and it's commonly used when writing unit tests to swap deep dependencies between versions or replace real I/O resources with fake ones. Let's take a look at how we can write a function that uses monkey patching to call two different versions of the summing code.

We're going to add a test and a helper function that compares the two versions. We also need to provide the original Python implementation of the function here so that we can use it to override the Rust version.

> **Listing 7.17 Test comparing the output of Rust and Python versions**

```python
from pytest import MonkeyPatch

def test_compare_py_rust():
  compare_py_and_rust(
    ['{ "name": "Stokes Baker", "value": 954832 }']
  )

def python_sum(line):
  import json

  value = json.loads(line)
  return value['value'] + len(value['name'])

def compare_py_and_rust(input):
  rust_result = main.sum(input)

  with MonkeyPatch.context() as m:
    m.setattr(main.rust_json, 'sum', python_sum)
    py_result = main.sum(input)

  assert rust_result == py_result
```

We are not going to linger too long on the exact Python syntax that's required here, but let's break down what's happening a bit:

```
from pytest import MonkeyPatch
```

First, we need to import the `MonkeyPatch` class from `pytest1`. This class allows us to override the `rust_json.sum` function later:

```
def test_compare_py_rust():
  compare_py_and_rust(
    ['{ "name": "Stokes Baker", "value": 954832 }']
  )
```

The new test runs our helper comparison function with a single known input. In the future, we will update this test to pass in randomized inputs:

```
def python_sum(line):
  import json

  value = json.loads(line)
  return value['value'] + len(value['name'])
```

Next, we redefine the original Python implementation of our functionality to use as a baseline against which we can compare our new Rust code. In this case, we moved the functionality into the test file itself. This is not a requirement but rather something that we did because the original Python implementation is no longer used in the main program:

```
def compare_py_and_rust(input):
  rust_result = main.sum(input)

  with MonkeyPatch.context() as m:
    m.setattr(main.rust_json, 'sum', python_sum)
    py_result = main.sum(input)

  assert rust_result == py_result
```

Finally, we have the comparison function itself. This function runs the `sum` function using the `rust_json.sum` function and the `python_sum` function and then compares the results. It uses `MonkeyPatch.context` to create a small area in the code where we override the `main.rust_json.sum` function with our `python_sum` function. Let's run this test to validate that it passes as we expect:

```
$ pytest -v
=========================== test session starts ===========================
platform linux -- Python 3.8.10, pytest-7.0.1, pluggy-1.0.0
cachedir: .pytest_cache
collected 2 items

main_test.py::test_10_lines PASSED                                  [ 50%]
main_test.py::test_compare_py_rust PASSED                           [100%]

============================ 2 passed in 0.01s ============================
```

Let's also briefly reintroduce a bug in our code to validate that the assertion fails when Python results don't match Rust results. This time we'll add the bug to our Rust code. Let's change the return value of the sum function in lib.rs.

Listing 7.18 Rust library with a bug added

```
use pyo3::prelude::*;

#[derive(Debug, serde::Deserialize)]
struct Data {
  name: String,
  value: i32,
}

#[pyfunction]
fn sum(input: &str) -> i32 {
  let parsed: Data = serde_json::from_str(input).unwrap();

  parsed.name.len() as i32 + parsed.value + 10      ◁── Notice the extra + 10.
}

#[pymodule]
fn rust_json(_py: Python, m: &PyModule) -> PyResult<()> {
  m.add_function(wrap_pyfunction!(sum, m)?)?;

  Ok(())
}
```

Now let's rebuild our Rust code and rerun the Python tests:

```
$ cd rust_json
$ cargo build
$ cd ..
$ pytest -v -k test_compare_py_rust
=========================== test session starts ===========================
platform linux -- Python 3.8.10, pytest-7.0.1, pluggy-1.0.0
cachedir: .pytest_cache
collected 2 items / 1 deselected / 1 selected

main_test.py::test_compare_py_rust FAILED                          [100%]

================================ FAILURES =================================
_____ test_compare_py_rust _____
...
>       assert rust_result == py_result        ◁── The output is truncated for brevity.
E       assert 954854 == 954844                ◁── Notice the difference between the values.
E         +954854
E         -954844

main_test.py:38: AssertionError
========================= short test summary info =========================
FAILED main_test.py::test_compare_py_rust - assert 954854 == 954844
===================== 1 failed, 1 deselected in 0.02s =====================
```

The test fails after running because of the extra + 10 we added to the Rust code. Notice that the result from Rust, the `rust_result` variable, is now 10 greater than the Python result, stored in the `py_result` variable.

Let's revert the Rust code back to a working state and rerun the tests to validate it's all working:

```
$ cd rust_json
$ cargo build
$ cd ..
$ pytest -v
=========================== test session starts ===========================
platform linux -- Python 3.8.10, pytest-7.0.1, pluggy-1.0.0
cachedir: .pytest_cache
collected 2 items

main_test.py::test_10_lines PASSED                                  [ 50%]
main_test.py::test_compare_py_rust PASSED                           [100%]

============================ 2 passed in 0.01s ============================
```

Now that we know how the monkey patching itself works, let's add some randomization to our test to validate that it works with unknown inputs. We'll once again write a helper function to run a single test case through our code and then call it from a runner test function.

This Python test function runs the `randomized_test_case` function 100 times. Each time we generate between 100 and 500 lines of JSON, with each of those lines comprised of a `name` value that's between 100 and 200 characters of lowercase ASCII and a `value` number that's a random integer between 0 and 10,000.

> **Listing 7.19 A randomized test comparing Python and Rust results**

```python
import json
import string
import random

...

def test_random_inputs(monkeypatch):
  for _ in range(100):
    randomized_test_case(monkeypatch)

def randomized_test_case(monkeypatch):
  number_of_lines = random.randint(100, 500)

  lines = []
  for _ in range(number_of_lines):
    number_of_chars = random.randint(100, 200)

    lines.append(json.dumps({
      'name': ''.join(random.choices(
        string.ascii_lowercase,
```

```
            k=number_of_chars,
        )),
        'value': random.randint(0, 10_000),
    }))

compare_py_and_rust(monkeypatch, lines)

...
```

After constructing this list of lines of JSON, we feed the list of data into our previously defined comparison function.

This test function with its high degree of randomness may find corners in our library that were not exposed by our manually written tests. This approach is a rather blunt-force way to randomized testing. Specialty libraries are designed to perform "property testing" that can more intelligently design input values to exercise specific code paths. For our purposes, this test function is sufficient. We can control the number of test cases easily by increasing the number of iterations in the `test_random_inputs` function, which also increases the test's run time. We'll ask our test runner to do more work when we increase this number, and we can easily make a test in this way that requires hours to run.

The interesting thing here is that we have an existing Python implementation against which we can test our Rust code. We can continuously generate random inputs and feed them to both the Python code and the Rust code to ensure that both libraries emit the same results.

This chapter contains a lot of information on testing and documentation. By applying these skills, we can have more confidence in our refactors as we deploy them into production systems.

Summary

- By convention, we should put Rust tests in a `tests` module close to the code it is testing.
- Adding `#[cfg(test)]` to an item will make that item compile only when tests are being compiled.
- We can test Rust code by writing functions with the `#[test]` attribute macro on them.
- The `assert_eq!` macro allows us to panic a test if two values are not equal.
- `cargo test` will compile, discover, and run all of our test functions.
- Adding doc comments (`///`) before an item will add information to autogenerated documentation.
- `cargo doc` will build the documentation for a crate.
- `cargo doc --open` will build the documentation for a crate and open it in the default web browser.
- Adding a code block (```` ``` ````) within a doc comment allows us to write an example within the documentation that will also be compiled and run as a test.

- Raw strings allow us to skip escaping characters that we would otherwise need to escape in string literals.
- Raw strings are prefixed with r and must have the same number of octothorpe (#) characters at the beginning and end (this number may be zero).
- Monkey patching can be used in many dynamic languages to perform dependency injection where it would otherwise be difficult. It can be used to test code with different versions of the same function.

Asynchronous Python with Rust

This chapter covers
- Writing computationally expensive applications in Python
- Improving the performance of applications by using threads
- Externalizing a module in Rust to increase asynchronous performance in Rust to scale

Python is the ultimate prototyping language. It holds this title due to its simplicity and flexibility. Designed by Guido van Rossum in the 1980s and released in 1991, its original aim was to build a better programming language (a successor to a language known as ABC). What van Rossum developed first was an interpreter and runtime for the language; then, he slowly designed the first versions of Python. From there, people started to see the power in a language that was easy to read and write. By forcing developers to use indention for code blocks, Python automatically provides some structure to an application's source code. Since it is an interpreted language, developers can see quickly whether their application works as intended without the need to compile their code, which, on large projects, can take time. Python became beloved by many as it grew, and it still is today. The flexibility and simplicity of the language have lowered the barrier to entry for those in academic and research fields, and thus many research projects and production systems run on Python. This has led to a plethora of mathematics and simulation libraries that are used in developing ML models and data mining.

Since the language is interpreted, the underlying interpreter can be written in many different languages, leading to projects like Jython, which allows you to access Java libraries, and IronPython, which supports .NET. However, you may be more familiar with CPython, or Python written in C, which is the default installation for many. When the interpreter is written in C, under the hood, Python can read and use C and C++ libraries. This ability alone provides Python with a host of libraries and some performance benefits.

Yet there are tradeoffs. Python is a simple language, which makes it fast for development but at the expense of performance speed, as we will see. Python also gives up some flexibility by not providing type safety out of the box. Since Python is interpreted, it must rely on the underlying interpreter to handle these various pieces. You may be wondering where Rust fits within this world of Python interpreters. We will be using Cython (the standard Python distribution), which, as mentioned, uses C libraries and, therefore, can interact with Rust. We will once again use PyO3 from chapter 6, but instead of having Rust consume Python, we will have Python consume Rust.

In this chapter, we will explore writing a computationally expensive function in Python. Then we will find ways to scale the application to call this function multiple times and measure our improvement over time as we slowly move toward Rust. We will see that Rust once again provides us with the safety we need to go fast—even in Python.

8.1 Generating a Mandelbrot set in Python

Benoit Mandelbrot is known in mathematics for his research on fractal geometry and was one of the first to use computer visualization as part of his research. Fractal geometry is a fascinating branch of mathematics that looks at the recursive nature of functions and the structures they create, as shown in figure 8.1. When zooming in on a fractal, you will find that it never ends but continues to generate shapes and patterns. This property can be highly useful in doing certain calculations—for example, calculating irregular shapes, such as coastlines. However, fractal geometry's reliance on recursive definitions and complex numbers makes it computationally complex and, therefore, computationally expensive.

Figure 8.1 Mandelbrot sets can include repeated patterns as you zoom in since they are recursive in nature.

With Python and its amazing mathematics libraries, an application generating a Mandelbrot set is relatively simple to create. What's interesting about many of Python's core modules and libraries is that they are sometimes written in C and C++ for performance reasons. So, computationally heavy modules like Pillow, which is used in mathematical calculations, are written in C and C++. In other words, the performance of the code we are using is not necessarily limited by Python but instead by how Python works.

Python is an interpreted language, and we will see the implications of that later in the chapter. Since it is interpreted, it requires an interpreter that takes Python byte code and runs the application. Compiled languages like C and Rust will compile the source code based on the operating system they are supposed to run on. This compiled code creates a special type of code known as *object code* that the operating system and processor can understand. Byte code is similar to object code in that it is interpreted by an underlying system. However, whereas object code is specific to the processor running the code, byte code is interpreted by the underlying virtual runtime. Languages like Python and Java provide an interpreter or runtime, an application that runs on a given system configuration; the byte code remains the same.

So, ultimately, Python is a language that can be interpreted by other languages that have implemented the Python runtime, allowing Python to interoperate with those other languages. The most common implementation of Python is CPython, where the Python code is run via an interpreter written in C and can, therefore, use C modules and libraries. Since Rust can interoperate with C as well, we will eventually see how these paths converge. In the meantime, we will use the existing Python and C relationship before we introduce Rust.

Let's see how we make a Mandelbrot set image like the one in figure 8.1 in Python using existing libraries and then refactor the application to become more performant. To start, let's create a new directory and a virtual environment to isolate our Python project. To do this, create a new directory and navigate there. Then create a virtual environment and install Pillow.

Listing 8.1 Console: Initializing the project

```
python -m venv venv
./venv/bin/activate
pip install Pillow
```

Once this is set, we can create our algorithm and render an image of our Mandelbrot set. Open a new file called `main.py` and add the following.

Listing 8.2 `main.py`: Using the Mandelbrot algorithm

```
from PIL import Image                    ⟵┐ Import Pillow
                                           │ mathematics library

def mandelbrot_func(size: int, path: str, range_x0: float, range_y0: float,
↳range_x1: float, range_y1: float):
    image = Image.new(mode='RGB', size=(size, size))    ⟵┤ Creates a new image

    size_f = float(size)

    x_range = abs(range_x1 - range_x0)
    x_offset = x_range / 2.0                    ┐ Creates the boundaries
                                                │ the Mandelbrot set will
    y_range = abs(range_y1 - range_y0)          │ use to calculate
    y_offset = y_range / 2.0
                                      ┐ Iterates for each
    for px in range(size):    ⟵──────┘ pixel of the image
        for py in range(size):
            x0 = float(px) / size_f * x_range - x_offset
            y0 = float(py) / size_f * y_range - y_offset

            c = complex(x0, y0)     ⟵┐ Creates a complex number to
            i = 0                    │ be contained within the set
            z = complex(0, 0)

            while i < 255:
                z = (z * z) + c
                if float(z.real) > 4.0:
                    break
                i += 1
                                              ┐ Places pixels in the image
                                              │ based on a calculation
            image.putpixel((px, py), (i, i, i))   ⟵┘
    image.save(path)             ⟵┤ Saves image to path

mandelbrot_func(1000, "single.png", -5.0, -2.12, -2.5, 1.12)
```

You will notice that the code takes a little while to run because we are using complex numbers to calculate the value of each individual pixel on a 1,000 × 1,000 pixel image. Each calculation is expensive, and all of the results are being written to a single image. Now, imagine that we want to create a service that generates multiple instances of these images. How would you design it?

8.2 Scaling

Refactoring decisions can be triggered by multiple reasons, but all are intended to improve our code in some way. Systems evolve quickly, and it soon becomes apparent where our code does not perform as well as we would like. These spots in our code where slowdowns occur are known as *bottlenecks*, named after the way the neck of a bottle limits the overall flow out of the bottle. In the same way, the slowest function often determines the throughput we can get out of a system. Once a system hits a limit on performance, there are two options: rewriting the code and scaling.

These two options often go hand in hand because systems can be scaled in two ways: horizontally and vertically. Horizontal scaling is adding more instances to an already running service. This is the equivalent of spinning up extra servers or some other machine or process. The point is that you are duplicating or cloning the existing system as it currently stands without changing the configuration of the actual machine. Vertical scaling is adding more resources to an existing machine instance. This is equivalent to adding a faster CPU with additional cores or additional memory. The point is that the system itself has more resources and, in theory, can thus do more if the application can take advantage of it.

However, in some cases, neither vertical nor horizontal scaling can happen without code changes. When scaling horizontally, you will need to change your code to work as a distributed system wherein a server must work as a group rather than as an individual instance. To get an idea of how this works, you can run more than one instance of your Python programs at the same time. On a Unix-like system, you would type the following.

> **Listing 8.3   Console: Running multiple processes at once**

```
python main.py & python main.py
```

This code asks the operating system to run the same application twice at the same time but in separate processes. If you were to look at the output, you would only see one result. While our system is scaled horizontally, it is not handling outputs as unique values. Therefore, when we run the application twice, the output will be `single.png`, and the processes will overwrite each other. While the mathematical function itself is *idempotent*, the service was not structured to write to a unique output. Idempotent systems will distinguish their tasks and outputs in a unique way. This can be done by the originating system, giving the entity some unique identification. In our example, we did not have a unique filename, so there was a conflict, and the files were overwritten. If we were to change the output to be idempotent, we could append a unique ID or a timestamp to ensure they aren't overwritten. When we execute these functions on a Unix-like system with a single `&` command, the operating system will execute these scripts at the same time. Running multiple versions of the same code without changing the resources is known as *horizontal scaling*.

Horizontal scaling happens naturally as our system grows because it builds redundancy into our system, as figure 8.2 shows. But when more than one server is running our application, a certain level of coordination needs to occur at both a routing level and a system level. First, to coordinate, an external mechanism needs to run to distribute the tasks to the running services. In web applications, this is typically done through the use of a load balancer. The load balancer's job is just as its name describes: to distribute the load of calls coming into our system among the various running processes. It accomplishes this through simple or complex logic, possibly alternating between services and inspecting their current load. We don't want two processors grabbing the same task and doing redundant work. That means checking for existing records or marking a task as in process.

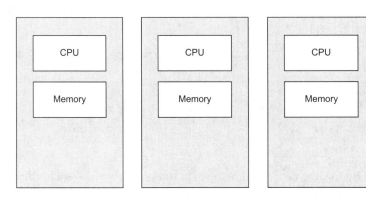

Figure 8.2 Horizontal scaling means adding more physical hardware

Since this discussion is more of an architectural nature, it doesn't particularly fit with what we are trying to do in this book. However, it is important to note that adding additional servers is one solution that works and is solved by load balancing and queues, but it doesn't necessarily take full advantage of the hardware it's running on. That is, the tradeoff with this particular solution is monetary cost rather than a time cost. In contrast, vertical scaling helps provide performance increases without additional monetary costs (which makes CEOs happy).

Vertical scaling means adding more resources to an existing system and finding a way to break up the work such that it can be processed in smaller chunks by separate processes to use your increased power as opposed to having multiple machines running individual tasks. It becomes a problem in how you break up your work. Vertical scaling is like opening up your PC to add more RAM or a CPU with more cores, as shown in figure 8.3. The point is to enhance the current system to process data more quickly. However, if your application is not developed properly, it becomes a Band-Aid solution. To get the benefits of vertical scaling, your application needs to be able to take advantage of the new resources properly. It becomes more of a software problem than what we saw in horizontal scaling. However, the solution to the problem is similar in that the work needs to be distributed

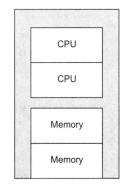

Figure 8.3 Vertical scaling means adding more resources to existing hardware

throughout the process. Instead of a load balancer or some external system managing the tasks being distributed, the application or operating system must split up the work. Now you have a coordination problem, possibly within the system. It's a complicated problem, and not all languages do it well.

Unfortunately, Python does not handle running multiple processes at once very well. Tradeoffs occur in every language, and this is one Python has made to keep its language simple. Let's explore how to refactor our code to scale vertically. To do this, let's modify our code to create multiple images at once during a single process. We are simply going to add a loop.

Listing 8.4 main.py: A simple loop

```
def main():
        for i in range(0,8):
            mandelbrot(1000, f"{i}.png", -5.0, -2.12, -2.5, 1.12)

if __name__ == "__main__":
   main()
```

Running this code locally, we get a time measurement of about 46 seconds. This isn't great, but it can be our baseline for improvement. Right now, our problem is that this entire process is being run *synchronously*, meaning each process is waiting for the others to finish before it can begin working. This is known as *blocking*, where a process cannot proceed until the provided resource is available. To improve our service, we want to allow our processes to be independent of each other without waiting. This is known as *asynchronous* processing, where work can be done without waiting for a response. Let's see how this works.

8.3 Asyncio

Converting our existing service into one that performs asynchronous tasks is fairly straightforward but requires a tool to manage it, as we discussed earlier. Asynchronous tasks are helpful because we are telling the system that we are okay waiting for a result, which tells the CPU we don't care which result is returned first. This gives the underlying system (in this case, the Python interpreter) the freedom to return results as soon as it has them. We don't need to wait for Task 1 to return before Task 2 does. Additionally, our system is no longer deterministic because we don't know which process will return first.

For Python to use fan-out and fan-in processes, we can add the `async` keyword in front of the method definition. This tells the interpreter that it can proceed, and a response will eventually come back when the function returns. We then need to do the same thing with our `main` function but add a method to run multiple tasks on multiple threads. In the end, we need all processes to finish before the application exits. Here, we will use a command that gathers the results into one comprehensive output. Finally, we need to have something to manage and run the tasks in this way. Let's take a look at the example in the following listing.

Listing 8.5 `main.py`: Using `async` and `asyncio`

```
from PIL import Image
import asyncio                      ◁─── Imports the async library

async def mandelbrot_func(          ◁─── Changes the function to be async
    size: int,
    path: str,
    range_x0: float,
    range_y0: float,
    range_x1: float,
    range_y1: float):
    ...
async def main():                   ◁─── Makes the main function async
    await asyncio.gather(*[         ◁─── Spins out multiple instances and waits
        mandelbrot_func(1000, f"{i}.png", -5.0, -2.12, -2.5, 1.12)      to return until all are completed
        for i in range(0,8)
    ])
asyncio.run(main())                 ◁─── Kicks off async run
```

When we run this command locally, the total time required to execute it on one author's machine is around 42 seconds. This time is an improvement over our initial 46 seconds, but not by much. Now, how do we know that this is running asynchronously? If you watch the output, you will probably see the tasks running in order, which is a bit disappointing, but let's see if we can force this to change. Let's add a few lines to our Mandelbrot function to test this out.

Listing 8.6 `main.py`: Adding sleep

```
from PIL import Image
from random import randint
import asyncio

async def mandelbrot_func(
    size: int,
    path: str,
    range_x0: float,
    range_y0: float,
    range_x1: float,
    range_y1: float):
    s = randint(1,5)                ◁─── Creates a random number for testing
    print(f"{path} sleeping for {s} seconds")
    await asyncio.sleep(s)          ◁─── Pauses the Python thread and
    ...                                  allows other processes to run
```

When we run this locally, we see this pattern:

```
0.png sleeping for 3 seconds        ◁─── 0.png is the first image created
1.png sleeping for 1 seconds             and needs to sleep for 3 seconds.
2.png sleeping for 4 seconds
```

```
3.png sleeping for 2 seconds
4.png sleeping for 1 seconds
5.png sleeping for 4 seconds
6.png sleeping for 1 seconds
7.png sleeping for 5 seconds
1.png created
4.png created
6.png created
3.png created
0.png created      ◁──┐  However, the 0.png image isn't
2.png created         │  created exactly when it is ready
5.png created         │  (more than 3 seconds have passed).
7.png created
```

All of these tasks were queued to work, but they were executed based on their availability when they were not blocked by sleeping. This is why you see results returning in a semi-random order. The first image (0.png) we schedule to create will sleep for 3 seconds. If we look at the sleep times of the various "completed" images that appear before 0.png is created (1.png, 4.png, 6.png, and 3.png) and add up their sleep times, we notice it adds up to more than 3 seconds. Somehow, just because 0.png was scheduled before all of these other images, Python isn't going to wait around for it to be ready. Instead, it will grab the next image that is not sleeping and ready to process. It eventually gets back to 0.png, but not until after it has completed some additional tasks. In fact, it needs to wait past its sleeping time and an additional 2 seconds for 3.png to be completed. What you aren't seeing is that Python is only still allowing one thread to run at a time. `asyncio` is eventually going to get faster as Python changes, but that requires the removal of a very special value that lives within the Python interpreter. Before we can introduce that topic, let's first understand how threading works in an operating system.

8.4 Threading

The first computers worked in a very procedural way. Input consisted of tape reels or punch cards that would get processed by the computer and output the results to a screen, paper, or back to tape. Timesharing systems were invented to break away from this tradition by allowing multiple people to use the system at one time. This meant that a very powerful computer could be used by many people and many applications all at once, suddenly reducing the cost per person per machine and opening up the computing world to what we experience today. Timesharing systems did this by allowing multiple processes to appear to run at once and then, by extension, allowing applications to break themselves up into smaller tasks called *threads*.

There are two different types of threads that we will get into later in this chapter, but at the core, a thread is a little package of information about a process. A thread includes memory and the actual instructions to run. Once the processor finishes the task it is working on, it will grab another task. After working on a thread, the processor will pause the work on the thread due to either a timer or a signal from the thread that it needs to wait on a resource (network, file, etc.). After a thread is paused, the processor will pick up another thread and begin working. When you have only one processor, it still ends up doing only one task at a time, but with threads and the speed of the processor, it appears that the computer is doing many things at once.

When an application cannot proceed because it needs a resource, we describe that application as *blocked*. Once blocked, an application is unable to advance, so the operating system takes this opportunity to take on another task (see figure 8.4). This method is efficient for the system as a whole but is often the source of the bottlenecks we discussed earlier.

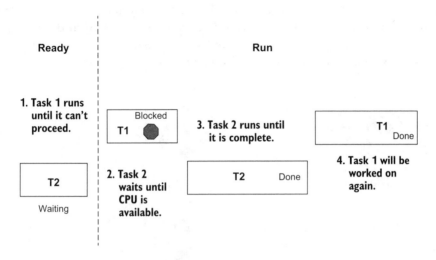

Figure 8.4 The CPU will try to process tasks that are not blocked.

As machines evolved, we started seeing additional processors being added. Suddenly, there were dual-core, quad-core, and even eight-core processors! But did that mean that our applications became faster? Only if they were written to take advantage of these cores by dividing their work into multiple tasks. The core structure stayed the same: one thread can only be executed on one core at a time. Previously, applications could be written to start additional threads to spread out their work. For example, you could have one part of an application reading data while another part processes that data. This division of work in an application is known as *concurrency*. Concurrency is often confused with parallelism, but they are not the same.

Parallel systems mean that a system can execute multiple threads at one time. If you have four threads running and four cores on your machine, you are truly running in parallel. However, many systems don't have as many processors as they do threads, so applications will run concurrently. Concurrency, therefore, is having multiple executions running in the same application but not necessarily at the same time. For example, your email application can show you a message while concurrently fetching new messages from the server.

Here's another example: One author has a BlackBox Can Crusher. Cans go in one end, and compacted cans come out the other. We can measure the rate at which the cans are crushed to get an idea of how efficient it can be. After loading up the hopper with cans, we measure a rate of one can crush per second. Marking the cans with numbered stickers, we can see the order in which the cans are crushed. The cans come out in no particular order.

The next day, we get a new BlackBox Can Crusher 2, which promises faster crushing abilities. Now we measure a rate of two cans per second. Deciding to void the warranty, we open both machines. Inside the first machine, we see one hammer that crushes the cans with a funnel going in, while the second machine has two hammers to crush cans. This seems like a fairly obvious solution. The cans in this example are concurrent processes waiting to be crushed, but the machine can only crush as many cans as it has hammers, as depicted in figure 8.5.

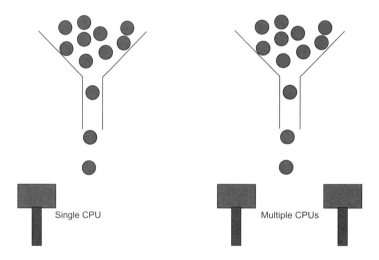

Figure 8.5 Within our box, we do not know how many crushers we have, and we have no guarantee of the order. Adding more crushers adds more throughput.

This type of concurrency at the operating system level is managed by POSIX threads, or pthreads. These threads are managed by the operating system. Alternatively, a language or runtime can create threads. These are known as *green threads*. While the main application runs in a single thread, the application then maintains its own set of internal threads to manage. This is common in interpreted languages and virtual machines.

Since Python is an interpreted language, it manages all of its threads when using the `asyncio` package. Python needs to know when a portion of the service is unable to run because it is waiting for a resource. In our example program, we were making calls to math libraries and graphics-rendering tools. Both of these tasks are often blocked by resource constraints or are called outside of the main Python code, making them great candidates for an asynchronous system and multithreaded computation. To do this, we will need parallelism and not just concurrency. Let's convert our code to use Python's threads to see whether we can get any sort of improvement over our asynchronous code. To begin, we need to remove the sleeps from our previous section and add the following code.

> **Listing 8.7** `main.py`: Adding execution threads

```python
from concurrent.futures import ThreadPoolExecutor
import asyncio

def mandelbrot_func:
    ...


executor = ThreadPoolExecutor(max_workers=4)

async def mandelbrot(size: int, path: str, range_x0: float, range_y0: float,
    range_x1: float, range_y1: float):
    return executor.submit(mandelbrot_func, size, path, range_x0, range_y0,
        range_x1, range_y1)

async def main():
    await asyncio.gather(*[
        mandelbrot(1000, f"purp{i}.png", -5.0, -2.12, -2.5, 1.12)
        for i in range(0,8)
    ])
```

Now each calculation is being put on an individual operating system thread created by Python. When you run it, you should see little to no improvement over our `async`-only implementation. Why? If we are running this on three additional threads, we should expect to see this run in about a fourth of the time, provided we have at least four cores on our machine. Yet, by design, we aren't. Python is a single process and, therefore, has some limitations. For us to see any improvement, we need to understand what is happening within Python and then see how Rust can help.

8.5 *Global Interpreter Lock*

Let's hop back to our discussion of threads. From the previous section, we know that there are two types of threads, one maintained by the operating system and the other by the runtime. Python creates and manages its threads through `asyncio` or through system threads using the `ThreadPoolExecutor`. Running the Python interpreter on multiple threads can cause some strange issues, and so in 2003, the creator of Python put in a Global Interpreter Lock (GIL). This tool, while simple, has vast implications for our concurrent programs. Its simplicity allows single-threaded Python applications to run fast while concurrent applications are safe. The GIL only allows one thread to run while all others sleep or await input or output resources.

Regardless of how expertly we try to distribute work onto threads in Python, the GIL will prevent us from running work in parallel because Python cannot guarantee that the code can be memory-safe, along with other issues that come about in parallel programming a shared memory space (see figure 8.6). If multiple threads were able to run at the same time, we could see multiple accesses to the same slots in memory, causing various memory problems.

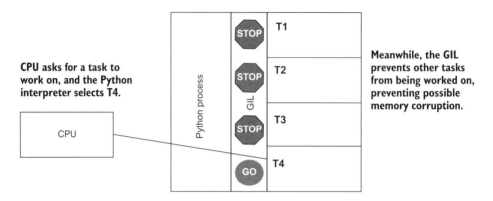

Figure 8.6 GIL is a lock that the interpreter gives out to allow tasks to run.

How does the GIL work? A global value within the Python interpreter is a *mutex* or lock on a given resource to prevent multiple threads from accessing it at once. Think of it as a hall pass. Only a single student can wander the halls at a given time. Having this key allows the thread within Python to access resources available to the interpreter but denies any other thread access to that resource. Python can then only proceed when the lock is given back. It can then give the key to another process if it is ready. Giving the GIL to another process allows it to run. Like a mutex, the GIL protects from two processes accessing a section of memory at the same time. Not having this key would allow two processes to access the same values, which can lead to various problems. In our can crusher example, we can imagine having two arms that can crush but only one hammer. You first need to grab the hammer before you can crush, preventing two hammers from hitting each other.

What we need is the ability to run parallel threads that bypass the GIL. To do that, we need memory safety within Python. For that, we need a module that can handle parallel threads. This can be done with C and C++, but we would like to take a safer route by using Rust.

8.6   PyO3

Throughout this book, we've seen how Rust is able to attach itself to applications written in other languages to slowly break down the problems, allowing those applications to use all of the safety and speed that Rust provides without needing us developers to overhaul our system completely. In chapter 6, we were able to use a library called PyO3, which provided us with the proper Rust bindings to run Python code inside a Rust application to improve our system. Now we are going to do the reverse: take Rust code and run it inside Python. Why would we want to do that? Because refactoring a system can be challenging, as we discussed at the beginning of the chapter. Often, teams will get into a flow or establish a base of engineers who are good at one particular language or have an ecosystem surrounding them that lends itself to a particular programming language. Yet when we hit a point where we need to scale and we identify a section of code as a bottleneck, it should be refactored. At this point, we have refactored our Python code for performance as far as Python will let us due to the GIL. PyO3 provides us with the tools we need to get improved performance from our application by using Rust's safety and speed to circumvent the GIL. Rust does this by providing the ability to release the GIL, which will allow other threads to run. Earlier we introduced a thread pool in Python, but we saw that the creation of threads didn't do much to help us with our overall execution time. CPython does not allow you to disable the GIL directly in your code, but as you will see, we can bypass this lock by using Rust.

Refactoring is an extremely powerful tool. Think about the evolution of many programs. We've already talked about refactoring in many contexts, but it is often easier said than done—especially with languages like Python, which are excellent at building prototypes but do not scale well. Ruby is another example of a scripting language that is easy to learn and use but has difficulties scaling. This problem has to do with the nature of the languages themselves. Trading performance for ease has always been the tension between these easy-to-learn languages and system languages like C, C++, and even Rust. While Rust positions itself among the replacements for C and C++, it still isn't as easy to write as Python.

Even so, if you own a business that you are looking to grow, it typically isn't best to throw away everything you've done to rewrite it in some other language. Using another language incurs additional overhead on staffing and also expands the knowledge required to fully understand the system. As we saw with C and C++, replacing a portion of the code with Rust can make this transition a little easier.

Type `maturin new` to start a project, hop into that directory, and type `cargo add image num-complex`. This is all we need to get started. Open `src/lib.rs`, and we will add our Mandelbrot function.

Listing 8.8 `lib.rs`: Initial Mandelbrot function

```
use image::{Rgb, RgbImage};                  ◁── Imports the image library
use num_complex::Complex64;                  ◁── Imports the complex number library
use pyo3::prelude::*;                        ◁── Imports the PyO3 libraries
use std::path::Path;

#[pyfunction]                                ◁── Adds a macro for the function to export to Python
fn mandelbrot_func(size: u32, p: &str, range_x0: f64,
    range_y0: f64, range_x1: f64, range_y1: f64) {
    let mut img = RgbImage::new(size, size);
```

```rust
    let size_f64 = size as f64;

    let x_range = (range_x1 - range_x0).abs();
    let x_offset = x_range / 2.0;

    let y_range = (range_y1 - range_y0).abs();
    let y_offset = y_range / 2.0;
    let path = Path::new(p);
    for px in 0..size {                    // Iterates through the pixels
        for py in 0..size {                //  to insert into the image
            let x0 = px as f64 / size_f64 * x_range - x_offset;
            let y0 = py as f64 / size_f64 * y_range - y_offset;

            let c = Complex64::new(x0, y0);

            let mut i = 0u8;
            let mut z = Complex64::new(0.0, 0.0);

            while i < 255 {
                z = (z * z) + c;
                if z.norm() > 4.0 {
                    break;
                }
                i += 1;
            }

            img.put_pixel(px, py, Rgb([i, i, i]));   // Places pixels into image
        }
    }
    img.save(path).unwrap();               // Saves the image to the filesystem
}
```

The `pymodule` macro at the top of the function allows us to call this method from Python. PyO3 will package this for us once we create a module for it to live in. To do that, we will add one more bit of code.

Listing 8.9 lib.rs: Creating the Python module

```rust
#[pymodule]                                // Creates a module for Python
fn mandelbrot(_py: Python, m: &PyModule) -> PyResult<()> {
    m.add_function(wrap_pyfunction!(mandelbrot_func, m)?)?;   // Adds a function to the module
    Ok(())
}
```

To compile this, we again rely on `maturin`. Type `maturin development` to compile the library and add it to your environment. Next, we will copy over our `main.py` from before and make a few modifications to call our new module.

Listing 8.10 `main.py`: Importing a new module

```
from mandelbrot import mandelbrot_func         ◁── Imports function
import asyncio                                      from module

# Remove Python implementation of Mandelbrot

async def mandelbrot(size: int, path: str, range_x0: float, range_y0: float,
↪range_x1: float, range_y1: float):
    return executor.submit(mandelbrot_func, size, path, range_x0, range_y0,
↪range_x1, range_y1)                          ◁── Calls Rust
                                                   function
```

When we run this code using a timing method, we find that just by using Rust, we shaved 25 seconds off of the compute time to 23 seconds! Still not ideal because we are still blocked by the GIL. We need PyO3 to tell Python to trust us—we are safe. To do this, we will make one extra function that we will export.

Listing 8.11 `lib.rs`: Adding a thread-safe function

```
#[pyfunction]
fn mandelbrot_fast(
    py: Python<'_>,
    size: u32,
    path: &str,
    range_x0: f64,
    range_y0: f64,
    range_x1: f64,
    range_y1: f64,
) {
    py.allow_threads(|| mandelbrot_func(size, path, range_x0, range_y0,
↪range_x1, range_y1))
}                                         ◁── Tells Python that this function
                                              does not need the GIL
#[pymodule]
fn mandelbrot(_py: Python, m: &PyModule) -> PyResult<()> {
    ...
        m.add_function(wrap_pyfunction!(mandelbrot_fast, m)?)?;

    Ok(())
}
```

Then we need to create some threads to run on in Python. Here, we will import a pool executor for threads. We will use four to see what sort of improvement we get. This method also works for the other function we created, but you will find that the execution times are the same since we haven't disabled the GIL. Running the fast function, however, disables that and allows us to use true concurrency.

Listing 8.12 `main.py`: Using a thread executor

```
...
from concurrent.futures import ThreadPoolExecutor    ◁── Imports the executor to
                                                         run on various threads
```

```
executor = ThreadPoolExecutor(max_workers=4)

async def mandelbrot(size: int, path: str, range_x0: float, range_y0: float,
➥range_x1: float, range_y1: float):
    return executor.submit(mandelbrot_fast, size, path, range_x0, range_y0,
    ➥range_x1, range_y1)           ◁──┐ Sends the function and parameters
...                                    │ to thread for future execution
```

When this completes, the total time is a blazing 6 seconds. That's a significant improvement from the original 46 seconds for pure Python and 23 seconds for our Rust implementation without disabling the GIL. Additionally, we iteratively migrated our code to allow for the incorporation of Rust into our existing Python application to get an almost 5x increase in performance.

As part of refactoring, we need to identify which aspects of our system can be improved without affecting the larger system. This application that we wrote is obviously not production quality, but it underlines the point that often, in a language like Python, we like the ability to be flexible and prototype. But the more we ask of our systems, the more complex they become. We could have extended this refactor to be entirely in Rust to bypass the limitations of Python altogether. However, this library may be used elsewhere. Or, possibly, we don't have the support to have a whole system written in Rust. We've explored how to refactor our systems to scale from prototype to product in this chapter. While Python is amazing at prototyping, we found that Rust can make it better. Finding the bottlenecks in your Python code can help you and your team determine whether Rust is a solution to your speed problems.

Remember, refactoring is a process, not a destination, and therefore, it is never complete. Rust allows us to take these tiny steps over time to increase the visibility of our changes and move toward a solution that works best for our project.

Summary

- Python is a great prototyping language but suffers from performance issues.
- Scaling can be done to improve performance by adding additional hardware or extending current hardware.
- Scaling requires developers to modify their code to take advantage of these changes.
- Python's ability to run concurrent processes is limited by a global lock.
- Rust can bypass this lock to increase overall performance due to its inherent memory safety.
- Using Rust and PyO3, we can bypass the global lock in Python to unlock concurrent processes.
- Refactoring Python applications to have memory-safe concurrency patterns using Rust can reduce latency and increase performance.

WebAssembly for refactoring JavaScript

This chapter covers
- Writing a Rust library to be used in JavaScript
- Integrating WebAssembly into an existing JavaScript project and component
- Writing a web component entirely in Rust and importing it into an existing project

Finding a single language with which to develop all parts of an application has been a goal for many who create programming languages. "Write once, run anywhere" was a tagline for Java because, at the time, it seemed like as long as a system could run Java's virtual machine, your application would run there, too. Obviously, this had its limitations, but in essence, it was what made Java such a popular platform, even to this day. This idea of cross-platform software isn't new; in fact, it was a goal of early compilers to allow programmers to write an application once and compile it to run on other machines.

Rust, as we have seen, follows this same pattern. Instead of working like Java—that is, having a virtual machine to run an application—Rust uses different compile targets. Additionally, the examples we have looked at so far have relied, on some level, on Rust's C integration for importing libraries. In this chapter, we are going to explore a new approach to "write once, run anywhere," but instead of writing Java (breathe a sigh of relief), we will be working with a technology that was built to be portable for the web.

9.1 What is WebAssembly?

In 2018, the World Wide Web Consortium (W3C) published a specification that would allow compilation to target a special sort of bytecode that could be run in the browser. The idea is that compiled languages such as C++, Go, and Rust could target their compilers to write binaries in Web Assembly (Wasm) bytecode instead of targeting an AMD or Intel processor. The target for Wasm is a WebAssembly System Interface (WASI), which essentially is the runtime to run Wasm bytecode.

Now, we are seeing several technologies spring up around Wasm, along with some pretty cool projects. Developers are finding that they can put almost anything in the web browser, including whole operating systems! Wasm is used to run code in cloud workers, and the developers of some JavaScript libraries are refactoring portions of their code to use Wasm. Loading Wasm requires JavaScript to pull the library in and initialize it, as shown in figure 9.1.

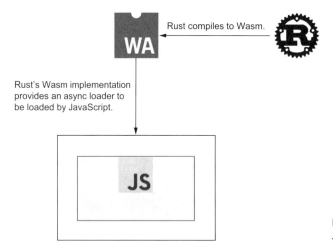

Figure 9.1 Wasm loaded into a JavaScript frontend

So why, as a Rust developer, should you care? Well, while a large portion of systems-level code is written in Java or a C-based language, the most-used programming languages are JavaScript-based languages that run in the web browser (figure 9.2). As mentioned earlier, Wasm was developed to be a universal binary that was targeted to run in the browser as well. This gives us the ability to write Rust code that can interact with or replace portions of JavaScript code, making it possible for us to refactor pieces of it to Rust.

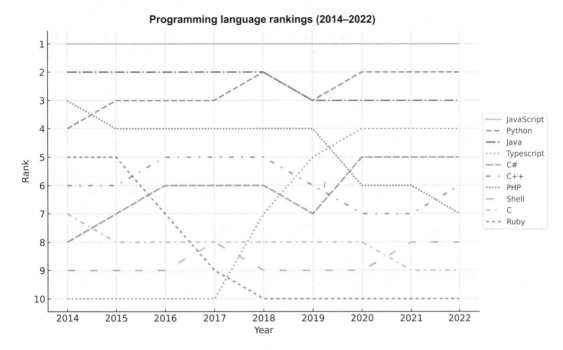

Figure 9.2 Github Octoverse Survey of most-used languages, 2022

There is also a flip side to this Rust/Wasm relationship: because Wasm is a universal binary that is supposed to run anywhere, we can run the Wasm library within Rust. Consequently, we can refactor old code by importing portions of it into Rust via Wasm. First, we will see how we can write a Rust function and import it into JavaScript via Wasm. Then, in the next chapter, we will take code that has been compiled to Wasm and run it within a Rust application.

9.2 Moving from JavaScript to Rust

Before we dive into the actual code, it is important to understand the world of JavaScript and how refactoring it differs from how we've refactored thus far. Up until now, we have focused on code that runs within a terminal rather than a web browser. C++ and Python are really C code underneath, whereas JavaScript is its own scripting language made for the web browser. Found on 98% of websites, it is an essential tool of the web. Originally developed back in 1995, the language has slowly changed over time. Yet its underlying purpose of being the "web browser language" didn't change until 2009, with the introduction of the Node.js runtime. Since then, the lines have really begun to blur between frontend and backend development with JavaScript. Additional tools have been written to help make JavaScript more robust, such as TypeScript, which added types similar to those in Rust to JavaScript.

So, here we are presented with another pervasive language that has slowly evolved (and, in some cases, devolved) over time and is lumped together with C++ and Python in the world of code that can become unmanageable and would benefit from refactoring. The difference is that instead of focusing on the backend code, we are going to focus on the frontend and refactor JavaScript to have the memory safety, speed, and type system that make Rust so robust.

How do you know when to refactor your JavaScript to Rust? What use cases should you be looking for? The answer is the same as for the decisions you would make for migrating from Python to Rust or C++ to Rust: safety and speed. The difference is that you will need to start thinking of the browser instead of the terminal (though Wasm can be used on Node.js runtimes as well). JavaScript is not type safe and is prone to runtime errors. Additionally, it can be slower than compiled programs. Wasm and Rust are also more secure than JavaScript in the way they manage the application's memory. So, consider refactoring if you are looking for any of these improvements or if you have backend logic that can be moved to the frontend to reduce the backend workload.

Developing a Wasm library for your site will typically follow the same process that UI developers follow anyway, but instead of using JavaScript and HTML, you will use Rust compiled to Wasm with HTML. In the future, you may develop whole components in Rust.

9.3 Rust in the browser

Most web components today are rendered on the client side using data transmitted over HTTP. Data is most commonly transmitted by sending JSON-formatted messages using a REST protocol. However, this is not the only way. In 1997, a data model known as RDF was created to help organize metadata around arbitrary objects. This became the foundation of RSS (RDF Site Summary) feeds, providing a passive way of notifying other systems of site updates. Tools are used to aggregate these various feeds and display them to users to read or save for later.

What we are going to build is a tool that takes an RSS feed (using RDF format) and creates a component to list and provide details of articles that are newly published to arXiv, an open-access repository of scientific papers. We will first write the method for retrieving papers based on a searchable term, providing links to the actual paper. Once this is written, we will export the function so it can be used in JavaScript and place it as a web component. To start, let's look at structuring the data and retrieving search results.

9.3.1 Requesting data

Let's first create a new Rust application by running the following commands.

Listing 9.1 Creating a new project

```
cargo new papers --lib
cd papers
```

9.3 Rust in the browser

Open up the `Cargo.toml` and add the following libraries.

Listing 9.2 `Cargo.toml`: Dependencies for our library

```toml
[package]
name = "papers"
version = "0.1.0"
edition = "2021"

[lib]
crate-type = ["cdylib"]
# See more keys and their definitions
# at https://doc.rust-lang.org/cargo/reference/manifest.html

[dependencies]
reqwest = { version = "0.11", features = ["json"] }         # Reqwest is a library for making HTTP calls.
serde = { version = "1.0", features = ["derive"] }          # Serde is the main encoding/decoding library for our various calls.
serde-wasm-bindgen = "0.5.0"
serde-xml-rs = "0.6.0"                                       # XML-parsing library
wasm-bindgen = "0.2.87"                                      # Converts Rust code to Wasm
                                                             # Wasm bindgen allows us to convert JSON objects from JsValue to a struct.

[dev-dependencies]
tokio-test = "*"     # Used in async testing
```

Now that we have a project, it's helpful to define our structures. To do this, we should first look at what an actual feed looks like.

Listing 9.3 arXiv: Example message from the service we are calling

```xml
<feed xmlns="http://www.w3.org/2005/Atom">
    <link href="http://arxiv.org/api/query?search_query%3Dall%3Atype"
     rel="self" type="application/atom+xml"/>
    <title type="html">
        ArXiv Query: search_query=all:type
    </title>
    <id>http://arxiv.org/api/MPA5fUXeKVs0FQAFaOfw4Eh7V44</id>
    <updated>2023-06-13T00:00:00-04:00</updated>
    <opensearch:totalResults
     xmlns:opensearch="http://a9.com/-/spec/opensearch/1.1/">
        229748
    </opensearch:totalResults>
    <opensearch:startIndex
     xmlns:opensearch="http://a9.com/-/spec/opensearch/1.1/">
        0
    </opensearch:startIndex>
    <opensearch:itemsPerPage
     xmlns:opensearch="http://a9.com/-/spec/opensearch/1.1/">
        10
    </opensearch:itemsPerPage>
    <entry>
        <id>http://arxiv.org/abs/cs/0507037v1</id>
```

```xml
            <updated>2005-07-14T08:58:31Z</updated>
            <published>2005-07-14T08:58:31Z</published>
            <title>Type Inference for Guarded Recursive Data Types</title>
            <summary> ... </summary>
            <author>
                <name>Peter J. Stuckey</name>
            </author>
            <author>
                <name>Martin Sulzmann</name>
            </author>
            <link href="http://arxiv.org/abs/cs/0507037v1"
                rel="alternate"
                type="text/html"/>
            <link title="pdf" href="http://arxiv.org/pdf/cs/0507037v1"
             rel="related"
             type="application/pdf"/>
            <arxiv:primary_category
                xmlns:arxiv="http://arxiv.org/schemas/atom"
                term="cs.PL"
                scheme="http://arxiv.org/schemas/atom"/>
            <category term="cs.PL" scheme="http://arxiv.org/schemas/atom"/>
            <category term="cs.LO" scheme="http://arxiv.org/schemas/atom"/>
    </entry>
</feed>
```

From this, we can see the root of the file is the `feed` tag, with each result being an `entry`. The details we want from an entry are a list of authors, an ID, a title, and a summary of when it was updated and when it was published. Given these fields, we can derive the following structures.

Listing 9.4 `lib.rs`: Defining our basic structures for searching

```rust
#[derive(Default, Debug, Clone, PartialEq, Serialize, Deserialize)]
pub struct Feed {
    pub entry: Vec<Entry>,     ◁── A list of entries to be displayed and wrapped in
}                                   a parent structure similar to the previous XML

#[derive(Default, Debug, Clone, PartialEq, Serialize, Deserialize)]
pub struct Entry {
    pub id: String,
    pub updated: String,
    pub published: String,
    pub title: String,
    pub summary: String,
    pub author: Vec<Author>,
}

#[derive(Default, Debug, Clone, PartialEq, Serialize, Deserialize)]
pub struct Author {
    pub name: String,
}
```

Given this structure, we can then create a function that retrieves paginated search results (*paginated* refers to data that is chunked by size and starting location). To do this, we will use the `reqwest` library (which has Wasm support) to retrieve our results. We will take those results and convert them from XML to JSON for our component. Using their RDF API, we can pass search queries as well as pagination data (start and max results). All of this functionality will be put into our library. Let's write the function now.

Listing 9.5 `lib.rs`: Fetching and parsing the results for searching papers

```
async fn search(term: String, page: isize, max_results: isize) ->
  Result<Feed, reqwest::Error> {
    let http_response = reqwest::get(                              ⟵ Calls the export
        format!("http://export.arxiv.org/api/query?search_query=      endpoint with a
        all:{}&start={}&max_results={}",                              given topic,
        term, page * max_results, max_results)).await?;              page, and count
    let b = http_response.text().await?;                          ⟵ Saves
    let feed: Feed = serde_xml_rs::from_str(b.as_str()).unwrap(); ⟵   the text
    return Ok(feed)                              Converts to a      response
}                                                Feed struct
```

Finally, we can write a test to verify that this is working as expected.

Listing 9.6 `lib.rs`: Adding unit tests for our search

```
#[cfg(test)]
mod tests {
    use super::*;                           Macro that allows for blocking
    macro_rules! aw {                   ⟵  within the async test
        ($e:expr) => {
            tokio_test::block_on($e)
        };
    }
                                                    Uses the macro to block
    #[test]                                      until you receive a response
    fn test_search() {                                 and verify the results
        let res = aw!(search("type".to_string(), 0, 10)).unwrap();  ⟵
        assert_eq!(res.entry.len(), 10);
        print!("{:?}", res)
    }
}
```

NOTE Blocking is when a system waits until a result is returned, as opposed to asynchronous calls, which switch to another process while waiting.

This is a pretty simple function that we can use to take advantage of Rust's asynchronous abilities and powerful parsing libraries. This method will be central to the components we build in this chapter and the tools we build in the next. While the method is simple, it can be used in a multitude of ways, making it ideal to demonstrate the powers of Wasm's portability.

9.3.2 Compiling to Wasm

Now that we have a function that performs the search functionality we want, we can see what it looks like in the web browser. To do that, we need to compile it to Wasm and use the JavaScript loading function. This is pretty straightforward once we have defined the function that we wish to export. There are a few different ways we can define our function, but to allow for a smaller interface, we are going to pass in a JSON object. Let's define that now.

Listing 9.7 `lib.rs`: Defining the object as a JSON object

```
#[derive(Default, Debug, Clone, PartialEq, Serialize, Deserialize)]
pub struct Search {
    pub term: String,
    pub page: isize,
    pub limit: isize,
}
```

Next, we need to define the function that the Wasm binding can generate to pass the JSON object. To do this, we will use a macro defined by the `wasm_bindgen` library. We will pass a special `JsValue` to the function and return a similar object. This function will also be asynchronous, meaning that it will return a JavaScript promise that needs to resolve before the data is returned.

Listing 9.8 `lib.rs`: Creating the search function

```
#[wasm_bindgen]                                    ◁— This attribute will be used at compile
pub async fn paper_search(val: JsValue) -> JsValue{    time to create a Wasm function
    let term: Search= serde_wasm_bindgen::from_value(val).unwrap();    that is exposed to JavaScript.
    let resp = search(term.term, term.page, term.limit).await.unwrap();
    serde_wasm_bindgen::to_value(&resp).unwrap()
}
```

Deserializes our JSON object into a Rust struct

Calls our search function and awaits the results

Encodes response to JsValue

Within this function, you see we are converting our `JsValue` into a `Search` struct. This is done by a special `serde` library. When a result is received from our `search` function, the values are then re-encoded to JSON and returned. That was all we needed! Now we can compile to Wasm using the following command.

Listing 9.9 Console: Building and compiling to Wasm for the web

```
cargo install wasm-pack
wasm-pack build --target web      ◁— The web target will provide us with the
                                     necessary bootstrap files to load the
                                     Wasm file into the browser and use it.
```

If you look in the output directory `pkg`, you will see that a special npm library was instantiated and is ready to use. If you open the `papers.js` file, you can see a bunch of bootstrapped code to help load the Wasm module. Similarly, if you open the file `papers.d.ts`, you can see the expected types and functions exported by this package. Next is verifying that this function works in JavaScript.

9.3.3 Loading Wasm in the browser

Now that we have a search function, let's see how it works in the browser. Before we add this code to our more sophisticated JavaScript component, let's first make sure it works through raw JavaScript. We'll create a lightweight HTML page, load the Wasm directly, provide it with a search element, and display the content as a list. To do this, we'll create a simple `index.html` file.

Listing 9.10 `index.html`: Calling the Wasm library from JavaScript

```html
<!DOCTYPE html>
<html lang="en-US">
  <head>
    <meta charset="utf-8" />
    <title>Feed example</title>
  </head>
  <body>
    <div id="listContainer">
      <ul id="list"></ul>
    </div>
    <script type="module">
      import init, { paper_search } from "./pkg/papers.js";          ⟵ Loads the JavaScript and Wasm file
      init().then(() => {                                             ⟵ Initializes the module and waits for the Wasm to be loaded
        var list = document.getElementById('list');                   ⟵ Once resolved, grabs the list element
        paper_search({"term":"type", "page": 0, "limit": 10}).then(   ⟵ Calls the search function and awaits the results
          (result)=>{
            result.entry.forEach((r)=> {                              ⟵ If successful, iterates through the results and adds items to the list
              var a = document.createElement('a');
              a.target = '_blank';
              a.href = r.id;
              a.innerText = r.title;
              var li = document.createElement('li')
              li.appendChild(a)
              list.appendChild(li)
            })
          },
          (error)=>console.error(error))                              ⟵ Otherwise, logs the error
        });
    </script>
  </body>
</html>
```

As you can see, we are using old-school JavaScript here to build our page. We have avoided the modern frameworks that many applications currently use to run JavaScript, but the code provides a great example of how to incorporate this function as a regular JavaScript library. Hopefully, this can start you thinking about some pesky JavaScript functions you are using internally that could be rewritten in Rust and loaded in this way. Raw JavaScript functions like this can be used almost anywhere, making this the first step toward refactoring. While this functionality is highly portable, it does not always fit into a larger JavaScript project. To do this, we can use a modern component library like React.

9.4 Creating a React component

Component-based development has been around since the inception of software engineering back in 1968. The concept is simple: separate concerns within a software system by building isolated packages, services, resources, or modules that have similar functions or data. Today, many languages, such as JavaScript, have frameworks or libraries that aid in creating components. One of the most popular of these is React.

React has been around for more than a decade and has changed the way people develop UIs. It has established itself as a great component-building tool and is all over the web. Other libraries, such as Vue.js, have become popular over the past couple of years, so the example we are about to write may be different for one of these other libraries.

To start, we are going to create a new web application using a tool called Vite. Vite is one of many modern JavaScript frameworks that provides tooling to bootstrap web applications. We will use it to bootstrap a new JavaScript app using the React component library. This will give us the minimum pieces needed to experiment with Wasm. First, you need to have npm installed, which can be done by following the setup instructions at npm Docs: https://mng.bz/eBMw.

Let's get started by opening up a terminal within your `papers` project and typing the following.

> **Listing 9.11 Console: Creating a new React app**

```
npm create vite@latest

Need to install the following packages:
  create-vite@latest
Ok to proceed? (y) y
✓ Project name: … papers-list
✓ Select a framework: › React
✓ Select a variant: › JavaScript
```

This will create our base application. Before we go any further, we need to change how our Wasm is being created. Right now, we have it set to be built using the `web` flag, which gives us a loader that must be called for the Wasm library to be used. We are instead going to use the `bundler` option, which takes our code and puts it in a module that can be easily imported and used within our JavaScript package.

Since JavaScript has been around for a while, there are different ways of building JavaScript code. Originally, JavaScript was built by loading multiple scripts via the browser, which required each page to track the libraries it was using and how they interacted. We did this in our earlier example using the `script` tag. Over the years, many libraries have been written in a modular format where a tool similar to a compiler takes all libraries and code written and assembles them into a single executable script. This compiler-like tool is called a `bundler` since it bundles the scripts together. This treats the code more as a library and less as a script. So, since we want to use our code as a library within our component, we are going to use the `bundler` flag when compiling our Wasm.

To use the `bundler` flag, we need to do the following.

Listing 9.12 Console: Bundling the library

```
wasm-pack build --target bundler
cd pkg
npm link
cd ../papers-list
```

Next, we will want to edit our `package.json` file to add our Wasm library as a relative import to our project. Add the following code under `dependencies`.

Listing 9.13 `package.json`: Adding local dependency

```
"dependencies": {
    "papers": "file:../pkg",
    ...
}
```

Then, add the following libraries and run the install.

Listing 9.14 Console: Linking our Wasm library and compiling

```
npm install vite-plugin-wasm vite-plugin-top-level-await --save-dev
npm link papers
npm install
```

Finally, there is one last configuration step before we can write our component. Open up `vite.config.js` and add the necessary Wasm modules.

Listing 9.15 `vite.config.js`: Configuring our app to use Wasm

```
import { defineConfig } from 'vite'
import react from '@vitejs/plugin-react'
import wasm from "vite-plugin-wasm";
import topLevelAwait from "vite-plugin-top-level-await";

// https://vitejs.dev/config/
export default defineConfig({
  plugins: [
    react(),
    wasm(),
    topLevelAwait()
    ],
})
```

240 CHAPTER 9 *WebAssembly for refactoring JavaScript*

Now, let's create that component. It's helpful to first create a component with static data so you can get the feel of it and make sure it works. Additionally, it provides a template that can easily be updated with variables. We are going to create a component called `List`. So, in the `src` folder, create a new file called `List.jsx` and add the following.

> **Listing 9.16 List.jsx: Creating a component with static data**

```
import React, { useEffect, useState } from 'react'
const List = () => {
    const [entries, setEntries] = useState([{id:"abc", title:"title"}])     ◁──┐
    const [page, setPage] = useState(0)     ◁──┐                                │
                                               │  The state          The state  │
    return (                                   │  management for     management for
        <>                                     │  the page count     our list of papers
        <ul>
            {entries?.map((v, i) => {     ◁──┐ Goes through the list of entries
            return <li key={i}>              │ and renders a link for each
                <a href={`${v.id}`} target='_blank'>{v.title}</a>
            </li>
            })}
        </ul>
        <button onClick={() => setPage((page) => page + 1)}>More</button>    ◁──┐
        </>                                                                     │
    )                                                           Uses a button to
}                                                               increase the page count
export default List;
```

Now, in a terminal window, type `npm start dev` and open a browser window to the host and port listed in the terminal. Hopefully, you see a link render. Let's add the Wasm file. Something to remember here is that our application needs to fetch and load the file. To do that, we need to add an `import` statement, which creates a JavaScript future that needs to be resolved before using the library. So, outside of the `List` component, we need to add an import statement.

> **Listing 9.17 List.jsx: Importing the Wasm library**

```
import React, { useEffect, useState } from 'react'

const wasm = await import('papers')
```

You'll notice that we have a `page` variable that is incremented as we click the `More` button. When this variable is changed, we want React to update the state of our component based on this `effect`. We will create a `useEffect` hook to do this.

> **Listing 9.18 List.jsx: Using Wasm to fetch papers**

```
const List = () => {
    const [entries, setEntries] = useState([])     ◁──┐ Creates an empty
                                                        list at the onset
```

```
        const [page, setPage] = useState(0)
        useEffect(() => {
            if(wasm){
                wasm.paper_search({"term":"type",
                    "page": page, "limit": 10}).then(
                    (result)=>setEntries(result.entry),
                    (error)=>console.error(error))
            }
        }, [page])
        ...
}
```

- An update watcher to the component so it knows to rerender when data changes
- Calls search function, passing the page and limit
- Sets entries from the search result
- Displays an error if an error occurs
- Watches and updates when the page variable changes

Save and watch the page reload. Now you should see some articles come across. When you click the More button, you should see the page update! We have fully integrated our Rust code into a JavaScript application with just a little configuration. Because of this marriage between Rust and JavaScript through Wasm, some tools have emerged to help with component creation that allow you to write your React component in Rust. Let's take a look at what that looks like.

9.5 Web components entirely in Rust

Yew is a library designed to create web UI components that compile into Wasm. Yew's intent is to bring all of Rust's safety goodness to web applications. Since most development patterns have migrated away from a server-side rendering model to a client-side model, most languages aren't able to bridge this gap from backend code to frontend code because most frontend code is done in JavaScript. With the introduction of Wasm, this is no longer true. Now, whole component frameworks are being written that act like those in React but are written in Rust.

The Yew library will help us create a component similar to the one we created in React; the major difference is in how we handle our components' states and actions. Our states will be `Fetching`, `Success`, and `Failure`, while our actions will be `IncrementPage`, `SetFeedState`, and `GetSearch`. Yew components then need to have three methods: `create`, `update`, and `view`. `create` and `update` are used to set the initial state and mutate the state, respectively, while `view` uses that state to render the component. This comes from the classic Model-View-Controller structure where a model holds the state, the controller controls the actions, and the view renders based on the state.

First, we should add Yew to our `Cargo.toml`.

Listing 9.19 `Cargo.toml`: Adding a Yew component library

```
[dependencies]
...
yew = "0.19.0"
```

Let's get started by creating our enums for our actions and state.

Listing 9.20 `lib.rs`: Creating enums for various states

```rust
use yew::prelude::*;         ◁── Imports Yew package

...

pub enum Msg {               ◁── Defines possible message types
    IncrementPage,
    SetFeedState(FetchState<Feed>),
    GetSearch(isize),
}

pub enum FetchState<T> {     ◁── Defines various page states
    Fetching,
    Success(T),
    Failed(reqwest::Error),
}
```

Our component itself must hold some sort of state. In this case, it will be the `Fetch` state, as well as what page we are currently on. The `List` structure will look like the following.

Listing 9.21 `lib.rs`: Creating the initial state struct

```rust
pub struct List {
    page: isize,
    feed: FetchState<Feed>,
}
```

Now, we need to implement the component type for our `List`. Here, we will define two values that will be used to help us render the component. Those are `Messages` and `Properties`. `Messages` are the type of actions that can occur on an update, whereas `Properties` can be values that will be monitored by Yew for updates. We provide a base struct `List`, which houses the properties of the basic values we want to use within the component. The `Component` implementation then requires us to implement functions to help the component render. We will not be using `Properties` in this example, but you can find more information about their use at www.yew.rs. Instead, we will be using this base structure `List`, which has a `feed` and current `page`. We also need to implement three methods: `create`, `update`, and `view`. So, let's create the basic skeleton, and then we will fill in the methods.

Listing 9.22 `lib.rs`: Basic component outline

```rust
impl Component for List {                    ◁── Implementation of a Yew Component
    type Message = Msg;         ◁── Defines the type of Message to be used
    type Properties = ();       ◁── Sets properties to None
```

```
    fn create(ctx: &Context<Self>) -> Self {
    }

    fn update(&mut self, ctx: &Context<Self>, msg: Self::Message) -> bool {
    }

    fn view(&self, ctx: &Context<Self>) -> Html {
    }
}
```

Let's first understand the flow of the component. We will start with an initial state established by the `create` method, which will also begin the search process with the page being 0. This causes the `View` stage to render in the `Fetching` mode, which will display a loading message. Any state change internally is managed by the update methods, which then will trigger changes to the view. A view can include a button that triggers an event and is handled by the update. A high-level map of what is going on can be seen in figure 9.3.

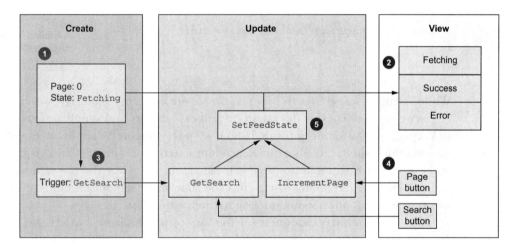

Figure 9.3 Component flow

We are going to start by creating the view and working backward to the update and initialization (create) phases. This will help us understand the different views we want and what actions will drive those changes. With this view, we will need to match the various states we established in our `FetchState` enum. Each state will then render HTML using a macro.

Listing 9.23 `lib.rs`: Implementing the view

```
impl Component for List {
    ...
```

```rust
fn view(&self, ctx: &Context<Self>) -> Html {
    match &self.feed {
        FetchState::Fetching => html! { "Fetching" },
        FetchState::Success(data) => html! {
            <div>
                <ul>
                    { for data.entry.iter().map(|e| html!{
                        <li>
                            <a target="_blank" href={e.id.to_string()}>
                                {e.title.to_string()}</a>
                        </li>
                    })}
                </ul>
                <button class="button" onclick={ctx.link().callback(
                    |_| Msg::IncrementPage)}>
                    { "More" }
                </button>
            </div>
        },
        FetchState::Failed(err) => html! { err },
    }
}
```

- The view function is required to display the component.
- Matches the various values of the page state
- If fetching, displays the word Fetching
- If there is data, processes and displays it
- Goes through each entry as we did in the React component to create the list
- Dispatches an IncrementPage method if the button is clicked
- If a failure occurs, displays the error

While fetching, we will let the user know we are fetching. Similarly, we display any errors we receive. These states are pretty self-explanatory and simple but are essential in keeping our customers informed about what is going on. When we receive data, we do something similar to what our React component does: iterate through the results and create a link with a button that calls an action to update the page state. The `ctx` variable gives us the ability to tap into the state management system that accepts a message and calls our update function to mutate the state.

With this in mind, we can now see the various mutations our system can undergo. One method will help us set the state, while the other two manipulate the state and request an additional update.

Listing 9.24 lib.rs: Implementing the update functions

```rust
impl Component for List {
    ...
    fn update(&mut self, ctx: &Context<Self>, msg: Self::Message)
        -> bool {
        match msg {
            Msg::SetFeedState(fetch_state) => {
                self.feed = fetch_state;
                true
            }
            Msg::IncrementPage => {
                self.page += 1;
```

- The update function changes the state of the page through message passing.
- We need to match all possible message dispatches.
- SetFeed will mutate the state of the component by setting the current feed state.
- True is returned so the component will rerender since the state has changed.

```
                    ctx.link().send_message(Msg::GetSearch(self.page));
                    false
                }
                Msg::GetSearch(page) => {
                    ctx.link().send_future(async move {
                        match search("type".to_string(), page, 10).await {
                            Ok(data) => Msg::SetFeedState(
                                FetchState::Success(data)),
                            Err(err) => Msg::SetFeedState(
                                FetchState::Failed(err)),
                        }
                    });
                    ctx.link().send_message(Msg::SetFeedState(
                        FetchState::Fetching));
                    true
                }
            }
            ...
}
```

- **IncrementPage will increment the page count and send a new message to the search.**
- **False is sent so an update doesn't occur until the state is updated.**
- **Sends a future call that will be resolved and handles the state change**
- **Calls our search function and checks the returning value**
- **If successful, passes the data to be rendered**
- **Otherwise, sends the error message to be displayed**
- **While this is happening, we want to display a "fetching" state.**

You'll notice that this method returns a Boolean. This is used by the component to determine if it should rerender, which should only occur when the state has changed. So, in the first method, we just assign the state, nothing special. This will, in turn, trigger the view to update based on the state. The second method mutates the page state but then sends a message to call the `GetSearch` function. This could be controlled using properties, but instead, we want to demonstrate how to call updates from other updates along with returning a false so the view does not update. `GetSearch` is the main method that we will use to call our original feed retrieval. This call is wrapped in an `async` method, meaning we need to provide a closure to run when it resolves. Once resolved, the state will be updated, providing either our data or an error message. While this is happening, we set the state to fetching so the user understands what is happening.

Hopefully, at this point, you are seeing how this whole component flows from the view state and the ways to affect the view. To review, we have a function that defines how the component looks based on a given state; this is the view. Changing the state in the update function happens through an external trigger. This, in turn, affects the state, causing the view to be run, changing the appearance. The final piece we need is to set up the initial state of the component when it is created. This will do two essential tasks: create the initial struct and set off the initial fetch request.

> **Listing 9.25** `lib.rs`: Implementing the initial state

```
impl Component for List {
    ...
    fn create(ctx: &Context<Self>) -> Self {
```

- **The Create method sets the initial state of the component.**

```
            ctx.link().send_message(Msg::GetSearch(0));
            Self {
                page: 0,
                feed: FetchState::Fetching,
            }
        }
        ...
}
```

- `ctx.link().send_message(Msg::GetSearch(0));` ◁— At the start, we want to get the first page of results, so we are sending an update message.
- `Self { page: 0, feed: FetchState::Fetching, }` ◁— Creates the initial structure and set its values

That's it! The component is done, but we still have one final method to add to expose this to our Wasm module.

Listing 9.26 `lib.rs`: Creating the component function

```
#[wasm_bindgen]
pub fn list_component() -> Result<(), JsValue> {
    yew::start_app::<List>();
    Ok(())
}
```

◁— Exposes the component in Wasm

After doing this, we can rebuild our Wasm module.

Listing 9.27 Console: Building and updating the library

```
wasm-pack build --target bundler
cd pkg
npm link
cd ../papers-list
npm link papers
npm install
```

Open up our `App.jsx` file and change the code to the following.

Listing 9.28 `App.jsx`: Mounting the Wasm component

```
import './App.css'

const wasm = await import('papers')

function App() {
  return (<div>
    <div>{wasm.list_component()}</div>
  </div>
  )
}
```

◁— Just call the component method, and Yew should do the rest!

That's it! Start up your dev server and see how this works just like our React component.

9.6 Refactoring JavaScript revisited

To review, we were able to use a Rust library to help us create an `async` method to retrieve and paginate through an RDF document. We then added this to the web browser and used it as a Rust library for a data provider as well as a component. Rust provides us with a level of safety and code quality checks out of the box that JavaScript requires many tools to handle equally well.

When you consider the evolution of the various projects we completed here, it might be difficult to figure out where in the process you may be and what sort of solution you might need. The first use case appears where you have an algorithm or process that you have written in Rust or have rewritten in Rust to run within the browser as a script. This is the classic JavaScript or web model, where it is the job of the web page to make sure that scripts are loaded for other scripts to use, and the context is therefore loaded for only that page. The second scenario is exporting your Rust code as a module or library that can be imported into other JavaScript projects, such as a React component. This is a modern approach and the most likely scenario for developers to use. Modules are the way most large JavaScript projects are managed, and integrating Wasm modules will be a larger extension to this pattern in the future.

Finally, there is a whole web component being developed in Rust. This technology is still in its infancy, and it is thus difficult to determine the growth trajectory of this pattern. Nonetheless, the option of developing a web component in Rust is extremely useful for scenarios where developing a product using only one language or a limited number of languages is appealing. Table 9.1 outlines these various use cases and patterns.

Table 9.1 Wasm frontend use cases

Use case	Format	Tool
Simple web page	Script	`wasm-pack` web
Library integration	Module	`wasm-pack` bundler
UI element	Component	Yew

Now that we have Rust producing a Wasm module used on the frontend, we can look at how we can use Wasm on the backend for a much larger refactor pattern.

Summary

- Wasm is a universal language that can be run in most web browsers.
- Wasm can be written in Rust to be used in raw JavaScript via a `--web` flag when using `wasm-pack`.
- Wasm can be used to write JavaScript libraries that can be imported into large web applications written in Rust by using the `bundler` option when compiling using `wasm-pack`.

- Wasm can be used within components by loading the exported module, allowing for more portable code, and integrating into modern frameworks and libraries.
- Full web components can be written in Wasm and Rust using Yew.

WebAssembly interface for refactoring

This chapter covers
- Writing a WebAssembly (Wasm) module to run in a virtual runtime
- Integrating a Wasm module into a Rust executable for output
- Using Wasm memory for non-numerical data

Java was released as a programming language in 1995 with the bold slogan "Write Once Run Anywhere" (WORA). The concept of writing code that can run anywhere was not new; it had been done before in other languages like Smalltalk, and today it seems mildly unremarkable given the extensive package managers, interpreted languages, and sophisticated compilers available to developers. But what Java did was truly amazing. In the course of a few years, it became one of the most adopted languages; it remained so for two decades and nearly succeeded in inserting itself into every possible piece of software, including the web browser.

> **NOTE** Java was at one point so popular that it influenced the name of an up-and-coming web language known now as JavaScript, even though the two are completely unrelated.

When Sun Microsystems developed Java, it had an eye on the newly emerging World Wide Web. Sun realized that there was a lot of potential for growth in that area, along with the presence of new hardware like cell phones. Internally, Sun was having problems with C and C++ running on their custom hardware and decided to create a language with its own *virtual machine* (VM), which can interpret a custom assembly language known as *assembly code*. The VM translates assembly code into the host's *bytecode* to execute applications on almost any device that the VM supports.

Developing in Java allowed the developer to write an application that would be compiled into a module known as a JAR (Java ARchive), which is a zip file that contains Java bytecode grouped into classes, as shown in figure 10.1. This archive could then be shipped to another machine and executed or used as a library. The files could be executed as long as the runtime Java Runtime Environment (JRE) was present on the machine. The JRE could even run in your browser as a little application known as an Applet.

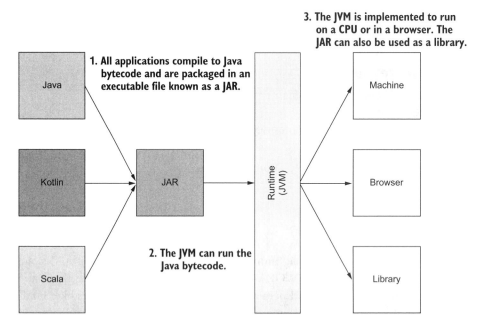

Figure 10.1 Languages compiled into a JAR and the ability to run in multiple locations

Java is still pervasive in the industry and is still one of the most prolific programming languages ever developed. Java blazed a trail for many development practices we use today. Notably, the important notion of being able to write code and run it anywhere remains. Java was able to create a new platform for others to develop on as well. Scala, Clojure, Kotlin, and several other languages all compile to Java bytecode and can run wherever a JRE is present.

The history of Java can give us a glimpse into the future of WebAssembly (Wasm). In the previous chapter, we looked at using Rust to write JavaScript code, but the process was really an introduction to a much larger opportunity to write code that runs anywhere in whatever language you'd like.

Every chapter in this book has demonstrated Rust's power to integrate into other languages such as Python, C++, and JavaScript, but this is only the tip of the iceberg. While the interoperability between Rust and various C-based languages is vast and impressive, the world of Wasm has made Rust one of the core languages for more extensive interoperability. Rust did this by creating WebAssembly modules, which are libraries or executables that are neatly packaged to be used by compatible Wasm runtimes or libraries, much like the JAR in Java.

In 2019, Mozilla announced an initiative known as the WebAssembly System Interface, or WASI. The initiative essentially lifted Wasm out of the browser and into virtually every runtime and language as long as there was a supporting library or binary. Like the Java JVM, WASI establishes a set of protocols that allow the assembly language to interact with the underlying system. This set of protocols is known as an *application binary interface*, or ABI, where two binary modules can interact via machine or assembly code. These protocols are very low-level compared to higher-level APIs.

So, what you have is a WebAssembly module that can run in a web browser or on the command line with the addition of one runtime binary or a module that can be imported and run by any supporting language. The power of this type of flexibility can be seen through the lens of how we use containers in development today.

Many are seeing Wasm + WASI as the next step in creating universally running applications. Some developers are moving to containers as a way of bundling their applications to run anywhere. However, Wasm and WASI are providing an alternative to help gradually migrate legacy systems by allowing developers to create their own runtime to embed old business logic or slower-performing code (figure 10.2).

Consider the current trend of writing applications in the form of functions as a service. Here again, a common runtime and target are created for a given language, and the code is loaded into a temporary container. The temporary container runs on an abstraction above the underlying operating system. In this scenario, the hosting application that executes your function constrains the container runtime to only execute in a predefined way. The limited API that these services provide for you typically requires a single entry point that needs to be implemented. The code is provided in raw form to the hosting system, and the system compiles it and mounts it in a container runtime. The host system then attempts to call the function based on the language and other configuration data required by the provider.

As we will see, Wasm requires us to define an interface. This interface will be used to allow clients to call specific functions within our runtime. Instead of a runtime like the JRE or a container runtime, we will have the ability to define the interfaces and how we interact with the underlying system. You can provide the scope necessary to make your system as flexible as you want, allowing anyone to create an API-like application, or as constrained as you want to cordon off a segment of legacy code. You get to choose the language for the Wasm runtime, and your users can choose to write the code in whatever language they are comfortable using.

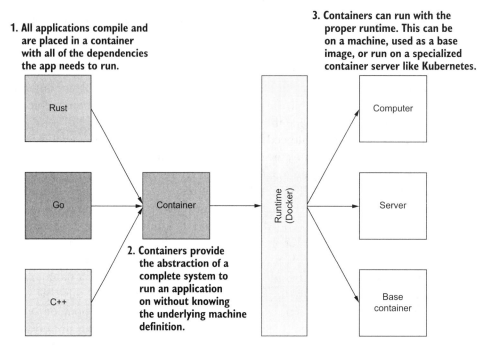

Figure 10.2 Container runtimes are similar to VMs.

> **NOTE** For an up-to-date list of supported languages, check out this link: https://github.com/appcypher/awesome-wasm-langs.

To underline this point, Solomon Hykes, one of the creators of Docker, tweeted in 2019,

> *If Wasm+WASI existed in 2008, we wouldn't have needed to create Docker. That's how important it is. Web assembly on the server is the future of computing. A standardized system interface was the missing link. Let's hope WASI is up to the task!*

Having a universal runtime is a problem that developers have been trying to tackle through various forms of technology, but Wasm seems to be the answer many have been looking for; it is now at the forefront, and Rust is one of its most important languages.

10.1 WASI universal runtime

So, what exactly is WASI? Well, in chapter 9, we explored how Wasm works in the context of a browser. WebAssembly code is in a compiled format that can be interpreted by a web browser or any runtime that can interpret this compiled code. The runtime that can interpret the WebAssembly code will do so using the WebAssembly System Interface, or WASI. Now, our code is liberated from the WebAssembly runtime within a web browser using JavaScript. We can instead write an executable or a library that can be used by any other language that supports WASI. WASI is the tool that allows us to write our own runtime or use a runtime provided by someone else. The interface understands the underlying WebAssembly code and interprets it just as the JRE does with bytecode. In this case, WASI interprets Wasm code just like the JRE interprets Java bytecode. The difference is that we will get to write our own VM, just like the JVM.

WASI allows a developer to define how external libraries will interact with the underlying code that the host provides. The *I* in WASI stands for *interface*, and that's what the developer will be defining for the host code they are writing. In software, we define interfaces but don't necessarily need to create an implementation. In the same way, the host is providing a way to interact with an external library or application without knowing how the library works. When we define our interface with a set of given parameters and outputs, we can implement other code to call it. In this fashion, a library can be written in Wasm that fulfills an interface defined by the host application. The library can then be swapped out without affecting the host application. We will be demonstrating this ability throughout the chapter. Additionally, the Wasm modules can be swapped out *without* stopping the host application. The creation of the interface allows us to execute anything as long as it implements that interface, as shown in figure 10.3.

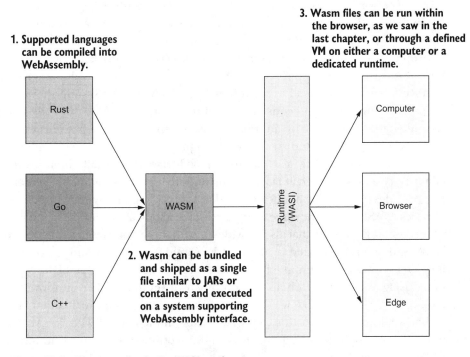

Figure 10.3 Wasm running in the WASI runtime

Executing arbitrary code within another piece of code can be dangerous. For years, we have been trying to prevent cross-site scripting attacks or SQL injection by limiting what users can input into various forms and fields. So, the idea of creating a runtime where any arbitrary Wasm file can be run seems dubious. However, a safety mechanism is built into the Wasm standard to prevent attacks from happening. Wasm modules are run in a sandboxed environment that receives input in only two forms: as direct argument inputs (like input for command-line functions) or through a memory buffer allocated solely within the external module's sandboxed environment. The host must ask the module to manage memory in some capacity and provide functions to read from this memory. Like containers, the JVM, and other virtual runtimes, the module runs as if it were the only application in the universe, with no concept of what lies outside of it. Because of this added security, we can execute Wasm files with little fear of the application doing anything malicious without the calling service explicitly permitting it.

The goal of Wasm is to allow code to become portable and modular. As a developer, you typically want to write code in the language you are comfortable with and use libraries that are helpful to you. Yet other languages have advantages in particular areas or libraries that you just don't have access to. As an example, take Python, which is very easy to write and a great language for machine learning. Yet Python is a scripting language and, as we saw in chapter 7, can be improved by replacing Python code with a module written in C++ or Rust. Yet we don't need to be limited to just those languages with the advent of WASI. Now we can share a function that was written in Go to do some performant operation without changing our underlying Python code.

Similarly, a Rust or C++ developer may want to use code from Python or a Go tool and make sure that the code is secure. We can use Rust's safety and Wasm's sandboxed environment to isolate and execute the insecure code in a locked-down environment. With Rust's extensive support of WebAssembly, we can get the "ultimate refactoring" with Rust. Since Rust has all of the tooling for Wasm and WASI support, we can refactor parts of our system and consume it in Rust, or we can rewrite our code in Rust and compile it to Wasm and have another language run it. Let's see how this works.

Let's look at WASI in terms of a VM. WASI provides the interface that allows another application to consume a Wasm module, much like we may install a binary within a containerized framework such as Docker. The underlying container may have a base image that provides the running application with resources like a filesystem, utilities, and even libraries. WASI can do the same thing. Let's take a look at WasmEdge as an example of a WebAssembly runtime that also provides us with some libraries to use in development.

WasmEdge is supported by the CNCF (Cloud Native Computing Foundation) to help create a standard runtime for WebAssembly code as well as an SDK. We are going to be using WasmEdge to help us with much of the boilerplate and low-level Wasm tooling that, as developers, we should not need to worry too much about. The caveat is that whatever we do in this example can be implemented with raw WebAssembly tools. If your application requires fewer abstractions, you may need to look into the WASI specifications more closely.

WasmEdge provides SDKs for Rust, JavaScript, Go, C, C++, Java, and several other languages, so it is a great choice for our refactoring needs for this book. The WasmEdge project is growing, as is the whole Wasm ecosystem, so it is important to stay up to date with the changing landscape. To get started with WasmEdge, we are going to install the library using the following command for Linux (or find your supporting OS at https://wasmedge.org/docs/start/install).

Listing 10.1 Command: Installing WasmEdge

```
curl -sSf https://raw.githubusercontent.com/WasmEdge/WasmEdge/master/
↪utils/install.sh | bash
```

Once WasmEdge is installed, you will have access to the WasmEdge runtime as well as some of its tooling. Follow any onscreen instructions to complete the setup. We will verify that the code is working by running a prebuilt Wasm module. To test it out, let's download the Wasm file and run it.

Listing 10.2 Command: Testing WasmEdge

```
wget https://github.com/second-state/rust-examples/releases/latest/
↪download/hello.wasm
```

You should see "Hello World!" printed on the screen. What happened? Earlier in the chapter, we likened Wasm files to JARs in that they are compiled, prepackaged code that can be executed on their respective runtimes without considering the underlying system architecture (Windows, Linux, 64 bit, 32 bit). We can go to the Rust source code for the module and see how it works, but we don't need to worry about how it is built or how it will be executed, since the runtime handles that for us. We can imagine a similar situation by downloading and executing a JAR file for Java.

Listing 10.3 Command: Executing a JAR

```
java -jar hello.jar
```

In the previous chapter, we used Wasm to run code within JavaScript in a web browser. With the compile target destined to be consumed by JavaScript, we were provided with some code to load the Wasm file into the browser runtime so we could execute the logic and retrieve values from an API. In a similar way, we can create a host environment outside of the browser to instead serve as a command-line utility. Let's see how we can break up our work to create an agnostic CLI tool that receives Wasm libraries for the CLI tool's business logic.

10.2 From the browser to the machine

Let's revisit our project from the last chapter. We decided to build a Wasm module that would call an external API and parse the results to display within the web browser.

256   CHAPTER 10   *WebAssembly interface for refactoring*

Often, when you consume an API endpoint and translate the data into a format that your business can use, you then have the power to extend it into other areas. If we take this same concept and combine it with Wasm/WASI, we should be able to construct a very portable and extensible system.

To start, we are going to create a new umbrella project called a *workspace* to house a library and a binary. A workspace shares the same `Cargo.lock` file and output directory to help organize packages and keep related packages together. Let's create our new project.

Listing 10.4   Command: Creating a new project

```
mkdir journal
cd journal
```

We will then create the library and the binary.

Listing 10.5   Command: Creating a new binary and library

```
cargo new paper_search_lib --lib      ◁── Creates a library using the code from the last chapter
cargo new paper_search                ◁── Creates a new binary to consume the library
touch Cargo.toml                      ◁── Creates umbrella Cargo file
```

And we will add workspaces to the `Cargo.toml` file using the following contents.

Listing 10.6   `Cargo.toml`: Workspace file

```
[workspace]

members = [
    "paper_search",        ◁── Members are the libraries you want Cargo to manage for you.
    "paper_search_lib"
]
```

Finally, we need to make sure we have our target, which will be `wasm32-wasi`, installed.

Listing 10.7   Command: Installing the target

```
rustup target add wasm32-wasi
```

Open the `lib.rs` file. We will add some of the same code from the previous chapter to create our search function. First, we will add our structures.

Listing 10.8   `paper_search_lib/src/lib.rs`: Copying structures

```
use serde::{Deserialize, Serialize};
use std::env;
```

10.2 From the browser to the machine

```rust
use std::error::Error;
use std::fmt::{self, Debug, Display, Formatter};

#[derive(Default, Debug, Clone, PartialEq, Serialize, Deserialize)]
pub struct Feed {
    pub entry: Vec<Entry>,
}

#[derive(Default, Debug, Clone, PartialEq, Serialize, Deserialize)]
pub struct Entry {
    pub id: String,
    pub updated: String,
    pub published: String,
    pub title: String,
    pub summary: String,
    pub author: Vec<Author>,
}

#[derive(Default, Debug, Clone, PartialEq, Serialize, Deserialize)]
pub struct Author {
    pub name: String,
}
```

This code provides the XML structure for the returned items. Then we will copy over our search function.

Listing 10.9 `paper_search_lib/src/lib.rs`: **Copying our search function**

```rust
pub async fn search(term: String, page: isize, max_results: isize) -
> Result<Feed, reqwest::Error> {
    let http_response = reqwest::get(format!(
        "http://export.arxiv.org/api/
     query?search_query=all:{}&start={}&max_results={}",
        term,
        page * max_results,
        max_results
    ))
    .await?;
    let b = http_response.text().await?;
    let feed: Feed = serde_xml_rs::from_str(b.as_str()).unwrap();
    return Ok(feed);
}
```

With the code in place, we then need to add the dependencies by opening the file `paper_search_lib/Cargo.toml` and adding the following libraries.

Listing 10.10 `paper_search_lib/Cargo.toml`: **Library dependencies**

```toml
[package]
name = "paper_search_lib"
version = "0.1.0"
edition = "2021"
```

```
[dependencies]
tokio_wasi = { version = "1.21", features = ["rt", "macros", "net", "time"]}
reqwest_wasi = "0.11"
serde = { version = "1.0", features = ["derive"] }
serde-xml-rs = "0.6.0"
```

That created the library, which our module will then call. It is important to pay attention to how you isolate and separate various segments of work to make sure they don't conflict and that the business logic does not get buried in the application logic. Since a Wasm module is a shippable binary, we want to move toward making the binary independent. Our module will be compiled in Wasm format but will depend on some libraries from the WasmEdge runtime.

Let's see if we can make a simple executable Wasm file that we can run on WasmEdge. We need to add some content to our `paper_search/Cargo.toml` file.

Listing 10.11 `paper_search/Cargo.toml`: Binary dependencies

```
[package]
name = "paper_search"
version = "0.1.0"
edition = "2021"

[build]                              ◁── Always targets our
target="wasm32-wasi"                      build for Wasm

[target.wasm32-wasi]                 ◁── Specifically, we want our runner
runner = "wasmedge"                       to be defined for WasmEdge.
                                                                        Imports the
[dependencies]                                                          functionality from
tokio_wasi = { version = "1.21", features = ["rt", "macros", "net", "time"]}  the last chapter
paper_search_lib = { path = "../paper_search_lib" }   ◁──
```

Now, we can write a binary that calls our library function and prints the results to the standard output (which typically is the console). It will be compiled in Wasm, and we can then run it through the WasmEdge runner we installed.

Listing 10.12 `paper_search/src/main.rs`: Fetching search results

```
use std::error::Error;
use std::fmt::{self, Debug, Display, Formatter};
                                                              Retrieves search
fn main() -> Result<(), Box<dyn std::error::Error>> {         results using the term
    let res: Vec<String> = search("rust".to_string(), 0, 10).unwrap();   ◁──
    for entry in res.iter() {       ◁── Prints results
        println!("{:?}", entry);         out to the screen
    }
    Ok(())
}
```

We created a simple WebAssembly application that will be the basis for the rest of our tool. This module will only expose the `main` function, which WasmEdge will call. The `paper_search` module, in turn, will use the underlying business logic we wrote in the `paper_search_lib`. Later, we will expose functions so this module can be used as a library. Upon running the code, you will see the results printed to standard out. What does standard out mean in terms of a module? The answer depends on the underlying implementation. We don't know exactly how WasmEdge handles those results. The output is dependent on the underlying runtime, which for now will just be what WasmEdge provides us with. Defining WasmEdge as our target runner tells Rust to compile using some of the functions defined by the WasmEdge SDK, allowing for better interoperability with the system. Essentially, WasmEdge fulfills the ABI we mentioned at the beginning of the chapter, and our module will have the implementation of those interfaces.

We separated the search function so we can extend it later and use this module as a library as well. Thus, it is best to make it accessible early on.

Listing 10.13 `paper_search/src/main.rs`: Wasm function to fetch results

```
pub fn search(
    term: String,
    page: isize,
    max_results: isize,
) -> Result<Vec<String>, Box<dyn std::error::Error>> {
    let rt = tokio::runtime::Builder::new_current_thread()
        .enable_all()
        .build()
        .unwrap();
    let feed: paper_search_lib::Feed = rt.block_on(async {paper_search_lib::s
      earch(term, page, max_results)
        .await}).unwrap();
    let res = feed
        .entry
        .into_iter()
        .map(|e| format!("{} {}", e.title, e.id))
        .collect::<Vec<String>>();
    return Ok::<Vec<String>, Box<dyn std::error::Error>>(res);
}
```

- We do not want to run this async, so we are going to block the call. To do this, we need a thread.
- We will wait on this thread until a response occurs. This requires us to use Tokio's thread management to block for a response.
- Formats the feed values to strings

Now that we have built an entry point to our module, we will be able to call it, but first, we must compile the module to use the Wasm runtime. Then we can call the module through WasmEdge.

Listing 10.14 Command: Building Wasm

```
cargo build --target wasm32-wasi
wasmedge target/wasm32-wasi/debug/paper_search.wasm
```

- Compiles to Wasm
- Runs the Wasm file using WasmEdge

You should see some data printed on the screen! Behind the scenes, the WasmEdge binary mounts our Wasm module and calls the `main` function. That's it. Think of it almost as an interpreter like that used in Python, except the code is already compiled. When we use the generic runtime, we have access to simple functionality like executing the module and printing results. WasmEdge has no clue about the code itself but does know how to interact with our operating system. This VM-like structure allows for portability, provided we have this binary on other systems. You could ship your Wasm module to your phone or to a Windows or Mac, and it would all work.

This example leaves a little to be desired, though. Right now, we don't have a way to interact with our module. Let's fix that by passing arguments to the module. We pass in arguments just like with any other application or binary—through an `args` list.

Listing 10.15 `paper_search/src/main.rs`: Wasm module

```
use std::env;
use std::error::Error;
use std::fmt::{self, Debug, Display, Formatter};

fn main() -> Result<(), Box<dyn std::error::Error>> {
    let mut args: Vec<String> = env::args().skip(1).collect();
    args.reverse();
    let term = args.pop().unwrap_or("rust".to_string());

    let res: Vec<String> = search(term, 0, 10).unwrap();
    for entry in res.iter() {
        println!("{:?}", entry);
    }
    Ok(())
}
```

- Captures input arguments for a search term; otherwise, defaults to rust
- Retrieves search results using the term provided
- Prints results out to the screen

Again, this is a simple application but with a lot happening underneath. Here, again, we find that WasmEdge provides us with tools to grab arguments as a string within the `env` package. But here's an interesting fact about Wasm: it doesn't have a string type. As we will see in the next section, Wasm has no concept of strings or characters as primitives within the language; therefore, doing something as simple as passing a string actually puts the work of implementing and handling this task on the runtime binary itself. So WasmEdge gives you the string input for free if you run their binary, but it will be something we will implement on our own later on.

Let's see how passing the argument changes our results.

Listing 10.16 Command: Building Wasm

```
wasmedge target/wasm32-wasi/debug/paper_search.wasm test
```

- Passes in an argument

What we've accomplished this far is the equivalent of writing a standalone application. We accept input via arguments, and output is written to the console. What we've built already is a pretty powerful tool. The WasmEdge binary provides additional options to allow more interactions with the underlying system while being able to run any Wasm module. But what if we wanted to use the module as a library instead of calling a binary?

10.3 Wasm library

Let's consider our search function again. Right now, we are executing the search module as a binary, much like you would if you compiled a Rust application and ran it through the `main` function. But let's consider using WasmEdge to bypass `main` and instead execute an exposed function within the library. By doing this, we move outside of WasmEdge's abilities to pass us string values and instead must rely on the supported primitives Wasm provides. Let's start by creating a function that just provides a static search where we can provide a page and an offset value. We only need to pass in supported primitives and expose the function using the `#[no_mangle]` macro, which preserves the name of the function for us to execute.

Listing 10.17 `paper_search/src/main.rs`: Wasm library

```rust
use std::env;
use std::error::Error;
use std::fmt::{self, Debug, Display, Formatter};

fn main() -> Result<(), Box<dyn std::error::Error>> {
    ...
}

#[no_mangle]
pub fn static_search(
    page: isize,          // Passes in i32/i64 bit
    offset: isize,        // integers for pagination
) {
    let res: Vec<String> = search("rust".to_string(), page, offset).unwrap();
    for entry in res.iter() {        // Iterates through responses
        println!("{:?}", entry);     // and print results
    }
}

pub fn search(
    term: String,
    page: isize,
    max_results: isize,
) -> Result<Vec<String>, Box<dyn std::error::Error>> {
    ...
}
```

As mentioned earlier, this exposes the library functions rather than the `main` function. Later, we will see the work required for a VM to translate and insert a string into a module. So far, WasmEdge has done that for us when we are executing a module like a binary. But now, we will instead bypass this functionality by using WasmEdge's `--reactor` flag, which allows us to call an individual function. At this point, WasmEdge no longer provides you with the tools to translate your string into a format your library can handle. We aren't provided with a set of arguments passed into the main application, but instead, we are interpreting values inserted into our function. All of this is to say that we lose functionality when we call the function directly as opposed to executing the module. So, we are left with a set of primitives supported by Wasm:

- `i32`—32-bit integer
- `i64`—64-bit integer
- `f32`—32-bit float
- `f64`—64-bit float
- `v128`—128-bit vector of integer, floating-point data, or a single 128-bit type

Outside of the primitive types, the responsibility turns to the module and the runtime. We are given the ability to create our own contracts between how we want our system to run and the modules we choose to run on that system. So, if you expect a string or JSON or whatever passed into your runtime, you need to write the library or mechanism to handle this. Later on, we will explore how to add in memory management, but first, we will discuss complex data to explain where our application will be moving and why we are starting with a simple pagination process.

WasmEdge allows us to call these libraries directly from our Wasm module, although we lose our ability to use strings. Let's compile and test our module's new library by running the following.

Listing 10.18 Command: Building Wasm

```
cargo build --target wasm32-wasi
wasmedge --reactor target/wasm32-wasi/debug/paper_search.wasm
➥static_search 0 1
```
◁── reactor allows us to call functions directly within a module and pass in arguments.

You should see the same results as before, but now, you are calling the library directly instead of the main entry point to the binary. So, now we know how to build a Wasm file that functions both as a binary and a library. But how can we run it in Rust? While we still have a hardcoded string in our code, we can begin to see where we will be able to add flexibility to our system. We can define libraries that take arguments from a runtime and are passed into an arbitrary library. We are going to move beyond using an existing runtime and start writing our own.

10.4 Consuming Wasm

Steve Klabnik's talk "Rust, WebAssembly, and the Future of Serverless" (https://mng.bz/X7Yl) begins by talking about runtimes, how overloaded the term *runtime* is, and how misunderstood a concept it is within software development. Almost every language has a runtime unless the language is an assembly language. Even compiled languages provide some sort of runtime to do simple tasks like memory management or other low-level operations. A *runtime* is a piece of code that gets executed to help run other code, whether that is an assembly language or another intermediate language. In the case of our earlier examples, we used the WasmEdge runtime. In chapter 9, we used a JavaScript runtime in the browser. Yet with WASI, we have the ability to start writing our own runtime and embedding Wasm files like in figure 10.4. Here is where you get to change a refactoring story.

Most projects we have discussed in this book have demonstrated how to put Rust into another language, such as C or Python, or how to call one of these other languages from Rust. These methods are very conservative and excellent ways to refactor, but consider the power of writing our own runtime. Suddenly, we have the ability to run whatever code we want as long as it compiles to Wasm—meaning that pesky business logic written in C could be compiled into a Wasm module and run *within* your Rust code, just as if it were any other library. When you've built the tools to support a flexible structure using Wasm, you can think of your code as a platform rather than just a node in a larger web.

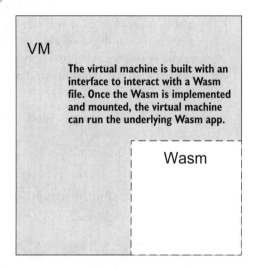

Figure 10.4 Wasm running with SDK

Considering the ability to embed external logic into a system you have built should raise concerns around how coupled systems can become. Design and architecture become important factors in how your system will utilize Wasm and the interfaces you develop to determine how flexible or rigid you need your platform to be. Yet, integrating any external language or library into your code provides a certain level of coupling and dependency management. In the previous examples of moving pesky C code, we could refer to a previous chapter and include it as part of our build, which would be tightly coupled. Embedding a Wasm file is also tightly coupled, but the module is isolated and safe. Here, we can run a module in isolation rather than rebuilding our system to consume the old and possibly insecure C code. The eventual goal will be to consider how to move completely off a given library or language or determine how the language can be adapted to your newer system.

If you find that you've established a common pattern that a singular runtime could support, you have found the ability to port or use any language within your company, merging C, C++, and Go, to run on a single Rust Wasm runtime. Or consider writing your runtime in any of those languages and using Rust to write a module! Rust can then be used in any other Wasm runtime provided it fulfills the proper interfaces. Describing how the runtime works and developing code supported by the runtime is very abstract, so an example will help us demonstrate these concepts. We are going to write our own runtime in the form of a CLI tool that accepts "searchable" modules. Our interface to our runtime will require a few functions that our CLI can call, and our CLI will have the ability to be flexible and import Wasm modules when the application starts. So, any module will run within our CLI tool as long as the module provides us with a search function that supports the following input: term, page, and offset. We can then mount Wasm modules that fulfill that interface without recompiling the underlying runtime application.

To start, let's create a simple binary that wraps this functionality together. We will call it the `journal_cli`. It will need to be in the parent directory, a peer to the `paper_search_lib` and `paper_search` projects we wrote before. Here, *journal* will represent resources we may want to collect in the future. This tool will rely on a Wasm file to provide its search capabilities and allow us to run the application without rebuilding it.

Listing 10.19 Command: Creating a new binary and library

```
cd ..
cargo new journal_cli
```

⟵ You will want to be in the parent directory (journal) with paper_search as a peer project and in the same directory as the workspace Cargo.toml file.

We want to exclude this from our other workspaces since it is a consumer of the Wasm file. To handle that, we need to edit the parent-level `Cargo.toml`.

Listing 10.20 `Cargo.toml`: Excluding the library

```
[workspace]

members = [
    "paper_search_lib",
    "paper_search"
]
exclude = ["journal_cli"]
```

⟵ We don't want our WasmEdge libraries to conflict.

Navigate into the `journal_cli` directory and add the following library to the `Cargo.toml` file.

Listing 10.21 `journal_cli/Cargo.toml`: Adding SDK

```
[package]
name = "journal_cli"
version = "0.1.0"
edition = "2021"

[dependencies]
wasmedge-sdk = "0.11.2"
```

The only dependency we need is the WasmEdge SDK. The SDK will allow us to create a virtual environment in which to run the Wasm file and provide us with the functions

10.4 Consuming Wasm

we will need to interact with the Wasm module. We can begin to think of this as our own version of the WasmEdge binary we used earlier to call our first Wasm module. But instead of `wasmedge` providing the interactions with the module, we are going to define how we want our inputs and outputs to be handled. The following code is a bit dense, but most of the code sets up our Wasm virtual environment for the module to run in. The flow of the application is first to find and load the Wasm file and then build the virtual environment. Once the file has been selected and loaded into the virtual environment, we will call the function that executes the Wasm as an executable. Open the `main.rs` file and add the following code.

Listing 10.22 `journal_cli/src/main.rs`: Calling the `main` Wasm function

```rust
use std::env;
use std::path::PathBuf;
use wasmedge_sdk::{
    config::{CommonConfigOptions,
        ConfigBuilder,
        HostRegistrationConfigOptions},
    params, VmBuilder, WasmVal
};

fn main() -> Result<(), Box<dyn std::error::Error>>{
    let mut args: Vec<String> = env::args().skip(1).collect();
    args.reverse();
    let target = args.pop().unwrap_or(
        "paper_search".to_string());

    let filename = format!("{}.wasm", target);
    let wasm_file: PathBuf = [
        "..", "target",
        "wasm32-wasi",
        "debug", filename.as_str()]
        .iter()
        .collect();

    let config = ConfigBuilder::new(CommonConfigOptions::default())
        .with_host_registration_config(
            HostRegistrationConfigOptions::default().wasi(true))
        .build()?;
    assert!(config.wasi_enabled());

    let mut vm = VmBuilder::new().with_config(config).build()?;

    vm.wasi_module_mut()
        .expect("Not found wasi module")
        .initialize(None, None, None);
    vm.register_module_from_file(target.as_str(), &wasm_file)?
        .run_func(Some(target.as_str()), "_start", params!())?;

    Ok(())
}
```

- Dynamically loads the Wasm file we created before via arguments, allowing us to swap out Wasm files in the future.
- Creates a configuration to load WASI
- Loads the host configuration for the WasmEdge VM
- Creates a new VM with the configuration so we can load our Wasm file
- Calls the main function and passes no parameters. The function is similar to calling `wasmedge hello-world.wasm` from the terminal.

Now, go into the `journal_cli` directory, type `cargo run`, and you should see the results pop up. The `journal_cli` runtime executed the underlying "main" function in the module just the same as when you call the WasmEdge binary directly using `wasmedge paper_search.wasm`.

Our CLI shows you how much goes into what WasmEdge has developed in their custom runtime, and how we can start building our own. What's interesting, though, is that what is printed on the screen is not the output from our CLI code but, instead, the output is from the Wasm module. Our runtime does not capture or manipulate this output in any way; instead, it provides a mechanism to the Wasm module (through the VM we set up) to give functionality to the `print` function, which goes to STDOUT. The virtual environment we created does a lot for us, and we can manipulate the runtime to change how we want our system to work. We can imagine a scenario where we want to use the same search module but have the virtual environment write to a file or compress the output.

What about the library we wrote? How do we access that? Again, the code requires a little tweaking, but we need only to change "_start" to "static_search" since that is the name of the function, and we can include parameters.

Listing 10.23 journal_cli/src/main.rs: Calling the main Wasm function

```
fn main() -> Result<(), Box<dyn std::error::Error>>{
...
    vm.register_module_from_file(
        target.as_str(), &wasm_file)?
        .run_func(
            Some(target.as_str()),
            "static_search", params!(0, 1))?;
    Ok(())
}
```

We use the params macro to encode values to pass to our search function.

With the change in the run target, we can now access the search method we used earlier. The functionality is the same as when we used the `--reactor` flag earlier with WasmEdge. Instead of hitting the `main` method, we are now calling a function directly within the module. Now we have a runtime and a Wasm module to run, but let's add another module to demonstrate the power of writing your own runtime and the flexibility the runtime offers.

Before moving on, let's revert our code from `static_search` to `_start` since this is how our next Wasm file will be called.

Listing 10.24 journal_cli/src/main.rs: Calling the main Wasm function

```
fn main() -> Result<(), Box<dyn std::error::Error>>{
...
    vm.register_module_from_file(target.as_str(), &wasm_file)?
        .run_func(Some(target.as_str()), "_start", params!())?;
    Ok(())
}
```

10.5 More Wasm

Our Wasm file is loaded and registered to a virtual runtime defined by the WasmEdge SDK, allowing us to safely execute code and providing a barrier between our CLI application and the search library provided in the Wasm module. As a result, we can swap out our Wasm file with another, without changing our underlying CLI code, by pointing to a different Wasm module. To demonstrate, let's throw together another quick search library and test this functionality out. Instead of searching for papers as we did in the previous section, we will search for books. We will implement the same type of search functionality as in the paper search library. We can then use this example to demonstrate how Wasm modules can be swapped out without changes to the CLI, as shown in figure 10.5.

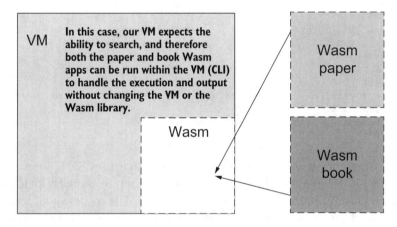

Figure 10.5 Wasm running additional modules

Let's go back up to the parent `journal` directory and create another Wasm library called `book_search`. Here, we will build a library similar to the `paper_search`.

Listing 10.25 Command: Creating a new binary

```
cd ..
cargo new book_search
```
You need to be in the root directory of the project (journal).

Open the parent `Cargo.toml` file and add the new library.

Listing 10.26 `journal/Cargo.toml`: Including the new library

```
[workspace]

members = [
    "paper_search_lib",
```

```
        "paper_search",
        "book_search"      ◁──┐ Adds a library to the
]                             │ workspace members
exclude = ["journal_cli"]
```

We are going to add several libraries similar to our paper search in `book_search/Cargo.toml`.

Listing 10.27 `book_search/Cargo.toml`: Book search dependencies

```
[package]
name = "book_search"
version = "0.1.0"
edition = "2021"

[build]
target="wasm32-wasi"

[target.wasm32-wasi]
runner = "wasmedge"

[dependencies]
tokio_wasi = { version = "1.21", features = ["rt", "macros", "net", "time"]}
reqwest_wasi = "0.11"
serde = { version = "1.0", features = ["derive"] }
serde_json = "1.0"
```

The biggest difference is that, although our paper search uses XML, we will be consuming JSON for this request. Again, we are taking different business logic and producing APIs that fit into our generic search tool. The code should be pretty straightforward. First, we will define the elements of the JSON object we expect to be returned.

Listing 10.28 `book_search/src/main.rs`: Book search core entities

```
use serde::{Deserialize, Serialize};
use std::env;
use std::error::Error;
use std::fmt::{self, Debug, Display, Formatter};


#[derive(Default, Debug, Clone, PartialEq, Serialize, Deserialize)]
pub struct SearchResult {
    pub results: Vec<Book>,
}

#[derive(Default, Debug, Clone, PartialEq, Serialize, Deserialize)]
pub struct Book {
    pub id: i32,
    pub title: String,
}
```

10.5 More Wasm

After that, we will write a very similar `main` function that calls a search function and prints the results.

Listing 10.29 `book_search/src/main.rs`: Book search `main` function for search

```rust
fn main() -> Result<(), Box<dyn std::error::Error>> {
    let mut args: Vec<String> = env::args().skip(1).collect();    // Captures the
    args.reverse();                                                // term from the
    let term = args.pop().unwrap_or("rust".to_string());          // input argument

    let res: Vec<String> = search(term).unwrap();    // Runs the search term
    for entry in res.iter() {                        // Prints results for each
        println!("{}", entry);                       // value to STDOUT
    }
    Ok(())
}
```

Next comes a copy of our search function.

Listing 10.30 `book_search/src/main.rs`: Book search `http` call

```rust
pub fn search(
    term: String
) -> Result<Vec<String>, Box<dyn std::error::Error>> {
    let rt = tokio::runtime::Builder::new_current_thread()
        .enable_all()
        .build()                    // We do not want to run this async, so we are going
        .unwrap();                  // to block the call. To do this, we need a thread.
    let searchresult: SearchResult = rt.block_on(async {call_api(term)
        .await}).unwrap();          // We will block this thread until a
    let res = searchresult          // response returns from the API.
        .results
        .into_iter()
        .map(|e| format!("{}", e.title))    // Formats the book
        .collect::<Vec<String>>();           // values to strings
    return Ok::<Vec<String>, Box<dyn std::error::Error>>(res);
}

pub async fn call_api(term: String) -> Result<SearchResult, reqwest::Error> {
    let http_response = reqwest::get(format!(
        "http://gutendex.com/books/?search={}",
        term
    ))                              // Calls the book API with
    .await?;                        // a given search term
    let b = http_response.text().await?;
    let res: SearchResult = serde_json::from_str(b.as_str()).unwrap();
    return Ok(res);
}                                   // Serializes output into the
                                    // previously defined structs
```

Looks familiar, right? JSON definitions are provided and deserialized from a book search result. Let's build the Wasm file and then test our CLI call.

> **Listing 10.31 Command: Building Wasm files**

```
cd ..
cargo build --target wasm32-wasi
```

← Be in the root project directory (journal).

Compiles all Wasm targets (paper_search and book_search)

Now, go back to our CLI tool. Since we made the CLI dynamic in terms of which library it uses, you should be able to run the command but pass the new library name.

> **Listing 10.32 Command: Running a book search**

```
cd journal_cli
cargo run book_search
```

When the code executes, you should see some results that are different than the ones from the `paper_search` library because our CLI tool is loading a different Wasm module than before. Passing in `paper_search` should give you results from the `paper_search` Wasm module we used before. Without recompiling, we can change the underlying behavior of the CLI tool by fulfilling the simple API definition defined by the `vm` object that we created. This loads the module and calls the desired function to do our search. Each underlying function acts the same but calls entirely different endpoints in entirely different formats. Right now, this works because we are executing Wasm modules directly, but what if we want to use the underlying functions like we did earlier? To do that, we will need to dive into Wasm memory.

10.6 Wasm memory

To begin, we should cover how Wasm and WASI manage memory. As mentioned before, Wasm operates in a *sandboxed* environment, meaning that it relies on the underlying VM for access to the actual machine's hardware and services. Additionally, each Wasm module manages memory within the module. The VM then has the ability to reach into the module to both write to and read from a memory address. This requires the VM to be responsible for the data being read from the module without the fear that the execution within the module will affect the underlying system. Nor do we need to worry about multiple Wasm modules grabbing or manipulating memory within another module. The onus falls on the VM, thereby making the design of your VM extremely important.

Wasm's memory structure is a simple, resizable `ArrayBuffer` that stores raw bytes of data. As we mentioned earlier, the Wasm standard has a few primitive types, but none of them are string or character primitives. These values vary from system to system and often take the form of byte data, which again varies from machine to machine. Yet, you might recall that there was a fifth value that Wasm supports: `v128`, or a vector with 128 bits; the VM uses it for data like strings. Module memory can grow and be changed through various memory instructions or the host runtime.

10.6 Wasm memory

To use memory within the module, we need the ability to allocate memory, retrieve its location, write to that memory slot, run a function, and read the results from a location in memory. Low-level operations like these are normally outside the scope of many developers, so this may seem a little tedious, but remember that we are building a VM and will therefore need to write some lower-level, systems-like code to manage memory. However, libraries and tools can be written to mitigate the need to rewrite these functions and reduce repeated code. This is complicated because Wasm is an assembly language that runs on a specific target without knowing the underlying architecture of the machine it is running on. The way an application or program represents a value in memory can differ based on whether it's running on a 64- or 32-bit machine. Wasm doesn't try to fit all of these different use cases because it needs to be simple and low-level.

The calling application and the Wasm file itself need to agree on how to allocate the data and how to read the data from memory. With each instance of a Wasm file running, the module will be given a certain allocation of memory, with a pointer to that data being known only to that module. The memory module is shared between the VM and the module, as shown in figure 10.6.

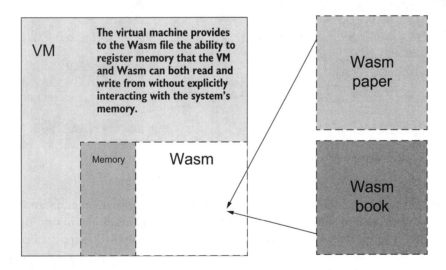

Figure 10.6 Wasm memory

The module needs to provide a way to allocate the memory and return the pointer of the address to the calling function. Let's add this method to our code. Open both `paper_search/src/main.rs` and `book_search/src/main.rs` and add the following.

Listing 10.33 [paper_search|book_search]/src/main.rs: Allocating function

```
use std::os::raw::{c_void, c_int};
use std::mem;
```

```rust
#[no_mangle]
pub extern fn allocate(size: usize) -> *mut c_void {
    let mut buffer = Vec::with_capacity(size);      // Allocates the buffer based on the size provided by the calling service
    let pointer = buffer.as_mut_ptr();               // Finds the pointer in linear memory
    mem::forget(buffer);                              // Clears its contents

    pointer as *mut c_void                            // Returns pointer value
}
```

Now, the host application can allocate a specific amount of memory for whatever it needs to pass in, as shown in figure 10.7.

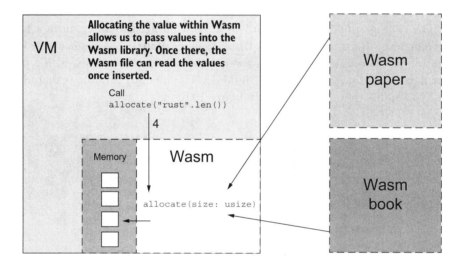

Figure 10.7 Wasm memory allocation

Having this tool in place will allow us to pass a string into a function and have the function write the results back to memory, where the calling function can then extract the data. To do that, we need to open that functionality up within our CLI runtime. It will be the responsibility of the runtime to expose memory to the module and provide the ability to read and write to that memory. So, open `journal_cli/src/main.rs` and rewrite the `main` function.

Listing 10.34 `journal_cli/main.rs`: Rewriting the CLI call to function

```rust
fn main() -> Result<(), Box<dyn std::error::Error>>{
    ...
    let term = args.pop().unwrap_or("type".to_string());
```

10.6 Wasm memory

```
let config = ConfigBuilder::new(CommonConfigOptions::default())
    .with_host_registration_config(HostRegistrationConfigOptions::default
().wasi(true))
    .build()?;                          ◄── Creates a config with the
assert!(config.wasi_enabled());              wasi option enabled

let mut vm = VmBuilder::new().with_config(config).build()?;  ◄── Builds a new VM just like we did previously

vm.wasi_module_mut()
    .expect("Not found wasi module")
    .initialize(None, None, None);              This time we want to
let m = vm.clone()                              grab the module object.
    .register_module_from_file(target.to_string(), &wasm_file)?;  ◄──
let env_instance = m.named_module(target.to_string())?;  ◄──

let exec = vm.executor();  ◄── Grabs the executor    Using the module, grabs
                               for the VM            the environment to grab
                                                     functions and memory

let mut memory = env_instance.memory("memory")?;       ◄── Grabs the memory object
let allocate = env_instance.func("allocate")?;         ◄──      from the environment
let search = env_instance.func("memory_search")?;     Grabs the allocation function
                                                      from the environment
```
Grabs the search function from the environment

```
let term_len: i32 = term.len() as i32;
let iptr = allocate.run(exec, params!(term_len))?[0].to_i32();   ◄──
let uptr: u32 = iptr as u32;      Writes the term    Runs the allocation function with
memory.write(term, uptr);    ◄──  to memory          the length of our search term


let iresptr = search.run(exec, params!(iptr))?[0].to_i32();  ◄── Runs the
let uresptr: u32 = iresptr as u32;                               search
let val = memory.read_string(uresptr, 1024)?;   ◄── Reads the    function with
let val = val.trim_matches(char::from(0));          return string a pointer
                                                    value from
println!("{:?}", val);                              memory
Ok(())
}
```

You can see that this is a little complicated for a setup, but we've seen a good portion of it before. For us to access the memory modules, we need a more complex VM, so we had to unwrap a few more tools. By grabbing our module's instance, we can then extract functions and abstractions like memory. We then allocate the space we need to pass in our value. Calling the allocation function can then ensure we can write to the memory without overflow, as shown in figure 10.8. Once the value is loaded, we can call our search function (yet to be written!) and await the pointer to where the response is written. We will read 1 KB of data and print the results from the host. There are more dynamic and sophisticated ways of returning response data, but we will not explore them here.

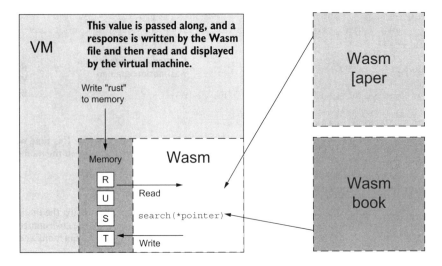

Figure 10.8 Wasm reading and writing to the memory buffer

If you run this, you will get a runtime error from the Wasm library because we don't have the search function written yet. So, let's do that for both paper and book searches. Starting with `paper_search/src/main.rs`, we will add the new memory search method.

Listing 10.35 `paper_search/src/main.rs`: Adding memory search

```
use std::ffi::{CStr, c_char, CString};

#[no_mangle]
pub fn memory_search(term: *mut c_char) -> *mut c_char {
    let t = unsafe { CStr::from_ptr(term).to_bytes().to_vec() };
    let mut output = t.to_vec();
    let search_term: String = String::from_utf8(output).unwrap();
    let res_string = search(search_term, 0, 1).unwrap();
    let mut res: Vec<u8> = res_string.into_iter().nth(0).unwrap().into();
    res.resize(1024, 0); 3((CO22-3))
    unsafe { CString::from_vec_unchecked(res) }.into_raw()
}
```

- Reads the term string from memory
- Calls the search function with the term
- Gets the vector pointer response
- Expands the vector to 1 KB for the result

This function will receive the pointer we passed from the VM that was returned as part of our allocation call. We will then read the string from memory and then pass it to our search function. We are only interested in returning one value, so we limit the results and pop the value from our vector. We then write this to the same memory slot, just increasing the size to 1 KB. When we are done, we need to return the new pointer in case the memory address is moved. We will write a similar function for `book_search`.

Listing 10.36 `book_search/src/main.rs`: Adding memory search

```
use std::ffi::{CStr, c_char, CString};

#[no_mangle]
pub fn memory_search(term: *mut c_char) -> *mut c_char {
    let t = unsafe { CStr::from_ptr(term).to_bytes().to_vec() };
    let mut output = t.to_vec();
    let search_term: String = String::from_utf8(output).unwrap();
    let res_string = search(search_term).unwrap();
    let mut res: Vec<u8> = res_string.into_iter().nth(0).unwrap().into();
    res.resize(1024, 0); 3((CO23-3))
    unsafe { CString::from_vec_unchecked(res) }.into_raw()
}
```

- Reads the term string from memory
- Calls the search function with the term
- Gets the vector pointer response
- Expands the vector to 1 KB for the result

These functions are *almost* the same: the only difference is that our search function in this library doesn't support pagination. Since we have both functions written and the CLI up to date, we can recompile our Wasm modules and test them out! From the root directory of the project, run the following.

Listing 10.37 Command: Building Wasm files

```
cd ..
cargo build --target wasm32-wasi
```

- Root of the project (journal)
- Recompiles Wasm targets

Then change directories to `journal_cli` and run the search.

Listing 10.38 Command: Running a book search

```
cargo run book_search rust
cargo run paper_search rust
```

You should see results! While this section of code around memory management seems complicated, you can always write a shared library that simplifies that process or uses a library that helps. The Wasm ecosystem is shifting fast, and various tools and libraries are coming out to aid in this process. Unfortunately, listing them here would only provide an outdated list. Despite this, you can hopefully start to see the flexibility that Wasm provides.

10.7 Just the beginning

Unlike C, C++, Python, and JavaScript, WebAssembly is on the front edge of technology, with standards continuing to be written and changed. What we've explored over the last two chapters uses current technologies but with already established Wasm standards. We are at the beginning of the possibilities of this technology, and it is poised to become much more influential as time progresses. We include WebAssembly as part of the refactoring process because it demonstrates how well Rust is positioned to refactor almost anything that is out there today. It may not always be an easy fit, but plenty of tools are available that allow us to move code toward Rust or at least help put Rust in our code.

Summary

- WASI is the standard for integrating Wasm modules into a universal runtime, as demonstrated through the WasmEdge SDK and runtime.
- WasmEdge is one implementation of this runtime and provides an SDK to write applications that consume Wasm, like the CLI search tool we constructed.
- Wasm's type system provides vector definitions and manual memory management, which can have tools wrapped around it for higher levels of flexibility without maintaining a complex type system.
- The Wasm runtime provides a shared, sandboxed, linear memory module for the VM and the module to use to allow for a secure runtime.
- To use the memory model, functions must be created to allocate and deallocate memory within the module to communicate with the defined VM.

index

Symbols

? operator 47–48, 56
/calculate endpoint 108
& command 216
&str type 33
#[test] attribute macro 189
-> operator 122

A

ABI (application binary interface) 251
absolute paths 147–155
add function 193–194
admire_art function 18, 22, 24, 26–27, 29–31
allocation 20
App.jsx file 246
args list 260
art1 variable 22, 24, 27
Artwork variable 24
as_ prefix 36
as_ptr method 63
assembly code 250
assert_eq macro 189, 191
assert! macro 189
async keyword 218
asynchronous processing 218
asynchronous programming
   Python with Rust
      Global Interpreter Lock 223–224
      PyO3 225–228
asynchronous Python
   scaling 216–218
   threading 220–223
asynchronous Python with Rust
   Global Interpreter Lock 223–224
   PyO3 225–228
asyncio 218–220
auto-initialize feature 176
automated memory management 20

B

bananas.rs file 144
bar function 45
bench_py function 181
bindgen 103–109
bindings 99
black_box function 178, 182
blocking 218
borrowed_art reference 31
borrowing 26–27
bottlenecks 216
browser to machine 256–261
browser, Rust in 232–238
   compiling to Wasm 236–237
   loading in browser 237–238
   requesting data 232–235
build scripts 100–103
build target 97
build_art function 32

build-dependencies section 104
build-script-test crate 100
builds, optimized 184–185
bundler 239
buy function 148
bytecode 250

C

C FFI (C Foreign Function Interface) 60–63
C, linking to Rust 98–109
calculate
  crate 124–125, 127
  library 94, 99
  package 125
calculate crate 124
calculator library 124–128
calculator, writing HTTP response 128–136
cargo new command 16
cargo run command 17
Cargo.toml file 125, 256, 264
cdylib 71–72, 107, 125
cfg attribute macro 188
CNCF (Cloud Native Computing Foundation) 254
component implementation 242
concat! macro 106
concurrency 221
configure script 97
ConsumedTreat type 149
consuming Wasm 263–266
Content-Length header 130
Copy trait 19
crate keyword 147
crate-type field 125
create method 241–243
Criterion crate 176
criterion_group macro 178
criterion_main macro 178
CStr helper struct 122
ctx variable 244

D

data processing in Python 164–165
day_kind module 144, 152, 155
deallocation 20

Debug trait 56–58, 138
dependencies section 104, 177
dereference operator 113
derive directive 56
destructuring 41
Display trait 138
doc comment 194
dynamic languages
  benchmarking in Rust 176–184
  integrating with Rust, optimized builds 184–185
dynamic memory 19

E

eat function 149
enums 37–59
  error handling with 41–43
  error types 45–49
  overview of 37–41
  panicking with errors 53–59
  transforming errors 49–53
  unit type 43–45
env package 260
env! macro 106
Err arm 48
err value 51
Err variant 45, 47, 50–51
Error type 46, 56–58
evaluate function 124–126
expect function 58
extension-module feature 176

F

feed tag 234
Fetching mode 243
FetchState enum 243
FFI (foreign function interface) 61, 93–137
  calculator library 124–128
  NGINX, creating module 94–98
  reading NGINX requests 109–124
  writing HTTP response 128–136
fmt module 138
forest crate 157–158, 162
format! macro 38, 128
free function 21

G

garbage collection 20
get function 131
get_day_kind function 144
get_name function 139–140, 154
get_value function 116–118
GetSearch function 245
GIL (Global Interpreter Lock) 223–224
goodbye function 139–140
GotNegative 58
GREET_LANG environment variable 101
greetings project 139

H

heap memory 20
hello function 139–140
horizontal scaling 216
how_was_day function 154
http module 144
HTTP response 128–136

I

idempotent function 216
ignored line 180
import statement 240
include directives 104
include! macro 102, 106
index.html file 237
input module 139–140, 143–144, 153

J

JAR (Java ARchive) 250
JavaScript
    creating React components 238–241
    refactoring 247–248
    refactoring to Rust 231–232
    Wasm (WebAssembly), web components entirely in Rust 241–246
journal_cli 264, 266
JRE (Java Runtime Environment) 250
json module 181

L

lambdas 52
language, string types, mutable strings 34–37
let statement 17
lib.rs file 144, 256
libraries, structuring
    paths 146–159
    upward visibility 159–162
libsnack crate 147–148
lifetime annotations 33, 115–120
    in NGINX plugin 120–124
lifetime graph 23
lifetimes 23–32
    controlling mutability 28–30
    references and borrowing 26–27
    references and lifetimes 30–32
List component 240
locals dict 182

M

main function 37, 140, 152, 196, 261–262, 266
main method 266
main_test.py file 203
main.rs file 144, 155, 265
malloc function 130
Mandelbrot set, generating in Python 213–215
manual memory management 20
memory bitfield 131
memory management, in other languages 19–23
mod bananas 144
mod day_kind 144
mod forest 144
mod keyword 139, 142
mod statement 144
modular format 239
module.rs file 143
module/config file 95, 108
modules 138–145
    multiple files 143–145
MonkeyPatch class 207
monkey patching 206–210
More button 240
mutability 28–30

mutable strings 34–37
mutex 224

N

NGINX
   creating module 94–98
   downloading source code 94
   reading requests 109–124
no-op 146
NotDivisible variant 40–41
NotUnique 50
null values 43–44
num variable 41

O

object code 214
offset_from method 123, 132
openssl library 99
output module 139–140, 143–144, 152
output.rs file 143, 145
ownership and borrowing 16–19

P

package.json file 239
page variable 240
panic function 54
panic! macro 54
paths 146–159
   overview 146–147
   path aliases 155–159
   relative vs. absolute 147–155
pipe characters 52
POSIX Threads 222
post_handler type 112
print function 266
print_day_kind_message function 144
print_fizzbuzz function 38, 45, 47, 54, 56
printf function 18
println! macro 18, 40
pthreads 222
pub keyword 126, 141–142, 148
pub use keyword 155
py_result variable 209
py.run function 182

PyDict 181
pymodule macro 226
pytest file 203
Python
   asynchronous 218–223
   asynchronous with Rust 223–228
   data processing in 164–165
   generating Mandelbrot set in 213–215
   planning move to Rust 165–166
   testing Rust code using 202–210
python_sum function 207

R

randomized_test_case function 209
raw pointers, unsafe Rust 62–63
raw strings 199–202
re-export 155
React, creating components 238–241
read_body_handler function 111–112, 127, 133
reallocation 34
reborrowing 113
refactoring
   browser to machine 256–261
   consuming Wasm 263–266
   defined 2–4
   Wasm (WebAssembly) interface for, modules 267–270
refactoring to Rust
   process 9–11
   when not to 9
references 26–32
regret function 149
relative paths 147, 149, 151
request variable 120
reqwest library 235
Result type 42, 45, 47, 49–50, 58
rlib 125
RPN (Reverse Polish Notation) 94
runtime 263
Rust 15–59
   asynchronous Python with 212–228
   benchmarking in 176–184
   enums and error handling 37–59
   in browser 232–238

integrating with dynamic languages, optimized builds 184–185
language, string types 33–37
lifetimes 23–32
linking C to 98–109
memory management in other languages 19–23
ownership and borrowing 16–19
planning move from Python 165–166
refactoring JavaScript to 231–232
structuring libraries 146–162
testing code using Python 202–210
testing integrations 187–211
Wasm (WebAssembly), web components entirely in Rust 241–246
rust_json library 182
rust-json virtual environment 202

S

sandboxed environment 270
scaling 216–218
script tag 239
Search struct 236
serde library 236
set function 131
shop module 148–149
solve function 99, 126
stack memory 20
std crate 138
string slice 121
string types 33–37, 44
   mutable strings 34–37
String, with_capacity function 35
structuring libraries
   modules 138–145
   paths 146–159
sum function 204, 206–208
super path segment 147, 152
switch statements 39

T

test module 198
testing
   adding tests to existing code 198–202
   documentation tests 193–197

Rust code using Python 202–210
   writing tests with Rust 188–193
testing crate 188
tests module 188, 193
threading 220–223
ThreadPoolExecutor 223
to_ prefix 36
toString method 57
Treat type 149
treats module 148
try/except block 41

U

u128 values 177
u8 values 177
unchecked 61
unit type 43–45
update method 241–242
upward visibility 159–162
useEffect hook 240
UsernameError type 50–51
usize type 123

V

v128 270
validate_lowercase function 50
validate_unique function 50
validate_username function 50, 52
value variable 117
view method 241–242
View stage 243
VM (virtual machine) 250
void function 45

W

W3C (World Wide Web Consortium) 230
Wasm (WebAssembly)
   browser to machine 256–261
   consuming 263–266
   creating React components 238–241
   defined 230–231
   interface for refactoring 249–276
   library 261–262
   loading in browser 232–238

Wasm (WebAssembly) *(continued)*
    memory 270–275
    modules 267–270
    refactoring JavaScript 247–248
    WASI universal runtime 253–255
    web components entirely in
        Rust 241–246
wasm_bindgen library 236
welcome function 21–22
with_gil function 181

workspace 256

X

x character variable 62
x parameter 52

Y

y character variable 62

RELATED MANNING TITLES

Code Like a Pro in Rust
by Brenden Matthews

ISBN: 9781617299643
264 pages $59.99
February 2024

Rust Servers, Services, and Apps
by Prabhu Eshwarla

ISBN: 9781617298608
328 pages $59.99
July 2023

Learn Rust in a Month of Lunches
by David MacLeod

ISBN: 9781633438231
568 pages $69.99
February 2024

Rust Web Development
by Bastian Gruber

ISBN: 9781617299001
400 pages $49.99
December 2022

For ordering information, go to www.manning.com

A new online reading experience

liveBook, our online reading platform, adds a new dimension to your Manning books, with features that make reading, learning, and sharing easier than ever. A liveBook version of your book is included FREE with every Manning book.

This next generation book platform is more than an online reader. It's packed with unique features to upgrade and enhance your learning experience.

- Add your own notes and bookmarks
- One-click code copy
- Learn from other readers in the discussion forum
- Audio recordings and interactive exercises
- Read all your purchased Manning content in any browser, anytime, anywhere

As an added bonus, you can search every Manning book and video in liveBook—even ones you don't yet own. Open any liveBook, and you'll be able to browse the content and read anything you like.*

Find out more at www.manning.com/livebook-program.

*Open reading is limited to 10 minutes per book daily